RETHINKING TIME

———

SÖDERTÖRN
PHILOSOPHICAL STUDIES 9
2011

Rethinking Time

ESSAYS ON HISTORY,
MEMORY, AND REPRESENTATION

Hans Ruin
& Andrus Ers (eds.)

SÖDERTÖRN
PHILOSOPHICAL STUDIES
9

Other titles in this series

Phenomenology and Religion: New Frontiers (2010)
Jonna Bornemark and Hans Ruin (eds.)

Phenomenology of Eros (2012)
Jonna Bornemark & Marcia Sá Cavalcante Schuback (eds.)

Ambiguity of the Sacred (2012)
Jonna Bornemark & Hans Ruin (eds.)

Foucault, Biopolitics and Governmentality (2013)
Jakob Nilsson & Sven-Olov Wallentein (eds.)

Translating Hegel (2013)
Brian Manning Delaney & Sven-Olov Wallenstein (eds.)

Södertörns högskola
2011

Södertörn Philosophical Studies 9
ISSN 1651-6834
ISBN 978-91-86069-32-2
© The authors
Cover painting: "Incidents of Granma's Travel in America", Jan Håfström, 2009.
Graphic design: Johan Laserna

Distribution: Södertörns högskola, Library
S-141 89 Huddinge
Phone: + 46 (0)8 608 40 00
E-mail: publications@sh.se

Table of Contents

Preface
HANS RUIN & ANDRUS ERS   9

1. CONCEPTS OF TIME

On the Historical Representation
of Contemporary Art
DAN KARLHOLM   19

The Productive Dilemmas of History
PETER ARONSSON   29

Is Every Tale a Fairy Tale?
STAFFAN CARLSHAMRE   39

Aporetics of Time and the Trace of the Other
HANS RUIN   51

Hermeneutics of Tradition
MARCIA SÁ CAVALCANTE SCHUBACK   63

Requirements of an Aesthetic Concept of the Canon
ANDERS OLSSON   75

2. MONUMENTS OF TIME

Social Dreams of History: Museum, Utopia, Mythology
JOHAN REDIN   97

*Walking Through History: Archaeology
and Ethnography in Museum Narration*
JOHAN HEGARDT   109

*Creative Confusion: Modern Ruins
and the Archaeology of the Present*
MATS BURSTRÖM   119

*Claiming Makunaima: Colonisation, Nation,
and History in the Northern Amazon*
PATRICIA LORENZONI   129

*The Times of Television: Representing, Anticipating,
Forgetting the Cold War*
STAFFAN ERICSON   139

3. POLITICS OF TIME

*Year Zero: The Temporality of Revolution
Studied Through the Example of the Khmer Rouge*
ANDRUS ERS   155

Ways of Warmaking
JENS BARTELSON   167

On the Historicity of Concepts: The Examples of Patriotism and Cosmopolitanism in Ellen Key

REBECKA LETTEVALL   179

Network and Subaltern: The Antinomies of Global History

STEFAN JONSSON   189

Historians' Picnic in Kurdistan

DAVID GAUNT   199

4. LITERATURES OF TIME

Ambivalent Evolution: Euclides da Cunha, Olive Schreiner and the (De)Colonising of History

STEFAN HELGESSON   217

Histories Matter: Materializing Politics in the Moment of the Sublime

KRISTINA FJELKESTAM   227

History and Mourning

VICTORIA FARELD   237

Derrida on the Poetics and Politics of Witnessing

IRINA SANDOMIRSKAJA   247

Event, Crack-up and Line of Flight – Deleuze Reading Fitzgerald

FREDRIKA SPINDLER   257

5. REWRITING TIME

Rethinking the Industrial Revolution and the Rise of the West: Historical Contingencies and the Global Prerequisites of Modern Technology
ALF HORNBORG   269

Enlightened Prejudices: Anti-Jewish Tropes in Modern Philosophy
JAYNE SVENUNGSSON   279

Identity and Collective Memory in the Making of Nineteenth-Century Feminism
ULLA MANNS   291

Temporality and Metaphoricity inContemporary Swedish Feminist Historiography
CLAUDIA LINDÉN   301

Atomic Hindsight: Technology and Visibility as Factors in Historical Periodization
TROND LUNDEMO   313

Index   323
Authors   327

Preface

Where are we located in time? Are we still modern? Or are we post-modern, perhaps even post-post-modern? Or are we something for which we still have no name? In what age are we really living: the age of the atom, the age of information, or the age of some other technology still in the making? And what is the nature and locality of this "we" in the name of which these questions about temporal and historical location are constantly being posed? All such queries and concerns demonstrate the relevance of what Foucault once pointed out in relation to Kant's pamphlet on Enlightenment, that this time – "our" time? modern times? – is uniquely preoccupied with its own present, with its actuality, and its now. It is a time for which the temporality of time constantly matters.

In recent decades, the question of the temporality and historicity of knowledge has assumed increasing urgency in the human sciences. There are many sources for this intensified theoretical preoccupation. The emergence of new theoretical-critical impulses within the humanities brought with them new ways of conceptualizing time and historical understanding, captured, not least, in Lyotard's proclamation of the collapse of the "meta-narratives". Hermeneutics, critical theory, and deconstruction pointed to how the subject of knowledge is always already inscribed within the historical field that it is seeking to interpret, and also how the conceptualization of the past implies questions of justice, of application, and of redemption.

Marxist and social history, Feminist history, and Subaltern or post-colonial studies emphasized the necessity of thinking about who writes history and for whom. Together, they have shown how social transformation and power struggles are always reflected in the writing of history. More generally, they have strengthened the interest in the "uses of history", that is, in how the writing of history and the formation of historical consciousness are somehow always related to the present, to questions of suffering and oppression, and of possible liberation.

The break-up of the Soviet empire and the unification of Europe did not only lead to the emergence of a new political order. It also opened up the frozen histories of the national states of Europe, prompting a rewriting of the history of the entire continent and a reassessment of the legacy of national memory and history with all its traumatic repercussions. The new political landscape has stimulated new ways of thinking about history, starting with the debate about the "End of history", followed by attempts to rewrite European history and memory in the subsequent decades. As the late Tony Judt, a British historian, wrote in his celebrated history of post-war Europe some years ago, recent modernity has in a very concrete sense resulted in the collapse of "master narratives".[1] And, in a passionate coda to the book, he documents the upsurge of politics of memory and the creation of new monuments and institutes devoted to handling the traumas of a century of suffering and destruction without precedent.

Moreover, increasing interest in the multifaceted phenomenon of globalization is influencing how history is thought and written. As global information technology expands rapidly, human culture has entered a new phase, in which presence is produced and mediated technologically, and in which everyone becomes potential witness and recorder of historical events. Throughout this intensified preoccupation with the historical and the temporal can be detected also a tendency towards the commodification of history. Finally, the symbolic arrival of a new millennium focused attention on the role of calendars and of time-measurement as cultural practices, and the way they constitute patterns of meaning and self-understanding.

These examples serve to highlight only a few of the reasons for an increased sensitivity to the temporal and historical situatedness of contemporary Western culture, its preoccupation with the nature of the present, and the forms of telling time and narrating history. The writing of history, the shaping of historical consciousness, and the very experience of time are never just matters of the past but always, ulti-

---

1. Tony Judt, *Postwar. A History of Europe Since 1945* (London: Vintage Books, 2005), 7.

mately, signs of a future in the making. To theorize critically the ways in which a temporal and historical awareness is constituted is therefore also to explore the conditions for the emergence of what is to come.

Some years ago, a group was formed at Södertörn university in Stockholm with representatives from philosophy, intellectual history, gender studies and cultural studies in the ambition of creating a larger platform for researchers from a wide range of disciplines to explore the inner temporal and historical organization of the humanities, and to consider how time is viewed, represented, and used in the wake of recent critical theorizing. The tentative idea was to combine efforts not only from a broad spectrum of academic disciplines, but also from theoretical and methodological perspectives that often move in parallel orbits such as philosophical hermeneutics, deconstruction, media studies, gender theory, systems theory, and cultural theory. The hope was to combine a deeper understanding of historical interpretation and its focus upon meaning, trace, and witnessing with theories of aesthetic and technological representation of time, while also examining the way that this blends into the study of memory culture, its ethics and its pathologies, as well as its monuments and institutions, such as the museum and the archive.

By bringing together representatives from many disciplines, and by combining philosophers with historically oriented researchers with theoretical interests, the hope was also to bridge the often artificial divide between theorists and practitioners in the field of historical studies, thereby revitalizing discussion of the forms of historical writing, its motives, and its responsibilities in both an ethical and an epistemological sense. It was time to move beyond the stale debate between relativism and realism, between the "post-modernists" and their critics, which had dominated theoretical discussion in the humanities for decades, and to explore in unbiased ways the ethical, existential, and institutional conditions for, and possibilities of, historical research, historical narratives, and the shaping of historical memory.

Having outlined a series of general concerns and research themes, a number of scholars representing a broad spectrum of disciplines and academic institutions in Sweden were invited to propose research projects which they wished to pursue in the context of the proposed research grouping. The result of this work was the formulation of the research program "Time, Memory, and Representations: Recent Transformations in Historical Consciousness", consisting of 25 researchers from 12 different academic disciplines and seven universities. In 2009 it was given support from Riksbankens Jubileumsfond to initiate a six-year research program, which got under way in early 2010.[2]

In the outline program, the term "historical consciousness" was chosen as an overall category for gathering together the many different strands of research represented in the group. The word carries a productive polysemy. It can signify the way in which a person or culture is aware of the past, how one has knowledge and a memory of the past. But it can also points to the way in which consciousness in itself is historical, in other words, how the present is bound to, and conditioned by, belonging to the past. In the second sense, "historical consciousness" is not something that can be separated from the academic study and interpretation of past events. Instead it describes the conditions for historical knowledge and for historical truth.

In the study of a broad phenomenon such as historical consciousness, a number of different general avenues open up. The program seeks to capture these by means of the tripartite structure of Time, Memory, and Representation. The first term is meant to designate studies concerned with the conceptual organization of time and history, such as the basic cognitive categories of "past" and "present", but also "time" and "history" as such. It also concerns the formation of more specific categories for organizing historical understanding, such as "modern", "pre-modern", "post-modern", and how time is labeled in accordance with different natural or artificial indexes, such as the age of stone, the age of the atom, or the age of information, etc.

Historical consciousness also has to do with how the present is guided by and preoccupied with the past, perhaps even obsessed with the past, as here indicated by the general heading of "Memory". Today, such phenomena are often explored as "uses" of history. The term "use" can be taken as indicating that history is an object of choice and perspective, which it sometimes is. But often this is not so, in which case history presents itself as interpellation, as an inner call to bear

---

2. For a more detailed presentation of the program, see www.histcon.se.

witness, to remember, and to preserve a certain past, often of a traumatic nature. History then appears as a primarily ethical and political domain in which memory, nostalgia, repression and forgetting overlap in forging what are essentially contested spaces of historical awareness.

Under the label "Representation", the program gathers a series of research projects relating to the representation and mediation of time and history, aesthetically and technically, in literature, art, and film, but also in the institutional and spatial arrangements that produce and maintain historical consciousness, notably the museum. It is essential for the program's comparative approach that the boundaries between these general different orientations are not adhered to strictly. On the contrary, they are in most cases inextricably intertwined. Therefore, the general headings should be seen as a kind of heuristic framework, to indicate the interconnectedness between different lines of research rather than establishing strict boundaries between them.

Multidisciplinary work on this scale is an idea to which many people can subscribe in principle. But the fact of academic research is that it is usually carried out and disseminated in relatively restricted circles. In order to make it work, it is first necessary to establish a common frame of reference. The seminars during this first year have been primarily devoted to exploring common theoretical interest by organizing discussions about key texts from within the different disciplines involved in the program. Some of the seminars have also been organized around the work of members from the international board of experts. So far the group has hosted meetings with Hayden White, Walter Mignolo, and Aleida and Jan Assmann. These sessions have been extremely valuable for distinguishing more clearly the current situation and for developing a combined effort in exploring historical consciousness. They have all been taped and filmed, and will be eventually be made available in some format.

The present volume is the first collective publication from the group. The idea behind it is to present short samples of the kind of work that is to be carried out. The overall thematic here is Time and different ways of understanding and articulating the temporal, as organized along five different trajectories. These concern the conceptuality of time, monuments of time, the politics of time, the literatures of time, and, finally, the critical rewriting of time. Like the organization of the overall platform, these sections have a tentative character. There are several texts in this volume that could just as well have been put under a different heading. The structure of the book constitutes one possible map of a territory with many intersections and possible constellations.

The first section, "Concepts of Time", consists of six contributions which all raise fundamental questions concerning the conceptualization and understanding of time. It starts with Dan Karlholm's critical discussion of the problem of "The Contemporary" from the viewpoint of how it functions today as an organizing temporal principle of production and display in the art world. Peter Aronsson and Staffan Carlshamre develop different ways of defining History and the historical. Aronsson argues for a transhistorical concept of history on the basis of its basic defining dilemmas, and Carlshamre addresses the problem and possibility of historical truth. Hans Ruin contributes a text on the philosophy of time, comparing different ways of capturing the basic experience of the temporal. In the last two texts, Marcia Sá Cavalcante Schuback and Anders Olsson explore the nature and problem of tradition and canonicity from the viewpoint of philosophical hermeneutics.

The second section, "Monuments of Time", consists of five essays which circle in different ways around material monuments of time and ruins as well as museums, satellites and modern visual representations of times past. Mats Burström shows how the ruin presents a paradox for archaeology and its sense of time. Johan Hegardt critically analyses the linear narrative representation of history in Swedish national history museum displays. Johan Redin interprets the messages from human civilization directed toward the future included in the Voyager- and KEO-satellites and the "Crypt of Civilisation" at Oglethorpe University, as different ways of trying to salvage the present. Patricia Lorenzoni takes her point of departure in a historical monument to settlers in a region of the Amazonas which can be seen as legitimizing colonialism. In the last contribution, Staffan Ericson explores the temporal implications of a visual monument to a recently concluded historical era, the CNN-series "Cold War".

"The Politics of Time" contains five texts which concern the relation between time, history, and power. Andrus Ers focuses on the idea of "Year Zero" as a historical-philosophical category, taking examples from the French Revolution and the Khmer Rouge in Cambodia. Jens Bartelson and Rebecka Lettevall analyze the concepts of war, patriotism, and cosmopolitanism in critical adaptations of conceptual history. Stefan Jonsson discusses the contemporary political-philosophical concepts of "network" and the "subaltern", and how they enable us to think historical subjectivities in new ways. This section ends with a personal and more literary account by David Gaunt about his encounter with political power in conjunction with his investigation of a mass grave from the Armenian genocide in Turkey.

The fourth section, "The Literatures of Time," brings together five texts which all approach issues of time, narration, and history through works of literature. Stefan Helgesson studies strategies of decolonization through the work of Euclides da Cunhas och Olive Schreiner. Kristina Fjelkestam approaches the literary sublime as a historical-philosophical category in a reading of Fanny Lewald. Irina Sandomirskaja discusses the problematic nature of historical witnessing through the works of Paul Celan and Derrida. In an analysis of the work of Jean Améry, Victoria Fareld presents Mourning as a legitimate category for understanding and relating to traumatic history. And in the last text, Fredrika Spindler discusses how the concept of "event" in Deleuze's thought is developed through his reading of Scott Fitzgerald.

The fifth and final section, "Rewriting Time," combines texts which expose established historical narratives and confronts them with possible counter-narratives. Alf Hornborg gives an overview of, and makes a critical contribution to, the continuing attempt to write world history from a non-Eurocentric perspective, focusing on the role of technology in historical narratives. Ulla Manns raises the issue of inclusion and exclusion in First Wave feminist history writing, using the example of Alexandra Gripenberg. Claudia Lindén discusses critically how the history of the second wave feminism is written and understood. Jayne Svenungsson exposes the anti-semitism hidden within traditional, progressive Enlightenment narratives of historical development. In the final contribution, Trond Lundemo explores the historical classification of our age as "Atomic" and suggests an alternative way of viewing the relation between technology and time using an analysis of visualization.

PREFACE

The cover of this volume is an original adaption of an artwork by contemporary Swedish artist Jan Håfström. In his work, Håfström has often returned to the enigma of time, as memory and as history, combining painting, drawing and sculpture in excavations of both real and imaginary pasts. He has moved between monumental abstract representations of historical events and childhood drawings, exploring the intersection between personal and collective myth. The cover image comes from a recent series of collage drawings entitled "Incidents of Granma's Travel in America". The underlying surface is made up of pages torn from an old encyclopedia from the time of his grandmother's journey. Onto these pages have been glued painted figures which create a personal pattern of hidden meanings and constellations on the surface of an alphabetically organized collection of human knowledge from a time past.

An encyclopedia is a strange combination of order and chance. It is organized according to a strict, sequential logic by which every entry can be located alphabetically. But on every page aleatory constellations emerge, creating uncalculated combinatorial meanings, as on the present page, where mourning, moving, and movie come together. This organized randomness is then broken up by Håfström's images and drawings so as to create a new imaginary encyclopedia, disturbing the significance of a presumably systematic order of knowledge. The artistic work thus also permits us to see and receive the given order as both gift and event.

It is hoped that the texts gathered here will also be read as such an imaginary encyclopedia, that is, as a systematic yet randomly organized body of voices and perspectives trying in different ways to think and to rethink what it means to exist and understand in and through time, to struggle with and against given orders of time, to tell new stories, and to anticipate new futures.

Stockholm June, 2011

Hans Ruin
Andrus Ers

1. *Concepts of Time*

On the Historical Representation of Contemporary Art

DAN KARLHOLM

> The 'contemporary' is a cultural élite... So the 'contemporary' has nothing to do with time, nor with age.
> *Wyndham Lewis* (1954)

This essay, which derives from my project "Art and the Passing Present: Contemporary Art in Time" considers some examples, and consequences, of representing contemporary art historically. What are the implications and effects of comparing "contemporary" art with "historical" art? How did these loose categories emerge, and when? How is representation linked to documentation? Rather than following the currently most authoritative account of contemporary art, according to which the epithet "contemporary" is reserved for new art that matches "the conditions of contemporaneity,"[1] I suggest an understanding of contemporary art as *actualized* art. I conclude by examining an artwork that proposes a wider application of the label "contemporary."

Diverging References of "Contemporary Art"

The attribute "contemporary" has been used in the Western-based art world throughout the twentieth century, and even earlier, either to denote someone or something of the same time, or as a synonym for "modern". In the last couple of decades, however, "contemporary art" has come to signify a specific kind of art situated within a specific historical space. The thrust of my argument in the following short essay is to complicate and, ultimately, question so restrictive a usage of this term. One clear merit of the rapidly evolving scholarly interest in issues of art and contemporaneity in recent years – specifically in the wake of massive investment in this sector of the art market since the 1990s, and the gradual demise of postmodernism as a definitional paradigm for contemporary art – is that it invites us to rethink the domain of art history, both from the vantage point of its past-present and that of its continuously-expanding present "past."

The two dominant usages of this adjective in the discourse on art since the 1990s are: 1) the most conventional, roughly chronological use, according to which "contemporary" art is new, recent, current or modern, or pertains to the present moment, era, etc: and, 2) a historical usage, relating to art that belongs in a specific space in time more or less explicitly historicized as the contemporary period.[2] While the first usage relates principally to us, and the second to other periods, application of the former within the historical space of the latter makes it difficult to tease out their various implications. The former usage discriminates synchronically among co-existing contemporary candidates, while the latter, more absolute, use discriminates diachronically within a putative succession of movements or periods. The first of the two is the more normative, offering itself as commonsensical, while the second is more descriptive. Even so, such a clear-cut distinction is ultimately impossible since both are constrained by the evaluative decisions that underpin all modes of historical discourse. The first usage operates with a relative chronology that has existed for all of the period now known as modernism, while the second usage, based on an absolute chronology, has only been applied quite recently, since the putative demise of modernism and postmodernism. In short: the former, "contemporary" usage of "contemporary" is old, while the latter, "historical" usage of "contemporary" is new. What could thus be identified as contemporary art in the first sense of the word, that is, recently produced – presented at a gallery, perhaps, and reviewed in a recent issue of an art journal – may conflict with the latter usage of the word, which could cover a key work, say, by Jackson Pollock from the late 1940s, that would appear "historical" rather than "contemporary" according to our first definition. Not all specialists would draw the line at 1945, however, but rather extend the threshold to the 1950s or 1960s, or even the 1980s or 1990s.[3]

HISTORICAL REPRESENTATION & CONTEMPORARY ART

Comparatively contemporary

Every work of art that is represented as contemporary is brought within a *pantemporary* sphere of history, which is also, by definition, competitive by being comparative. An isolated work or artifact cannot be con-temporary. There is no such thing as a contemporary artwork per se, since the very term presumes a frame of reference: except for the category of art, it is compared either to time or to us. The latter two terms have often been sandwiched into *our time*. Within the spectrum of historical representation (as embodied in books, courses, exhibitions, and so on) a work effectively competes for attention with every other unit in the system. Like its contemporary relevance, the work's historical meaning and literal originality are only established, however implicitly, by this comparison. A work deemed contemporary is thus directly related to other equally contemporary, or radically non-contemporary, works. Its singular identity is the fruit of a comparison, however unconsciously or reluctantly established, with the entire category of historical works of art. Many advocates of contemporary art would, of course, assign it to a liminal space outside or beyond history altogether, but to make a designation such as "contemporary" meaningful, history is arguably the unavoidable other term. Moreover, explaining why something counts as (contemporary) art at all requires a historical framework for the gradual transformation of the concept and practice of art in the postwar period. The value attached to the contemporary and the historical derives from their respective positions at opposite ends of a spectrum ranging from "new" to "old" (the parameter of age, which is relative to the object as such) and from "now" to "then" (the parameter of temporal modes, which is relative to us and to time). Furthermore, the value and status of much art today hinge not only upon its organic relationship to history, but upon its space of exhibition or topological representation, which, in turn, depends upon a historically conceived and continuously maintained definition of art that defines, in turn, all the spaces of art – whether pavilions, fairs, galleries, or art museums.[4]

DAN KARLHOLM

The historical emergence of the contemporary

Let us consider "contemporary" as the correlated offspring of history, and vice versa. Between the late eighteenth century and circa 1870 in Europe, "contemporary" became the differing other of a new, coherent unity; history (often capitalized as "History" in order to distinguish it from mere histories). As Reinhart Koselleck has noted, the gradual establishment of a "new time" congealed into a unique period: *Neuzeit*. As a consequence of this semantic innovation, the very word for "time" in German came to connote "contemporary": *Zeitgeschichte* is the counterpart of "contemporary history".[5] Given that all history is at some point literally contemporary with those experiencing or remembering it (i.e. in the first sense above), history is established in the modern period as non-contemporary, non-present: past. History, in the new understanding of the word, a *Kollektivsingular*, produces itself, and this object or product – history itself – is preconditioned by its non-historical other: the contemporary. This is to suggest that *the contemporary* is not just a relational universal but historically produced during the period of so-called Enlightenment. According to Michel Foucault, Immanuel Kant's response to the question "What is Enlightenment? (1784)" amounted to "a reflection on 'today' as difference in history and as a motive for a particular philosophical task."[6] For F.W.J. Schelling, too, it seems that the past is only constituted when it has been forcibly separated from the present, and that the present, likewise, only assumes its final form by means of this disjunction.[7] Friedrich Nietzsche's critical observation in 1874 that historical consciousness threatened to pervade and overwhelm contemporary life highlights a problem unique to this historical period, which has been called *the* historical period in a qualitative (i.e. new) sense.[8] It is during this period that contemporaneity begins to assert itself in new ways, because of the way history was increasingly experienced as burdensome by its then-"contemporary" subjects. Those now theorizing about this development would benefit from extending their frame of reference in this way since the post-1945 trajectory is arguably too long, too obviously historical to make sense to young artists now working with "contemporary art," and far too brief to allow the discourse on the contemporary vis-à-vis the historical to be put into perspective. While the latter half of the nineteenth century was the *historical* period, giving way to the *modern* or *modernist* period of the twentieth century, we have supposedly entered a period or state beyond both of these terms. Not historical, modern, or postmodern, this *contemporary* period is stamped by a hegemonic synchronicity which is partly literal and partly a sign or projection. Taken to its logical extreme, however, an all-embracing synchronicity ultimately ceases to be counterposed to history, since the historical or recent past, what remains of it, will also be covered by and included within the synchronous spectrum. What is left behind is rather the diachronic framework of analysis itself, which conceived of identities according to their place within a developmental scheme of things.

The Precession of Representation

Representation may be thought of as re-presenting a previous presence, but my argument is that representation does not succeed but rather precedes the making of a contemporary work of art. No work of art, that is, is born contemporary (or is, again, contemporary *per se*); it belongs, not to the natural, but to the symbolic; not to the plainly temporal, but to the social and cultural order of things, being dubbed "contemporary," i.e. represented as contemporary, only if it succeeds in meeting the relevant criteria of the day. If so, from that moment on, it may be labeled "contemporary" as a token of its artistic ennoblement. One of the forms taken by representation is exhibition; another is documentation, which is not just an operative mode that preserves works of art for posterity. Documentation increasingly forms part of the medium by which art presents itself to the world. In such cases, documentation is not a *post hoc* enabler of artistic appreciation; rather, it actually produces the art. And it does so with the future history of the piece in view. In an environment replete with threats of extinction, extending the life-expectancy of the work beyond the next generation of soft- and/or hardware updates (to which *all* works today are ultimately subsumed, whether digital or analogue) requires the work to formulate a survival plan, a strategy for ensuring its existence beyond its immediate, merely contemporary, being.[9] This forces contemporary artists to take history into account in a very material way, indeed, much more so than their professional predecessors were required to do. These latter could rely on an academic training in which issues of duration, skill and the longevity of art were absolutely central. History was projected into their works from the beginning. Today, even artists who object to preserving the materiality of their work have to think about burial procedures. No-one can afford to ignore completely the afterlife of their art.

The Prospect of Actualization

The established understanding of contemporary art is not only in tune with the market vogue for art marked contemporary, it is also historicist and essentialist in a way that perpetuates the modernist conception of history that became dominant in the nineteenth century. On this view, in order to be regarded as "contemporary", a work of art must have a recent provenance since its historical essence, originality, or ontology is perceived as indissolubly linked to its particular historical emergence, that is, its origin, as first theorized by Hegel. This has been the model, by and large, for the academic discipline of art history from the mid-nineteenth century to our own time – a "metanarrative," indeed, that was supposedly shelved by "the postmodern condition."[10] Transformations of the avant-garde art scene between the 1950s–1960s to the present have come to disassociate – in theory at least – the work of art from the immediate circumstances of its material production or origin in a specific moment in time. With the idea – derived partly from a kind of "Duchamp position" that only became established in the postwar period – that an artwork can constitute whatever the artist chooses, new or old, the historicist myth of origin of the work of art itself or the object of art, has effectively been made parenthetical; the balance has shifted from the work to the creative beholder – whether artist, public or curator – from object to subject, from work to text and context in the here and now.

While Hegel was prone to contextualize the work in its unique historical environment, Hans-Georg Gadamer locates the understanding of the work within us, at a historical distance from the work that can only be bridged by our creative contribution. Another important facet of Gadamer's thinking relates to what he calls "effective history" (*Wirkungsgeschichte*), from which it follows that there is no work of art as such, only works of art that are continuously formed, and even transformed, within their different interpretative environments. A work of art is peculiarly non-temporal, according to Gadamer,[11] a claim which can be read as non-Hegelian. Paradoxically enough, the work is also *only* temporal, i.e. without a fixed identity or centre of gravity in its historical position, since it is determined by shifting readings and usages over time. The artwork is thus established by a performative gesture that, in turn, presupposes acknowledgement by the art world. The artist activates as "art" something that previously was not art, because it was either unfinished (the craft-based principle) or just an ordinary object (the "readymade" principle). The artist's position mimics that of the curator, who has the power – a power that inheres in the position, not the person – to put something on show *as* "art." The most distinguished artistic embodiment of this artist-as-curator model, upon which a great deal of contemporary art today depends, is, of course, Marcel Duchamp, whose tilted urinal of 1917, inscribed with the pseudonym R. Mutt and entitled *Fountain*, is arguably one of the most important works of art of the twentieth century. This piece has gone down in history as un-exhibited since, shortly before its disappearance, it was excluded from the exhibition of the Society of Independent Artists in Paris to which it had first been submitted. It survives and thrives, however, with all the power of myth, and, more concretely, in a contemporary photograph by Alfred Stieglitz as well as in several signed copies authorized as "originals" by the artist in the 1960s. Paradoxically, this historical non-event was eventually to inaugurate the exhibitionist paradigm by which the status of "art" is *de facto* bestowed on anything that is exhibited to the art world, provided that it is received and acknowledged as such. The so-called "institutional theory of art" that emerged in the United States in the 1970s can be seen as a response to the conundrums which the belated arrival of "Duchamp" in the 1950s and 60s presented to the art world.[12]

As a corollary to the "readymade" principle, I would like to suggest a different understanding of contemporary art, as *actualized* art. Since the current state of art theory allows for anything in principle to be or become "art" – subject to certain circumstances that are, in practice, defined by the art system or art world – there is no reason why old art could not be included on the list of current candidates for artistic status.[13] It is not only found objects, consumer items, concepts or organic matter that can become art; historical art, no matter its age, can now also become "new" art, i.e. "contemporary" art, if it is brought to the attention of the contemporary public and presented as having contemporary relevance. Such an understanding would, once and for all, abandon Hegel as a theoretical model for defining art, by historicizing it in terms of its specific birthplace. It would be more attuned to that phenomenological procedure by which an encounter with art is always new insofar as it makes the work seem new upon each encounter, thereby crossing the boundary between subject and object, or present and past, which the old dichotomies had established and upon which the entire modern discipline of analyzing art and images relies. The modern and modernist art historian did not deal with modern or contemporary works at all. The privileged imagery of art history was historical works of art, which demanded that the analyst carefully calibrate the historical distance between object and viewer in order to avoid falling into an anachronistic trap or proceeding unhistorically. Spatial distance was also required since the works were meant to be seen from a certain angle or ideal point of view. Phenomenology contributes to the disrupting of such notions and the crossing of such boundaries.

Almost always contemporary?

My concluding remarks take their cue from a "contemporary" artwork by Maurizio Nannucci. The work, which consists of a sentence in capital neon letters mounted on a preexisting wall, says: "all art has been contemporary." Nannucci works within a conceptualist tradition, in obvious proximity to Joseph Kosuth and Jenny Holzer. This particular work, however, strikes me as interestingly flawed, although I might be accused of taking it too literally (i.e. literally reading it). Whatever wit or novelty this proposition may have stems, arguably, from the more conventional sense of "contemporary art" that it ostentatiously questions yet ultimately reinforces: only new or recent art is contemporary. Not so! What seems like a quaint proverb from the seventeenth century reminds us that once upon a time all the old stuff was also young and "contemporary." "Contemporary" in this sentence becomes synonymous with "new," i.e. literally devoid of content. Is this to provoke a debate about the temporal limits of contemporary art, to make old art relevant, or to challenge the hyped-up presentism of contemporary discourse? My first reformulation of this sentence would simply be: *some art has been contemporary*. The adjective here refers to a highly valued contemporaneity that differs from the past which has preceded it as well as from accumulated history turned relatively obsolete by default. A historical qualification of this reformulation would be: *some art has only been contemporary for some time* (since the eighteenth century). To proclaim all art "contemporary" in this (past) sense is to ignore the power relations operating in any current field of art, only a small part of which is defined as "contemporary," as well as to disregard the historical contingency involved in establishing the contemporary in its still current sense. My second reformulation seeks approval on different grounds: *all art is contemporary*. The adjective here refers not to contemporaneity or the contemporary, as a distinct construct of interests and a point of identification within a certain society, but to mere contemporaneousness, a relative synchronicity of all the art that still remains and thus shares the same time. Shifting the tense from past to present is key here. What "has been" is automatically no more, it is the mode of history and memory, rooted in Hegelian historicism. My second reformulation aims to substitute this historical mindset for a phenomenological procedure in which not merely each encounter with the work is new but the work itself remains always new, no matter its age, in the encounter. My final twist is that this second sense of contemporary (relating to contemporaneousness) may be coordinated with or superimposed upon the first sense (relating to contemporaneity) if we can accept the notion that "contemporary" art means actualized art – that is, any art, regardless of its physical genesis, which is actively brought into "contemporary play."[14]

Notes

1. Terry Smith, *What is Contemporary Art?* (Chicago & London: The University of Chicago Press, 2009).

2. The third, neutral use mentioned above according to which "contemporary" simply means "relative to someone or something of the same time" is used irrespective of period and warrants no further commentary here.

3. Dan Karlholm, "Surveying Contemporary Art: Post-War, Postmodern, and then what?," *Art History* 32:4 (September 2009).

4. Cf. Boris Groys, "The Topology of Contemporary Art," in *Antinomies of Art and Culture: Modernity, Postmodernity, Contemporaneity*, in Terry Smith, Okwui Enwezor, and Nancy Condee (eds.) (Durham & London: Duke U.P. 2008).

5. Reinhart Koselleck, *Futures Past: On the Semantics of Historical Time*, trans. Keith Tribe (Cambridge, Mass. & London: MIT Press, 1985), 231–66.

6. Michel Foucault, "What is Enlightenment?," in Paul Rabinow (ed.) *The Foucault Reader* (New York: Pantheon Books, 1984), 32–50.

7. Fredric Jameson, *A Singular Modernity: Essay on the Ontology of the Present* (London & New York: Verso, 2002), 24–25.

8. Friedrich Nietzsche, *On the Use and Abuse of History for Life* (1874), trans. Ian Johnston, rev. ed. 2010: http://records.viu.ca/~johnstoi/nietzsche/history.htm (2011-04-29).

9. Boris Groys, *Art Power* (Cambridge, Mass. & London: MIT Press, 2008).

10. Jean-Francois Lyotard, *The Postmodern Condition: A Report on Knowledge*, trans. Geoff Bennington and Brian Massumi (Minneapolis: University of Minnesota Press, 1984).

11. Hans-Georg Gadamer, *The Relevance of the Beautiful and Other Essays*, trans. Nicholas Walker and ed. by Robert Bernasconi (Cambridge: Cambridge U.P. 1986).

12. George Dickie, *Art and the Aesthetic: An Institutional Analysis* (Ithaca: Cornell U.P., 1974), Hal Foster, *The Return of the Real: The Avant-Garde at the End of the Century* (Cambridge, Mass. & London: MIT Press, 1996), Thierry de Duve, *Kant after Duchamp* (Cambridge, Mass. & London: MIT Press, 1998).

13. An example is *Documenta 12* (2007), the mega-exhibition of contemporary art in Kassel which featured art from the 1500's.

14. These Gadamerian terms are taken from Donald Kuspit, "The Contemporary and the Historical" (2005): http://www.artnet.com/magazine/features/kuspit/kuspit4-14-05.asp (2011-02-12).

The Productive Dilemmas of History

PETER ARONSSON

A concept's tenacious core

Both as word and concept, *history* in its broadest sense refers partly to the past itself and partly to narratives about the various realms of the world, natural as well as cultural. It can take the form of the rise and fall of nations, but also of strange customs, natural features, and animal life. Practical, useful knowledge.

This range of meanings, together with the applicability and contemporary relevance of historical knowledge, evokes all of the theoretical concerns that currently preoccupy Western thinkers, complicated by the additional factor that the past no longer exists. What can we know about events which took place before our time? Why should we know? Why and for whom should we narrate the past? These questions lie at the root of the enduring topicality of historical thinking and its *tenacious dilemmas*.[1]

My first thesis will be that the concept of history has a very general and tenacious core of formalized and communicated knowledge about the world. The framework of this general significance accommodates a series of essential, productive, and tenacious negotiations in the form of different kinds of history, scientific and otherwise. My second thesis will be that a very large part of this historiographical development takes place within these stable parameters The often dramatic emphasis on change in the historiographical tradition is the result of a focus upon transformational processes and a (successful) strategy of professionalization within the discipline of history. Traces of this duality are captured by commonplace expressions such as "nothing new under the sun" and "history never repeats itself" as well as in various theoretical paradigms. Here they will be presented as stable parts of a productive and contradictory whole rather than as an ambiguity to be removed by theoretical cleansing.

Various individuals and professions have regarded themselves as having a vocation, and some as being authorized to confer general validity upon their own version of history. Institutions such as museums, scientific disciplines, and various modes of preservation, presentation, and mediation have served to stabilize and sanction the means by which traditions are carried on. As a cultural construction, historical narratives are a communal resource insofar as they lay claim to a validity that goes beyond mere personal opinion.[2]

As a field of enquiry, history seeks to produce solid knowledge, and claims on the basis of its methods to be a guarantor of historical truth.[3] Aesthetic, ethical, and utilitarian considerations pose a threat to objectivity. The history of writing history in this way became the history of how limits were placed on the improper influence of considerations that were seen as falling short of the evidentiary requirements of intersubjective analysis. The most important advances in history writing in the nineteenth century were tied to methodological developments, which in turn coincided with an era in which history became the overarching form of knowledge for the study of culture.

That which can be explained can also be altered. History became simultaneously a subject and an object, both for itself and for us humans. The dialectic which was thereby created, according to Reinhart Koselleck and many others, is something specific to the modern era.[4] Their principal claim is that a rupture occurred during the French Revolution and the Enlightenment. Where previously history had denoted a series of significant narratives, the concept of History freed itself as its own object and subject. In their account, it has always been the case that "ohne Geschichte keine Erinnerung, keine Gemeinsamkeit, keine Selbstbestimmung sozialer Gruppen oder politischer Handlungseinheiten, dis sich nur im Medium gemeinsamer Erinnerung zusammenfinden können." Yet is was not until the Enlightenment that History became a concept on a par with, and an alternative to, such forces as destiny, God, violence, justice – in short, a foundational social concept capable of explaining processes, progress, development, and necessity. In his highly valuable discussion of the relationship of "the space of experience" and "the horizon of expectation", Koselleck has himself contributed to our understanding of history as an activity or practice. It is this aspect of his argument that I find most useful in the present context.

However, I am convinced neither that it remains productive to focus on change brought about by the Enlightenment, nor that progress can be achieved only by focussing on methodological questions. This perspective ignores fundamentally significant usages of history that have a longer provenance. By focussing exclusively on methodological developments (in truth, only a handful of the methods that have actually been used), the space for self-reflection in professional historiography has been severely curtailed, and the space for moral, aesthetic, and utilitarian reflection has been left to actors outside the academic domain.

The overarching purpose of this essay is to open up a space for historical-theoretical reflection that can absorb the modes of historical representation that have been created within the broader field of historical culture, expanding what has largely been a narrow study of methodological advances and the writings of canonical historians by those working in the fields of academic historiography or historical philosophy.

History is an act of communication and, in two senses, a collective form of knowledge. Its object is always a collective even when represented by a person or, indirectly, by studying others, as in Herodotus' history of the Persians. It lays claim to universal applicability, at least for the group whose narrative perspective it favours, the reading subject of communicated history. Rhetoric of this kind requires a public. Thus it has been all the way from Pnyx, the meeting-place for rhetoricians and the populace, not far from the Acropolis in Athens, where the first historians sought to convince their audiences of the necessity for action (to unite and fight), through the Renaissance city-states and the educational ideals of Humboldt University, up to the virtual communities of the internet generation. Despite being underdeveloped, the media- and public-history perspective on history can draw inspiration from an array of contemporary historical theorists. History is told about something, for someone, for various reasons. When the audience changes from slaves to serfs to citizens or consumers, it also changes the conditions under which history needs to be, can be, and should be written.

The domains and tools carved out by historians over a hundred years ago in order to consolidate their professional status today need to be supplemented with more interfaces for communication with society and people. The specialist journals, conferences, and ranks of professional advancement need to be connected with and develop the needs of society in a self-reflexive and critical dialogue. Currently, the strategic visions of research policy place a value only on technology research, and adapt the system of meritocratic evaluation accordingly, with an exclusive focus on narrowly conceptualized innovation systems and intra-disciplinary professional exchanges at the international level. It is a dire omen for those studying culture and for a society that needs academic disciplines with premodern origins, holistic, and pragmatic ambitions, and a vital engagement with the human predicament.

What I am proposing – namely, a dynamic thematizing of the historical dilemma that can make historical narratives and hence communication and dialogue relevant for longer periods of time and for different fields – is intended to make possible a historical-theoretical evaluation of ethical and aesthetic dimensions that can make history more reflexive (and thus more scientific) and equip us to highlight more forcefully its relevance for knowledge production.

I will begin by noting that there are numerous parallels between contemporary controversies in cultural theory and debate and similar exchanges in the early modern period and antiquity. This stems, in turn, from the fact that the concept of history has a very general significance, making it a kind of rag-bag containing every epistemological problem under the sun. I base this statement on the fact that these issues, which have been argued over for a long time, need to be understood as productive dilemmas that deserve to be sustained rather than quashed. The aim is to include human and social perspectives that stand in a more authentic and multi-dimensional relation to the human environment than our highly specialized academic discipline are capable of appreciating. This communicative entity requires the creation of more roles, which will assume key functions in the creation of history. The old division of labour in the humanities, which was integrated within a national evaluative schema, needs to be replaced by a more complex framework that is responsive to the ongoing renegotiation of value, identity, and utopia at the individual, local, and global level.

To focus exclusively on change and renewal is to conceal the underlying continuity that characterizes history as both concept and discipline. By foregrounding continuities in the form of tenacious dilemmas, it becomes possible to view the subject and historical narrative from a perspective that has long been suppressed within the academy.

Productive dilemmas

As a concept, history reflects and represents occurrences from the past. Whatever their form, these embody a series of tenacious dilemmas, tensions that stem not from some intellectual incoherence but rather from epistemological preconditions, the phenomenon of time itself, and the transitory character of human existence. Using these dilemmas as the backdrop for a reading of historiographical representations ranging from the ancient Greeks to our own era, I contend that they have, to a varying degree, been prominent and relevant in every age. This approach towards understanding the dynamic relevance of historical representations may be able to effect a renewal of the way history is used in our own time.

1. *Reality or representation.* In what sense does the past exist? Did it have an unambiguously independent reality, or do our belated efforts to interpret its remains in fact create the past? For decades, arguments among cultural theorists have taken the form of a struggle between a majority of historians, who defend a realist approach to knowledge, and a provocative postmodernist position which insists on the fluid and uncertain relation of knowledge to anything beyond discourse. Between them, a constructivist position has emphasized the formative power of knowledge while nonetheless emphasizing that it is constructed by "something". The various positions intersect with long-standing ontological arguments between materialists and idealists.[5]

2. *Science or art.* The answers to the preceding question lead onto the debate over whether writing history is a science or a creative artistic activity. Can historical research and the writing of history be pursued in the same fashion as the natural sciences, or does it require its own norms? The ideal of truly transparent representation, or at least the verifiable intersubjective method, is being continually reformulated in light of its dependence upon the aesthetic qualities, particularly narrative form, of historical representations. The perspectival, situational, and empathetic connectivity of a narrative position which joins present and past must be weighed against the necessity of a detachment that guarantees intersubjectivity, not individual preferences, will dominate a history that must serve as shared experience. These are paradigmatic positions which all writers of history act upon.[6]

3. *Living or dead history.* What are the conditions for history to be a living reality in contemporary society, rather than being treated merely as an archaic and meaningless phase of passing time? The duty to remember, the fear of forgetting, the desire to learn and predict – each of these positions generates both lightness and darkness, stories and oblivion. What belongs in the light changes according to the vanishing point chosen, yet it is not arbitrary. An array of possibilities can be discerned, including Friedrich Nietzsche's distinction between useful and harmful history, in which the former increases our room for manoeuvre, wisdom, judgement, victories, or revenues.

4. *Unique descriptions or rule-governed patterns.* Is knowledge best presented descriptively, by means of illustrative narratives and accounts, or nomotetically, by means of general laws? Since Aristotle history has typically been seen as required to present unique occurrences, while science seeks out general laws. History teaches only the particular and superficial aspect of past events, while poetry and theory supply its wider underlying truths. As far back as the ancient Greeks, however, history was already associated with the chronological and sequential investigation of how significant events had entailed consequences, and with the rhetorical presentation of these events as a whole. This connection between active event and history creates historical narratives which are politically and ethically relevant.[7] Since the nineteenth cen-

tury, the needle has swung between the ideal of explanation or understanding, that is, to answer the question "why?" with a causal relation or by means of presenting a new context.

5. *The particular or the whole.* Is history a long series of single events with no inner pattern other than chance? Can every individual have his or her own account of history, or does that presuppose the existence of and participation in society? What does a relevant context look like? Demands for broader context are not a recent invention. More than two thousand years ago, Polybius held that history could only be written in relation to a central sequence of events, in his case the birth and rise to dominance of the Roman Empire. In a number of respects, this approach is one of the strong contextual imperatives that have lasted over time: the development of the state through war, politics, and territorial change remains the framework of history even if its scope is widened to include economics, culture, and the world of ideas.

6. *Freedom and determination.* What degree of freedom do human beings have to make their own way into the future? How constrained are we by the traditions and conditions into which we are born? This dynamic is to be found in every historical account, and represents both the desire to present an overarching coherence and continuity and the desire to liberate ourselves from precisely these forces by using history as the model for an alternative future of creativity, imagination, and freedom. The clearest instance of this tension comes in Nietzsche's attack on the destructive aspects of the fatalism that frequently accompanies history writing. He called for engagement – whether in the form of solicitude, criticism, inspiration, or individuality – in order to break the trammels of fate.[8]

7. Are traces of the past *relics or narratives?* Questions of methodology have a long tradition, too. What are the surest ways of using traces from the past, and how should they be used? Does the best path to historical knowledge lie in temporal, spatial, or cultural proximity, or, quite the reverse, is distance needed in order to see and judge fairly? Historians have always had opinions on these topics. The methodological advances by historians around 1900 largely comprised a deter-

mination of what were genuine historical traces and what were later accounts of the period under investigation. Artefacts were considered to be reliable testimony where narratives tend to give rise to systematic doubts.

8. What *use* is historical knowledge? Does it form the basis for wisdom about life, a *Magistra Vitae*, or is merely a factual reconstruction for neutral purposes, or is the point that individuals for various reasons should derive enjoyment from the past? Is its primary value that it legitimates the ruling order or that it is capable of supplying the tools for criticizing it? Thucydides wrote in order to teach the art of war. Polybius was more expansive, giving reasons for why general history, pursued through the personal research of a learned man, offered the soundest foundation. They were followed by a succession of thinkers who continued to argue that history was a source of wisdom: Machiavelli, Montesquieu, and Hume, right up to the historical sociologists of our own era, among them figures as diverse as Jürgen Habermas, Michel Foucault, and Charles Tilly. This holds doubly true for the historians of public debate: in our day conflicts and crises are invariably interpreted in the light of previous experiences that are more typically chosen on the basis of their ideological convenience than from any desire to acquire knowledge without preconditions. On the other hand, there are always the professional historians and their Stoic antecedents: a genuine seeker after truth demands an exactness and an objectivity that are not governed by a desire to divert or startle contemporary onlookers. It is harder to find principled defenders of history writing for pleasure, but its practitioners are numerous.

9. Critique or confirmation. A central aspect of the question of history's value relates to whether its overall purpose is to create a stable context of identity and stability, or, its opposite, the ability to criticize and the historicizing of all *a priori* considerations. Powerful forces confront each other at this point, with a hardening of the polemical tone and a reversion to political positions: the first tendency inclines towards conservative stability as a social logic, and the second hopes for radical changes driven by reform or revolution. Yesterday's critics and victorious revolutionaries easily become tomorrow's conservatives. The need to hold up positive, and occasionally negative, models capable of encouraging progress is among the most timeless characteristics which history telling shares with religious myths. Legitimacy and power rest on it.

Conclusions

The productive dilemma outlined here gives rise to fields of discussions with shifting centres of gravity, hybrids, and mixtures in which unqualified extremism is a rare occurrence. Our review thus does not result in a choice of the correct means of practising history but rather enables us both to appreciate in just how many forms it can take place and to assess the motivating forces and consequences which they entail at the level of individual and society. It creates the possibility for a richer perspective on the creations of history, their use and potential, than is typically the case with more educational history textbooks. In so doing, my aim has been to strengthen its scientific rigour by adducing new dimensions and a greater degree of communicative reflexivity, and thereby enhancing the relevance of history as a discipline within the framework of a broader, vital, and more diverse historical culture. This approach is intended to defend the most banal as well as the most ambitious intellectual concerns of historiography. Its purpose is not to rescue such practices for the university but to offer a serious reply to the wider historical culture.[9]

Position-taking in these dilemmas is determined to a great extent by the intellectual agendas at stake in various communicative contexts. They are always connecting and negotiating cognitive, normative, and aesthetic values. Within this matrix, the value of knowledge is continually being renegotiated. More specifically, the professionalization of history-writing with which we are familiar has benefitted from the need for a neutral arena where those in power negotiate the meaning and content of history. Instead of fearing such exchanges, we should increase our respect for the different forms of logic – existential, ideological, aesthetic, economic – that are necessary for the dynamic task of historical reflection. Reflexive care for these tenacious but productive dilemmas should increasingly attend to its deep roots in cognitive, ethical, and aesthetic dimension – or in order to follow Plato on the relation between the true, the just, and the beautiful. This reflexivity cannot be cultivated in isolation but must be shaped in a communicative context. History is knowledge of something that has been given form – for someone and for something. The former is explicit, the latter often implicit. Historical study, as I have argued, should be reflexive, representational, and knowledge-promoting in each of these directions.

Notes

1. Martin Kylhammar, *Den tidlöse modernisten: en essäbok* (Stockholm: Carlsson, 2004), 224.

2. For a longer analysis, see Peter Aronsson, *BeGreppbart – Historia* (Malmö: Liber, 2011).

3. Rolf Torstendahl, *Introduktion till historieforskningen: historia som vetenskap* (Stockholm: Natur och kultur, 1971).

4. Otto Brunner, (ed.), *Geschichtliche Grundbegriffe. Historisches Lexikon zur politisch-sozialen Sprache in Deutschland. Bd 3, H-Me*, (Stuttgart: Klett-Cotta, 1982); Reinhart Koselleck, *Critique and crisis: enlightenment and the pathogenesis of modern society* (Oxford: Berg, 1988); Reinhart Koselleck, *Erfarenhet, tid och historia: om historiska tiders semantik* (Göteborg: Daidalos, 2004).

5. Keith Jenkins, Sue Morgan, and Alun Munslow, (Eds.), *Manifestos for history* (Abingdon, Oxon ; New York, N.Y.: Routledge, 2007).

6. Hayden White's identification of different tropes has contributed to this discussion.

7. Per Landgren, *Det aristoteliska historiebegreppet. Historieteori i renässansens Europa och Sverige* (Göteborg: Acta Universitatis Gothoburgensis, 2008), s. 30f.

8. Friedrich Nietzsche, *Unzeitgemässe Betrachtungen. Zweites Stück: Vom Nutzen und Nachtheil der Historie für das Leben.* (Leipzig: E.W. Fritzsch, 1874).

9. Peter Aronsson, *Historiebruk – att använda det förflutna* (Lund: Studentlitteratur, 2004).

Is Every Tale a Fairy Tale?

STAFFAN CARLSHAMRE

Can stories be true? An affirmative answer seems so obvious as to be hardly worth stating. We know that some stories are lies and others, by contrast, are not. We know that some stories are fictions, as in a novel or a fairy tale, while others are factual, as in a news report or a history book.

Nevertheless, there are narrative skeptics, philosophers (starting perhaps with Louis Mink and Hayden White) who argue that, strictly speaking, a story is never true: narrativity implies fictionality.[1] Historians and journalists may, of course, aim for truth and factuality in the stories they tell, but they will, according to the skeptic, inevitably fail. Denying their own fictionality is just one more way in which purportedly factual stories falsify reality.

Such sweeping denials of the truth claims of narratives may seem over the top, but common sense is not without its own doubts about the trustworthiness of stories. We know that in telling a story we sometimes strain the truth to make the story better, while at other times we aim for accuracy, to the possible detriment of story values. We know that we have to be careful with stories that are "just too good to be true". So here is a sneaking suspicion: as we aim for more accuracy, story values shrink, and as we boost story values we need to take more liberties with the truth. The closer to the truth, the lesser the story, and at the limit there is no story left, just a mess of reality.

Starting from observations about history as an academic discipline, Mink and White take aim at what they see as a kind of naiveté about historical knowledge. If they are right, however, their thesis will apply to purportedly factual storytelling of all kinds, and presumably with greater force in contexts where the constraints of historical methodology are not applied. My subject in this article is factual storytelling as such, and I want to avoid side issues such as whether narrative form is really essential for historical knowledge.

It would be unfair to concentrate only on the negative argument of Mink and White, as if their primary ambition were to criticize or disparage storytelling. On the contrary, they are adamant that narration is an extremely important cognitive form, on a par with theory-building and metaphor. If anything, they want to defend it against being reduced to mere description of facts. They are less explicit, however, about the specific cognitive contribution of narrativity, often being content with metaphors and catchphrases about "configuring" reality or "giving meaning" to events.

The negative and the positive sides are not unconnected, of course. The fictionality thesis is important because stories are important, and, in particular, because factual stories are important. Why are factual stories important? Because they combine factuality with the power to motivate, to "sell" us actions and attitudes, and they do this precisely by virtue of their purported factuality.

Where's the story?

In order to consider whether narrativity implies fictionality, we must first be clear about what a story is. There are concepts of narrativity so austere and undemanding that they obviously leave no foothold for a fictionality thesis, and there are notions of a story that builds fictionality into the very concept, making the thesis a triviality. Here, I want a conception of narrative that makes the fictionality thesis worth considering but not a foregone conclusion. I will start at the minimalist end and then see what needs to be added to get the discussion going.

Trying to identify what every conceivable story has in common, the minimal condition that something must fulfill in order to be a story, we may come up with something like Gerald Prince's suggestion that "a narrative is the representation of at least two real or fictive events or situations in a time-sequence, neither of which presupposes or entails the other."[2] Let's take an actual example, a piece of historical writing that fits this description perfectly. Here's what one of the oldest Chinese annals tells us about a certain year in the history of the state of Lu:

IS EVERY TALE A FAIRY TALE?

In the twenty-fifth year, in spring, the marquis of Ch'in sent Joo Shuu to Loo with friendly inquiries.

In summer, in the fifth month, on Kwei- ch'ow, Soh, marquis of Wei, died.

In the sixth month, on Sin-we, the first day of the moon, the sun was eclipsed, when we beat the drums and offered victims at the altar of the land.

The duke's eldest daughter went to her home in Ke.

In autumn, there were great floods, when we beat the drums and offered victims at the altar of the land, and at the gates.

In winter, Duke Hwan's son Yëw went to Ch'in.[3]

Suggestive, to be sure, but hardly what we would usually think of as a story. Nevertheless, a technical notion of the annals is important as a sort of baseline for more ambitious conceptions of narrativity. When a story is supposed to configure or give sense to something, that something is precisely the annals, a collection of situations and events ready to be fashioned into a meaningful whole. We can even fashion, as a theoretical tool, the idea of the complete annals, a totality of facts from which the story is built through the dual operations of *selection* and *configuring*.[4]

So what must be added to the annals to make a story? Presumably, the relevant facts and events must not only be *listed* but must also be *connected* in a certain way, and the usual suggestion is that the pertinent types of connection are *causal*.[5] Causality would function both as a principle of selection and as a form of configuration: we select events that are important causal antecedents or consequences of things that we for some reason wish to focus on, and we display them in a way that highlights their causal significance.

Still, causal facts are just more facts. We are looking for a gestalt property of a discourse, something that makes it different from the sum of its parts. "So we know the facts", an editor would say. "but where's the story?"

The most time-honored, and still most popular, idea is that the relevant property has to do with "closure". A story has a beginning, a middle and an end, says Aristotle, and many have agreed. For Hayden

White, the *gestalt* properties of stories stem from the fact that a story always belongs to a specific genre, one that imposes an overall pattern on a chain of events. He is usually content to borrow the list of genres from Northrop Frye, who argued that every story is either a romance, a tragedy, a comedy, or a satire. I won't go into details about the defining characteristics of each genre. Suffice it to say that the most important trait of each is that it moves towards a specific type of ending or resolution. Mink is even more abstract: the defining property of stories is that they have endings at all, that they move from a beginning towards an end through a logic of development.

As has often been pointed out, however, many perfectly good stories lack closure without being deficit in narrative structure.[6] Some are just unfinished, such as Musil's *Man Without Qualities*, but others lack closure as a matter of principle. Sitcoms and traditional saga cycles are examples from the realm of fiction, while national histories, biographies, and chronicles, such as those of Froissart and Gregory of Tours, offer an equivalent in the realm of fact. Such stories may be rich in recurring patterns and intricate connections, but they end by accident or fiat, rather than because they reach a logical conclusion. Something similar may be said of the powerful overarching narratives that shape the mind of an epoch, such as the story of the Cold War or the War on Terror. The Cold War may have come to an epic end with the fall of the Berlin Wall, but that was also the moment when it lost its grip on us: the important stories are those in which we live, not those that are already closed. Such overarching stories also function as matrices, providing shape to subordinate plots that illustrate and contribute to the totality.

Another popular idea is that a story needs a unified subject – a person, a nation, a people, an institution, or an epoch. But what is a unified subject? Most accounts seem to think of it as a unified object: some one thing that the story is about. But even *The Spring and Autumn Annals* have that; they are about the state of Lu. To get any further, we must take the notion of a subject in a stronger sense, as the one *whose story* it is, something that has interests and desires and can sustain the identification and emotional investment of an audience.

To elaborate on this idea, I will explore the French Connection. The French narratological tradition, with its roots in Vladimir Propp's work on fairy tales, is rich in ideas about the gestalt properties of stories.[7] In Greimas, we find, among other things, the theory of *actants* – direct descendants of Propp's heroes and villains, donors and helpers (not forgetting the Princess and the King) – according to which each story is structured around the striving of a *subject* to attain an *object* for the sake of a *recipient*, helped by *allies* and opposed by *enemies*.[8] In Lévi-Strauss, we find the observation that stories revolve around value-laden conceptual oppositions that are fundamental to a culture.

To get an interesting story going, we need *conflicts*, a system of *values*, and a number of *agents* assigned to dramatic *roles* within the narrative structure. These things are not unrelated. Values are most often organized into oppositional pairs – freedom versus oppression, wealth versus poverty, modernity versus tradition, East versus West, North versus South, good versus evil – and dramatic conflicts take place not just between people, but between people representing the contrary poles of such oppositions. Agents take up their narrative roles in the pursuit of values, helping and opposing each other, to end up as winners or losers.[9]

The War on Terror is a near-perfect example of a story structured in this mold: America (subject) wants Freedom (object) for the sake of Humanity (recipient), helped by her Allies and opposed by the Terrorists.

We might say that there is something essentially human about stories, or at least about the kinds of stories that we are here trying to nail down. They are about human agents, or about anthropomorphic entities conceived in the image of human agents, which are taken as having goals and desires that may be fulfilled or frustrated. Some have gone even further in this direction, arguing that narrative structure is essentially identical with the structure of action. Each agent, says Claude Brémond, is the hero of his own story.[10] To act is to situate oneself as a subject in relation to a desired object, weighing up one's allies and opponents (animate and inanimate), and asking for whose sake the act is undertaken. This is also a way of understanding the importance of our narrative abilities: the complexity of the actions I can undertake is proportional to the complexity of the stories I can understand.

This parallelism between stories and action description must not be taken too far, of course. Perhaps we might think of an action description as a *basic story*: an action is the smallest chunk of reality that can serve as the subject of a complete story. Most actual stories – for example, most literary stories – are more or less complex interweavings of basic stories.

From its connection with action, we can understand much of the power and poverty of narrative. To act, I must situate myself in a story. To act collectively, we situate ourselves as partners in a shared story; again, the potential for action and the potential for narration go hand in hand. As we do so, however, we forget that other people are not there to play supporting roles in our stories, but are the heroes of their own.

Fictionality

It may seem as if we have already cut the discussion short by concentrating on a conception of narrativity for which the fictionality thesis is trivial. In terms that White, Lévi-Strauss and Barthes would recognize, stories are Myths, tools for organizing reality in terms of a value system. But according to a venerable tradition, values themselves are not real, but projections of human affections and attitudes. And if values are not real, it seems to follow that neither are stories.[11]

But, wait, hasn't something gone wrong here? Actions are real, surely, but then some action descriptions must presumably be true. And if stories are action descriptions, some stories must be true as well. Where's the catch?

White's basic idea is that it is the historian's values which give shape to the story, and that rhetorically effective historians manage to convert their audience, where necessary, to their own value perspective. But nothing in the above argument makes this necessary. What the story must have are *agent values*: driving factors that start the action and keep it going as long as the story lasts. But such values are inside the world of the story, so to speak, not projections from the outside, and are as real as the agents themselves.

Once we distinguish between agent values, author values, and audience values, it is obvious that there are many possible combinations to take into account, – and even more if we consider the possible clashes of value between different agents within the story. Many narrations presuppose the harmony of all three value systems: the author and the audience wish for the protagonist what she wishes for herself. And the defender of objectivism may point to the possibility of a "view from nowhere," a narration where the author imposes no external value frame at all.[12] The historian can tell the story of Napoleon as a tragedy, without subscribing to the values of the Emperor or to any branch of French nationalism; it suffices to ascribe certain goals and values to Napoleon and see them frustrated at the end of the tale. And if Napoleon actually had those goals and values, then the story is indeed a tragedy – for him, of course. We would avoid ascribing merely relative truth to absolute stories by ascribing absolute truth to relativized stories.

Perhaps matters are not so simple, however. One of the dangers of good stories is that they don't leave us cold. Stories work by identification and immersion, and if these things do not happen, the story has failed. Stories are not only based on values but are used to transmit and strengthen values, not by stating them explicitly but by putting them to work and forcing us to identify with them. This is the dilemma of the mafia film. You know that everything the hero does is wrong, and that he should go to jail, but that's not what you want to happen while you watch the movie.

There are two ways to explain this phenomenon. One is that, faced with an engaging story, we at least temporarily forget our own values and adopt those of the hero. The other is that we find a deeper level of values which we already share – values connected with striving, surviving, caring for our children, winning the respect of others – and which in the context justify the villain's actions.

Maybe the reification of values is inherent to storytelling, explicit relativization does not work, and White is right: a story is a tragedy or a comedy only in the eyes of the beholder. Maybe in theory we can go from the relative truth of absolute stories to the absolute truth of relativized stories. But it does not work this way in practice.

Conflicting stories

Whichever way we cut the cake, the gist of the problem seems to be that there are many stories to be told about the same piece of reality, stories that do not manifestly differ in truth value, once we have got the basic facts right. It does not even seem very important whether we say, with the skeptic, that none of these stories is true, or, we say, with the relativist, that all of them are true, each from its own perspective. And in many cases we readily accept such a plurality of equally valid perspectives. Any amount of fiction has been built around a polyphony of points of view – just consider *The Alexandria Quartet* or the novels of Dostoyevsky. In other cases, however, we do not accept such plurality, but strongly feel that we have to choose one story to the exclusion of others. Why? The answer, I think, is that we take stories to be in conflict when they relate to an underlying real conflict. Full-blooded stories are about conflict, and the conflicts between stories are part and parcel of the conflicts they are about.

The simplest form of conflict is what we may call *straight conflict*, in which two parties share the relevant values and this is precisely the source of the dispute. Territorial disputes between nations, rivalry in love, or inheritance struggles, are all straight conflicts in which the parties agree about what is at stake but have incompatible interests.

More interesting from the present point of view are *value conflicts*, in which the parties not only contest the stake but disagree about what that stake is. The classic example is the American Civil War, in which the Confederates claimed to be fighting for a constitutional principle and the Unionists claimed to be fighting for the abolition of slavery.[13] In a similar fashion, the American side in the War on Terror claims to be fighting for democracy and peace, but these are not the values which the other side professes to be against – instead basing their story on religious values and political independence. In value conflicts, opponents are fighting past each other in much the same way that the sides to a verbal dispute may be talking past each other.

Perhaps it is part of our contemporary dilemma that we no longer accept straight political conflicts? To justify our actions, we must rise above self-interest and base our claims on a higher value, one that the other ought to acknowledge; his failure to do so turns a conflict of interests into a conflict of values. But the other makes the same move from the other side, and from an impartial point of view one set of values may seem as noble as the other. To make my case, I must not only assert my own story but deny the story of my adversary. This generally takes one of two forms. Either I simply portray the other as the Dark Side, someone who actually wants Evil and is against the Good, as in *The Lord of the Rings*. But, as Plato pointed out, it is hard to imagine anyone really striving for Evil as such. The other option is to deny the sincerity of the avowed motives of the other: my own motives are as noble as can be, but the other just wants the oil.

In a value conflict, each side casts itself as the hero, and the other as the villain of a story he refuses to accept. For the neutral, both parties may appear to be within their rights and the conflict thus to be tragic in a profound sense. Once the opponents themselves come to admit this, it becomes hard to insist on fighting to the end; violence may give way to talk. By the same token, however, the parties' resolve to fight on depends on not admitting the view from the other side. And our gut reaction in the presence of an opposing story is not to deny it but to refuse to listen: "I don't want to hear it! And you certainly can't tell it to my children!"

It is easy to see the importance of such "story blindness" from the point of view of stories as guides to action. To be able to act, I must stick to the structure that my guiding story imposes on the situation. Even when we are not in the thick of action, following a story has a certain lived, almost perceptual quality that compels my full attention, and crowds out the competition. Perhaps an analogy with ambiguous images such as Jastrow's duck/rabbit is illuminating here. A duck cannot be a rabbit, but one picture may be a duck-picture and a rabbit-picture at the same time. And yet, although I know this perfectly well, I can only see one picture at a time. Seeing the rabbit-picture crowds out seeing the duck-picture.

Truth and stability

The fact that stories are relative to value-frames is one of the main reasons why we do not all read the same newspaper and watch the same TV channel. We want to send our own witnesses to every conflict because we want to hear the stories that we are prepared to believe and that can guide our actions and attitudes. We want to avoid those other stories, which would only confuse us and disrupt our ability to tell right from wrong. We reject those other stories, not necessarily as false, but in a more violent way: as non-stories.

We may strive for a more inclusive worldview, trying to encompass different viewpoints in a less partisan perspective, but, as we do so, we may have to modify our commitment to some of our strongest values, running the risk of ending up with no perspective at all.

Even short of that, however, we should resist the facile conclusion that, given factual accuracy, no story is absolutely true and all stories are relatively true. In fact, truth is not such an easy thing, even if we presuppose our own perspective. Our own storytellers can lie to us, can let us down, and make us regret that we ever believed them. How?

They can get the annals wrong, of course, whether by invention or mistake, and thereby mislead us about details. But, once again, this is not the sort of falsity that concerns us here. How can they get the story itself wrong? Mainly in the following way, I think: by omitting the details that would blow the story for us, had we been told about them. We know that they cannot tell it all. Of course they must choose what to include. But they are my eyes, and are supposed to tell me the story I would have seen if I had been there. The picture they give should be stable with regard to improved information. Better knowledge of the facts should fill in the details, but not disrupt the pattern.[14] If it does, the story is false, and if the narrators know the disturbing facts but don't tell me, then they have deceived me.

Comparison with ordinary inductive reasoning may perhaps be helpful. Suppose that I am presented with a certain conclusion supposed to be based on a body of inductive evidence. For the truth of the conclusion, it is not enough that it be supported by the evidence that is actually presented. It must also be stable with regard to all "future" evidence – all further facts that are relevant to it. If you are aware of the existence of damaging further evidence but fail to present it, you are guilty of deceit. Even if you are not aware of it, it will still undermine the conclusion.

The difference between inductive validity and narrative truth is that the criterion of relevance for potentially damaging evidence is in the latter case relative to a value frame. I venture the following definition:

> Factual story S is true for A = A would accept S if A had access to all the relevant factual information.

IS EVERY TALE A FAIRY TALE?

C.S. Peirce famously suggested that truth should be defined as acceptability in the long run: what is true is what an ideal community of observers would believe when all the evidence is in and has been processed according to the best scientific method. Story truth, I suggest, should be defined as acceptability in the long run for some more specific community of subjects, demarcated by their adherence to some persistent frame of values. There is no guarantee against bigotry, of course, but for most of us, maybe our roads will start to converge as we struggle to adapt our stories to the details of reality.

Notes

1. On Mink, see "Narrative Form as a Cognitive Instrument," in *The Writing of History: Literary Form and Historical Understanding*, ed Robert H. Canary and Henry Kozicki (Madison: U of Wisconsin P, 1978), 129–140. White has stated his views on numerous occasions since the publication of *Metahistory* (1973). Cf. for example "The Historical Text as Literary Artifact," in *Tropics of Discourse* (Baltimore and London: Johns Hopkins University Press, 1978) or "The Value of Narrativity in the Representation of Reality," in *The Content of the Form* (Baltimore: Johns Hopkins University Press, 1987).

2. Gerald Prince, *Narratology: The Form and Functioning of Narrative*. Janua Linguarum Series Maior 108. (Mouton 1982), p 4.

3. *The Spring and Autumn Annals*, translated by James Legge. Vol 5 of The Chinese Classics, p 109. Shang Hai 1935.

4. This is itself a metaphor, of course, which must not be taken too seriously. There is no temporal sense in which the annals are always given "before" the story, and perhaps no logical sense either; both Mink and White stress the holistic dependence of descriptions of events on the stories to which they belong.

5. This idea has a long history, but the best recent version of it is Noël Carroll's. See, for example, his "The Narrative Connection" (2000).

6. Noël Carroll, "Narrative closure." *Philosophical Studies* 135, no. 1 (August 2, 2007): 1–15.

7. Vladimir Propp, *Morphology of the Folktale*, 2nd edn (Austin: University of Texas Press, 1968).

8. A. J. Greimas, *Sémantique structurale* (Paris, 1966).

9. In *Du sens I* (Paris, 1970), Greimas develops this idea into a difficult but suggestive "generative grammar" of narratives, which starts from a "deep structure" of concepts organized into squares of opposing terms, and proceeds through various intermediate levels to the surface, where concrete agents perform concrete actions in relation to each other.

10. Claude Bremond, *Logique du récit* (Paris: Ed. du Seuil, 1973).

11. A big "if," to be sure. White's obvious willingness to conclude from something being value-laden to its not being fully real has lead some to describe him as a positivist in disguise, but I will not pursue this possible objection here. Cf. Lorenz, C. "Can Histories be True? Narrativism, Positivism, and the 'Metaphorical Turn'." *History and Theory* 37, no. 3 (1998): 309–329.

12. White would probably respond that the view from Nowhere is inevitably the view from Now-Here, from a present perspective left invisible by its very obviousness. But this is a thread that I must leave dangling at the moment.

13. I do not assert that these were the true motives on either side, of course. But they will do as an example.

14. Simon Blackburn gives a similar account of moral knowledge, in "Securing the nots," in Walter Sinnott-Armstrong and Mark Timmons (eds.), *Moral Knowledge?* Oxford: Oxford University Press 1996.

Time as Ek-stasis and Trace of the Other

HANS RUIN

How can we know and speak about time *as* time? Does time as such exist? Is time a *thing*? From its inception philosophical thought has been driven by the conceptual and experiential riddle of time. The attempts to master it have generated impressive conceptual constructions. Is it still meaningful to try to articulate something like a philosophical account of time? Is time not already dispersed into a multitude of *constructions* of time? From comparative anthropology we are familiar with the many different ways in which humanity has sought to master time through calendars and chronometers.[1] Merely broaching the task of a general theory of time seems to accept a questionable metaphysical premise. Yet there is a "Time" to which we continue to refer as an index when speaking of its different modes of representation, construction, and articulation, and to which standard scientific and political discourse is still unreflectively committed. Posited in this way, it requires continual scrutiny.

Here, I will rehearse briefly the two basic ways in which time has been understood philosophically – as measureable movement, and as consciousness of past, present, and future – represented by Aristotle and Augustine. My discussion stresses the critical potential of the Augustinian legacy, especially for a culture so obsessed with technical mastery over time as ours, and how it was taken up and developed in phenomenology, from Husserl to Derrida via Heidegger. Through the phenomenological attempts to describe fundamental time consciousness, Time or Temporality emerges instead as an original *ek-statis*, as dislocation and dispersion, and as synonymous with the event of meaning. Following the radicalized phenomenological analysis of time leads us beyond an understanding of subjectivity as interiority, toward the phenomenon of an intersubjective bond between the living and the dead, and to the constitution of tradition as both active memory and social coercion.

The historical account partly follows that of Paul Ricoeur in his magnum opus *Time and Narrative* (1985).[2] His account pays great homage to phenomenology, Husserl, and, in particular, Heidegger. His ultimate conclusion is still that the phenomenological account of time leads to an aporia, a dead-end of time, between the subjective and the objective, between the individual and the cosmic, which needs repairing or healing through a theory of narrative imagination.[3] Unlike Ricoeur, the present essay emphasizes the inherent discrepancy of time, what might even be called an original and unbridgeable "chasm" or "wound" of time.

The etymology of the word itself, *time, tid, zeit, temps, tiempo*, is considered by linguists to originate from the Indo-European root *di*, relating to "partition" (Sanskrit *dayate*, Greek *daiomai*). In recalling this origin of the word, we can sense the gesture by means of which we circumscribe and delineate a period and a sequence. When referring to time – any specific time – we reach for a shape and a contour, a horizon around what takes place. It is noteworthy in this respect that in the Homeric vocabulary the standard Greek term for time – *chronos* – is not used in the abstract sense of time as such, but only ever to denote a passage or sequence of events. For example, in the beginning of the *Iliad* when Odysseus takes the lead among the tired Achaeans, he urges them on with the words: "courage my friends, hold out for a time [*epi chronon*]" (Il B 299). By gesturing toward "time" he refers here to a phase of life to come. It is in the magnificent declaration of Anaximander (c. 600 BCE) that the world is described as happening "according to the assessment of Time [*kata ten tou chronou*]".[4] Here, at the outset of Western philosophy, the ancient divinity of *Chronos* (who in Orphic mythology is the son of Gaia and the father of Zeus) is transformed into a non-anthropomorphic and general cosmic *order* of things.

When Aristotle in his *Physics* addresses the problem of movement, he develops a sequence of concepts, the tenacity of which can be measured by the extent to which we still use them, when referring to "potentiality" (*dynamis*), "actuality" (*energeia*), "fulfillment" or "realization" (*entelecheia*), etc. It is also in Aristotle's *Physics* that we find the earliest attempt to define time itself, as the "measure (or number, *aritmos*) of motion".[5] The purpose of this whole vocabulary is not primarily to come to terms with time as such, but to handle *movement* and *change*, the event of things becoming different from what they are and yet somehow remaining the same. It is the logic of this ongoing transformation of being in general and the question of agency and causation in particular that occupies his attention. For the Greek philosophers, the question of passage and change, and the logical dilemmas to which it gave rise, such as the paradoxes of Zeno, was an urgent challenge. But no Greek philosopher seems to have explored the problem of the *experience* of time in the sense of temporal awareness of the arc of time and the passing of time.

The paradigmatic example of such an attempt is to be found in Augustine's *Confessions*, written half a millennium later. Here Augustine takes on the metaphysical challenge of thinking time from the viewpoint of how it is experienced. He notes that we usually refer to time by observation of the changing face of nature. But time is neither the objective measure of movement nor the outer framework of change. Augustine instead focuses on the *experience of time* as the sense of past, present, and future, and on how things such as a "before" and an "after" are possible.[6] When we contemplate changes that have taken place, in nature as well as in human life, we are inclined to say that "time passes" or that "time flows" or even that "time flies", using metaphors of bodily movement in space in order to capture the general dimension of a specific event or passage. But what is really taking place is physical change.

All so-called registering of time is performed by correlating one change in nature to another periodically recurring change, such as the circular movement of heavenly bodies or rhythmically moving human artifacts (clocks). Modern physics has established an objective, observer-neutral framework for determining and measuring the movement of bodies, what Newton referred to as an "absolute time" and defined in his *Principia* as "the absolute true and mathematical time that passes equably without reference to anything external". But this framework also betrays its constructed and relative nature since its reference to "passing" and "equably" already implies another posited framework within which it supposedly takes place. There seems to be no way to define an objective time of nature without implying yet another framework.

The extraordinary level of precision with which time is today "measured" should not deflect us from seeing the general condition of what it means to measure time: namely to relate the movement of one natural phenomenon to that of another periodical movement. For humanity in the era of Augustine cosmic processes such as the movement of the sun, the earth, and the moon remained the index. More recently, techno-science has correlated its desire for continuity and mastery of change with atomic frequency, the so-called "atomic time" that follows the "caesium standard" based on the emission rate of caesium 133. Yet, for all its remarkable ingenuity this technology in itself does not really bring us closer to the phenomenon of time. It merely increases radically the precision with which movement can be registered and mastered for technical purposes.

The Augustinian perplexity vis-à-vis the being of time thus remains valid also in the age of modern physics and its sophisticated chronometers. To say that an hour or a year has passed is to have noted a repeated natural movement. Even though we are naturally inclined to say that whatever happens to us happens *in* time, we should realize that in fact it does not happen anywhere else than where it happens. The great temporal framework – Time – within which things are supposedly enacted is a nature-relative cultural construction. How long does it take for the earth to rotate once upon its axis? The correct answer, "one day," is ultimately tautological, since it means that it takes the world one rotation upon its axis in order to rotate once upon its axis.

In order to understand Time in this cosmic sense, there is no need to look deeper into nature, as if there were a more fundamental hidden true periodicity behind the relative chronometers and calendars of humans. The temporal organization of life arises from the need to determine what happens in relation to a fixed measure, and to harmonize social existence with stable and recurring events in nature. The fascinating recent discovery by biologists of what appear to be natural, congenital temporal rhythms (often correlated to the movement of the moon) in living creatures as simple as oysters does not contradict this; it just shows that the living partly move with and are attracted by non-living matter.[7] Time, in the cosmological sense of a universal order of things, is a socially motivated cultural construction by means of which, and using various technical means, all great civilizations have sought to adapt themselves culturally to observed regularities in nature.

In his continued search for the nature of time, Augustine turns to contemplate not the measure, but the very act and possibility of measuring. He asks how and where something like a measuring of time takes place. And to this question he responds: "it seems to me that time is nothing else but a stretching out [*distentio*] in length; but of what, I know not, and I marvel, if it be not of the very mind [*animi*]".[8] Time is a stretching of the soul, for were it not for this inner extension or intentionality, the individual moments would be but individual moments, without any coherence, order, or sequence. Time in the sense of past, present, and future is nowhere to be found in nature, for in nature we find only change. It is in and through the activity of the human intellect that something like time emerges. Thus Augustine in the third century arrives at the remarkable conclusion that Time is a creation of human intellect.

When Edmund Husserl turns his phenomenological analysis upon the problem of time in his seminal 1905 lectures on " inner time consciousness", he not only recalls Augustine but goes so far as to say that "no one has reached further than Augustine, not even in recent times".[9] The extremely detailed account of the structure of time consciousness which he then develops is based on the fundamental Augustinian presupposition, that the phenomenon of time is best understood through a self-reflexive exploration of intentional acts of human subjectivity. At the center of this act-analysis of time and temporality stands the intentional stretch of "retention" and "protention", the acts by means of which the experience of a stretch and continuity of time is constituted. The atom of time, the now, is established through this double intentionality, which reaches back and projects forward, so as to shape a dynamic present. Through these phenomenological analyses of the intentionality of time-consciousness, Husserl claims to have reached beyond so called "objective time" to the original source of the temporal as such.

Husserl's manuscripts on inner time-consciousness were edited by Edith Stein and Martin Heidegger, and published in 1928. The previous year, Heidegger had published *Being and Time*, which analyzes the ancient Aristotelian metaphysical question of the meaning of being in terms of time or, more specifically, in terms of the temporality of human existence and understanding. Heidegger's central thesis is that throughout its history, being has been posited and understood unreflectively according to temporal schema, namely, in terms of the *present*, or the *now*. In order to explore critically the meaning of being, we therefore need to reopen the question of time: what time is and, ultimately, how time itself *temporalizes*.

Heidegger does not refer to Augustine in *Being and Time*. However, the Augustinian legacy can also be clearly identified in his case from a lecture given in 1924 on "The Concept of Time".[10] In this lecture, he starts from the contemporary situation in physics in which time appears as a precise unit of measurement. He then asks on what this measuring is grounded. By way of answer he returns to Augustine and the idea that measurement originates in the human soul. Unlike Augustine, however, and unlike both Kant and Husserl, Heidegger does not want to confine this measuring or stretch of time to a human *interiority*, whether in a psychological or metaphysical sense. Instead, interiority and exteriority should be seen as two faces of a more original temporalizing movement, what in *Being and Time* he presents as original "ek-static temporality" [*Zeitlichkeit*] or "primordial outside of itself".[11]

Human existence does not exist *in* time. Rather, in and through its existence, it "temporalizes" [*zeitigt*]. Thus it opens itself up to the primary phenomenon of time that is the *future*, which is constantly released through its existence, as an anticipation of a not yet in a transcending and self-transcending movement. What we speak of as past or history is also, ultimately, just such a projection toward a future, in the form of a coming back to a possibility through a futural anticipation. In one of the densest formulations in *Being and Time*, Heidegger writes: "Having-been arises from the future, in such a way that the future that has-been (or better 'is in the process of having-been') releases the present from itself. This unified phenomenon of the future that makes present in the process of having-been is what we call *temporality*."[12]

TIME AS EK-STASIS AND TRACE OF THE OTHER

The ultimate sense and reality of this "temporality" recedes toward a shady ontological middle-ground for which speculative reason lacks adequate concepts. Heidegger tries to avoid the traps of previous metaphysical explorations of time by not referring to this fundamental level as "movement" or "flow", as do both Husserl and Bergson. All such metaphors of time implicitly recall a further exterior framework in which it supposedly takes place. It is for this reason that he speaks instead of how time "temporalizes", *die Zeit zeitigt*. One consequence is that one should not say that time *is* anything at all, or, in other words, that it belongs to the realm of *being* in a material or physical sense. Rather, time is what gives and enables being, out of which being comes to be. In *Being and Time*, the ontological locus of this phenomenon is human existence or *Dasein*. But Heidegger subsequently tries to dissociate it more clearly from "subjectivity" and to suggest instead a more neutral ground, what he was to refer to from the mid-thirties on as the "event" [*Ereignis*].[13]

In relation to this supposedly original, constitutive, and existential temporality, that which we normally call chronological or cosmological time emerges as a conditioned phenomenon. It is a temporal structure that rests on a shared horizon of common concerns and commitments, within which it emerges as a technical means of managing life. From the viewpoint of existential phenomenological analysis, the great cosmic wheel of chronological Time is a derivative construction in relation to temporality as an original projective domain. On the basis of Heidegger's account, the various technologies of time can thus be given a philosophical interpretation in terms of how they are generated from within this basic existential predicament.

To many subsequent readers, including those sympathetic to the general thrust of Heidegger's existential ontology, there is still something problematic about the aspiration to "ground" the phenomenon of time in existential temporality. In an early essay on the problem of time in *Being and Time*, Jacques Derrida argued that it is impossible to secure a foundational level of temporalizing.[14] For temporality itself, in its very mode of occurrence, does not constitute an underlying stratum of experience that is available to ontological description. Rather, it is the differential occurrence of a signifying procedure, the event of making sense. For this reason, he questions Heidegger's recourse to a strict separation between a supposedly "vulgar" and a more original or "authentic" temporality. Derrida agrees with Heidegger that the conventional concept of time is metaphysically naïve. But he does not see the possibility of returning to a more authentic concept of time, for, as he writes, "time in general belongs to metaphysical conceptuality".[15]

The criticism articulated by Paul Ricoeur twenty years later in *Time and Narrative* moves in a parallel direction. While recognizing the seminal contributions of Husserl and Heidegger to the development of a modern philosophy of time, he still refers to the phenomenology of time as ultimately a "failure". By this he means the inability of a phenomenology of time-consciousness to bridge the gap between the existential and the cosmic sense of time. The existential-phenomenological account of time-consciousness therefore needs to be complemented with a theory of narrative time, of how time is recounted, for which Ricoeur found support in the work of Koselleck and Hayden White, among others.

The failure of Heidegger's approach in Ricoeur's eyes had to do with what he sensed was the disappearance of cosmological, objective time in his analysis. In relation to the immensity of the universe, the development of biological life, and the evolution of cultures, the existence of an individual subject is certainly miniscule. But turning back to cosmic Time as an objective correlate, far from solving the problem, merely emphasizes the stakes for phenomenological analysis. Despite being a faithful scholar and reader of phenomenology, Ricoeur is too quick to interpret the Heideggerian approach as a form of transcendental subjectivism, an attempt to *ground* time in the life of the subject. The challenge posed by the existential-ontological approach instead lies in the attempt to think time as an "ek-static event", something located neither in the subject nor in nature, but constituting instead a kind of crack, fissure, or even wound in the self-identical through which it transcends itself in the direction of otherness, exposing itself to the arrival of the new, as promise or as threat, and as the trace of another.

In a text published after the completion of *Time and Narrative*, Ricoeur himself notes that the primary historical phenomenon with the help of which a historical space and a historical narrative are constructed is not the objective cosmic order, but the *trace*, understood as the indication of a "then" and, more specifically, of a "who and then".[16] It is on the basis of material remains of life in gradual decomposition, that the arc of time and history are first sensed as potential narratives of a once-having-been, in which we encounter ourselves from the outside, so to speak, as inhabitants of a story that we never occupied from the start but into whose passage we can fit our lives.

It is important to see what is at stake here. While we should be aware of how we are constantly building narratives by interpreting traces as testimonies from a life no longer there, we should not allow this to result in subjectivistic hubris, as if the evolving universe was a construction of the human mind. Nor should we fall prey to the objectivist illusion of an existing Temporal Order. The challenge for a phenomenological and philosophical account of time is not to provide one homogenous theory of time in order to escape conceptual entrapment. More importantly, we should try to grasp the opening within temporality itself, what we could perhaps call "the exit-character" of time, as an always already beyond itself. This is what Heidegger sought to convey when speaking of temporality as "ek-static", and what Derrida also pointed at when designating time as original *differance*.

Time becomes the name, then, for an opening from within itself, constituting both stretch and sequence. To speak of it as "original" is ambiguous since "origin" signals something stable and foundational. In this respect, Derrida's early criticism of Heidegger was appropriate. Still, his critique could be described as following the trajectory of Heidegger's own philosophical aspirations. The "original" phenomenon of time is not a stable ground upon which to build a system. On the contrary, it is something unmanageable and pre-chronological. Time is not temporal; time is what temporalizes.

*

In his survey of the various ways in which the human race has conceptualized and symbolized time, Anthony Aveni describes a decorated 30,000-year-old bone tablet found in the Dordogne valley.

This withered piece of bone bearing scratches from a sharp object is believed by some archeologists to be the first known human calendar.[17] The pattern carved on it could be a random effect of its having been used as some sort of tool, but it could also be a representation of the phases of the moon. We will never know with certainty what the purpose of this artifact was, but in all its ambiguity it invites a reflection upon the nature of temporal.

As a cultural artifact, it is a trace of human life once lived. As such, it opens a temporal "space" or "distance" which can be *measured* by being correlated to a fixed chronology of periodic movement (such as the earth's rotation around the sun). As a remnant of a past, something dead yet indicative of a life once lived, the tablet exemplifies the possibility of constructing historical time on the basis of a material trace. The present absence of a life no longer there is then projected as a possible meaning through the future-oriented temporality of the interpreter. If the object is indeed some sort of "calendar", it also marks the first known instance of a cross-cultural desire to "mark the time", to follow and master in and through symbols and technology the rhythmic movements and changes in nature, and thereby to give shape to the finite and ek-static happening of time itself.

Notes

1. See, for example, Anton Aveni's *Empires of Time. Calendars, Clocks, and Cultures* (Boulder: University of Colorado Press, 2002). The book makes a comparative survey of different methods of time-keeping and time-measurement across all the great civilizations.

2. *Temps et récit* was published in three separate volumes between 1982 and 1985 (Paris: Seuil), in English translation as *Time and Narrative* by K. McLaughlin and D. Pellauer (Chicago: Chicago University Press, 1988).

3. Ibid, see in particular volume III, which contains an extensive discussion of the phenomenology of time-consciousness.

4. *The Presocratic Philosophers*, ed. G. S. Kirk et al. (Cambridge: Cambridge University Press, 1957), 107f.

5. *Physics*, 219b.

6. See Augustine, *Confessions* (Cambridge: Loeb Library, Harvard University Press, 1912), Book 11.

7. For a good summary of these new findings, see Aveni, *Empires of Time*, s. 13f.

8. Augustine, *Confessions*, 269.

9. *Vorlesungen zur Phänomenologie des inneren Zeitbewußtseins* (Tübingen: Mohr, 1928), p. 2. In English translation by J. Churchill, *The Phenomenology of Internal Time-Consciousness* (Bloomington: Indiana UP, 1964).

10. This lecture to a group of theologians in Marburg was published posthumously as *Der Begriff der Zeit* (Tübingen: Niemeyer, 1989).

11. *Sein und Zeit* (Tübingen: Niemeyer, 1927/86), p. 329. In English translation by J. Stambaugh as *Being and Time* (Albany: SUNY Press, 2010), with original pagination in the margin.

12. Ibid., p. 326.

13. An important text here is the late essay "Zeit und Sein" from 1962, published in *Zur Sache des Denkens* (Tübingen: Niemeyer, 1969), in which he also elaborates critically upon his own earlier attempts. The thinking of the event, or Ereignis, is initiated much earlier, however, in the posthumously published *Beiträge zur Philosophie (vom Ereignis)*, in Gesamtausgabe 65 (Frankfurt am Main: Klostermann, 1989).

14. "Ousia et grammé – Note sur une note de Sein und Zeit", in *Marges de la philosophie* (Paris: Minuit), 31–78, in English translation by A. Bass "Ousia and grammé. Note on a Note from Being and Time", in *Margins of Philosophy* (Chicago: Chicago University Press, 1982).

15. "Ousia and grammé", 63.

16. Paul Ricoeur, "Le temps raconté", in *Revue de Metaphysique et de Morale*, vol 89 (1984), p. 436–452. For the revival of the concept of the "trace" in French phenomenology, the work of Levinas was seminal, in particular his article "La trace", in *Humanisme de l'autre Homme* (Montpellier: Fata Morgana, 1972), to which Ricoeur also refers.

17. *Empires of Time*, p. 58f. In discussing the bone tablet, Aveni relies on an analysis by A. Marschack, in his *The Roots of Civilization* (New York: McGraw-Hill, 1972).

Hermeneutics of Tradition

MARCIA SÁ CAVALCANTE SCHUBACK

Noch liegen die Schatten der Zeit wie Fragen
Über unserem Geheimnis[1]

Nelly Sachs

"The art of understanding" is a definition of hermeneutics proposed by Friedrich Schleiermacher[2]. It is the art of making incomprehensible texts comprehensible; an art which the ancient Greeks considered the domain of interpreters and translators. It is the art of reading the representations of time-memory. Since the earliest usage of the Greek word *hermeneia*, understanding has been related to interpretation, the decryption of hidden ciphers, and the translation of the unknown into the known. In his attempt to define the philosophical principles of this art of understanding called "hermeneutics", Schleiermacher insisted upon the decisive role of tradition. For him, every text, message, or work to be understood and interpreted not only belongs to a tradition but can only be understood and interpreted from within a tradition. However, if tradition is a condition for understanding and interpreting meanings, how should we understand the meaning of tradition? If tradition can only be understood from within tradition, how should we understand something from within itself? These questions indicate the difficulty of developing a hermeneutics of tradition insofar as one term already comprehends the other. Tradition is indeed a way of understanding and interpreting before and despite any understanding and interpretation; hermeneutics is, for the most part, a way of becoming aware of and legitimating tradition.

The word tradition comes from the Latin, *traditio*: the preservation of meanings, institutions, and practices through transmission. In its own dynamics, tradition is a conservative practice. However, it is also a condition for innovation. Thus every innovation coins new meanings from within already preserved meanings. This dialectic of preservation and innovation has determined the meaning of tradition in the history of practices and ideas in the West. It is also this dialectic that made possible the distinction between pre-modern and modern times. Immanuel Kant's paradigmatic definition of modernity as enlightened emergence from self-imposed immaturity, in which man acquires the courage to use his own understanding without the guidance of tradition [3], presupposes the dialectic between tradition and innovation which informed the famous *Querelle des Anciens et des Modernes*. It is still within the frame of this "querelle" that the task of understanding and interpreting contemporary history, a history that defines itself as both a history of atrocity and an acknowledgment of the atrocity of history itself, is divided between a defense of the hermeneutical necessity of understanding and interpreting the past, and a claim for critique against and without interpretation. Contemporary history has brought to light the obscure and aporetical dimension of tradition in which the defense of tradition was used to exterminate traditions. Indeed, it has showed how tradition appeared to be both reason of disaster and despair and a way of dealing with disaster and despair. Affirming that "the historical trace involving things, words, colors, and tones is always the suffering of the past", Walter Benjamin indicated the suffering of tradition in contemporary history: tradition as the most extreme danger and the only way not to forget "accumulated suffering". Contemporary history has exposed the inadequacy of the dialectic between tradition and innovation insofar as tradition and innovation showed their destructive power, on the one hand, and redemptive force, on the other, and thereby how oblivions of memory and the memory of oblivion are intertwined.

The main arguments against the "defense" of tradition, which hermeneutical claims for understanding and interpretation seem to sustain, rest on a critique of the normative character of tradition and the ideological dimension of the idea of temporal continuity and destiny that accompanies the concept of tradition.[4] Ranged against these critical arguments, there are today an increasing number of attempts to recognize the critical potential of the concept of tradition for a globalized, technological society which is entirely subject to neoliberal and capitalist imperatives of constant innovation. Tradition may well emerge as a new strategy for responding to the challenges of the present, in which case it may take the form of "active attitude" ("subaltern" traditions against hegemonic tradition), "freedom for the past" (as Gadamer proposed), or "memory of the unthought and forgotten" (as Adorno claimed, following Walter Benjamin)[5]. Rather than deciding whether to defend what is defensible in tradition, or to assume the necessity of critical innovation that would enable a way out of tradition, I would like to suggest another position. I would like to suggest the necessity of embracing the aporias of tradition as a starting-point for developing an understanding of tradition beyond the dialectic of preservation and innovation. This is the main scope of the present article.

Let us take as our point of departure the precept that tradition is that which one can neither live with nor escape from. Let us take as our point of departure the precept that tradition is a source of both life and death. The experience of tradition exposes, not temporal continuity and spatial enclosure, but the aporetical situation of trying to breathe while being suffocated: the suffocation of living in a tradition (not being able to exist within it) and the breathing in and of tradition (not being able to exist without it). This aporetical character of tradition can be described as *involvement*.

Tradition involves all of us as intimately as the air we breathe. The involvement of tradition is not like a mantle that can be taken away, but the involvement of a world of meanings, something that can never be taken away. Tradition involves each of us as intimately as the world in which we live. Assuming, on the one hand, that the world is not a sum of objects but a constellation of meanings and, on the other, that meanings are the play between what goes without saying (the known and the familiar) and the need to say what remains unsaid and asking to be said (the unknown or strange and the unknowable), then the world is always entangled in traditions. Each tradition is a world, the world each of us inhabit, the world without which we cannot breath, the world that suffocates, compelling us to search for worlds beyond. Considered in this way, tradition shows the worldliness of conceptualizing the world: there is no "outside" from which to understand, interpret, or describe the world. Only from within the world is it possible to conceive of the world. Tradition shows this in a dramatic way precisely in its attempts to evade tradition, presenting the very patterns from which forms of evasion and emancipation are formulated.

Being as vital to our existence in the world as air itself, tradition can be considered the world of meanings that already precedes us, giving each of us an already-understood and pre-interpreted world. The already-interpreted world of tradition is, indeed, never totally interpreted, being both interpreted and not interpreted, both an *already* interpreted world and a world *still* to interpret. In this sense, tradition precedes us going ahead of us, is both closeness and openness, being a closed openness and an open closeness.

Tradition shows the worldly condition for philosophical hermeneutics, which is one of *ontological involvement*. Ontological involvement means that only from within the world is it possible to conceive of the world; only from within language it is possible to conceive of language; only from within history is it possible to conceive of history; only from within nature is it possible to conceive of nature; and only from within being is it possible to conceive of being[6]. Ontological involvement means, not subjectivity or particularism, but the worldly condition of existence. Claiming that only from within tradition is it possible to conceive of tradition does not mean that each tradition is closed within itself, incomprehensible from outside. It means, rather, the impossibility of finding a position totally free from already existing meanings from which to conceive of meaning. Considered as an already-understood and interpreted world, tradition is a *sine qua non* for interpreting and understanding the world. That is why philosophical understanding and interpretation begin with estrangement: the already known and familiar must become strange and unfamiliar, the answers through which the world appears for the first time must become questions – questions that show the world, as if it were, for the first time.

From the viewpoint of what has been here discussed, tradition is ontological involvement in the sense of *being in a world of meaning*. Tradition presents the experience of already being grasped by the world of meanings when one seeks to grasp the world of meanings and the meaning of the world. This having been already grasped in order to grasp has its proper dynamics. As indicated before, tradition presents the world in a state of self-evidence. Self-evidence appears as the state in which everything both "fits well together" and can be "perfectly explicated", as Edmund Husserl claimed.⁷ It appears as familiarity and security. Meaning is self-evident when it seems familiar and certain. Faced by something self-evident, we say "of course", for it goes without saying. In the state of self-evidence, saying goes without saying. Tradition says without saying insofar as it grasps one both as what has already grasped one and as what grasps *for* him or her. Tradition, the world of habits and familiarities, the state of self-evidence thinks, says, understands and interprets *for* each one. It grasps for each one because it grasps beyond each one, grasping for *us*, "us", this "intimacy" with others, others before us and after us. Tradition is therefore ontological involvement, not only in the sense of presenting the being in a world of meanings, but also the evidence that the *self* is neither only itself nor entirely for itself, being a "being-with", as Martin Heidegger called it, and hence what in itself already is beyond itself. Tradition shows ontological involvement as being in togetherness. Tradition is a primary experience of a given togetherness, called world. It is a certain experience of the common that connects many meanings of the common: common as the same in many differences, common as the banal, familiar, and self-evidently not surprising, common as what belongs to many, building a sense of community. Tradition speaks from the perspective of plural personal pronouns such as "we" and "they", indicating the togetherness within and of a plurality.

But do these descriptions really correspond to our present? The way the "we" of traditions experiences today its meaning of having something in common with others and of recognizing meanings as "common", "familiar" and "self-evident" is, however, the very "loss of tradition". The historical situation for addressing the question about the meaning of tradition is today, in fact, the experience of the loss of its meaning. Loss of tradition does not mean, however, absence of tradition, but its absent way of being present, the presence of something fading away, of something that no longer possesses one and that no one entirely possesses. This is a further dimension of the aporetical structure of tradition revealed by contemporary history. Loss of tradition indeed means having tradition precisely in its fading away. Following Jean-Luc Nancy's and Maurice Blanchot's attempts to think through a possible meaning of the common from a situation of loss of common meanings of community, and trying to give some continuity to what Nancy discussed in terms of "inoperability of the community" (*communauté desoeuvrée*)[8] and what Blanchot exposed as "unavowable community" (*communauté inavouable*)[9], it would be possible to speak about inoperability of tradition and unavowable tradition. Using these expressions is a way of insisting upon how experience of broken traditions today can provide us with a means of developing a hermeneutics of the meaning of tradition beyond the dialectics of preservation and innovation, tradition and renewal.

The boundaries of tradition today appear broken, both in "sovereign" and "subaltern" traditions. In broken togetherness and dispossessed or inoperative traditions, the "common" is experienced negatively, in a sense close but not equal to what Maurice Blanchot called "negative community" (*communauté négative*).[10] This negativity does not appear as lack but as loss, as fading away, still there but almost absent, a thin and uttermost fragile link between presence and absence, between still being there and almost disappeared. This shows itself in the way the singular belongs to the common world of tradition, a tradition emptied of meaning but not without meaning, overwhelming the singular with the excess of traditional meanings and revealing the singular in its fragility and, moreover, the being in tradition or togetherness as fragility of being. The way of belonging to tradition is fragility insofar as tradition is itself transmission of what has faded away; indeed, fragility is the way one belongs to a fading away, dispossessed and loss tradition, showing the limits to tradition as fragile but, paradoxically, also presenting fragility as a "real bound" to tradition and to the common. Understood thus, it shows how another meaning of tradition and of the common can arise from it, the meaning of tradition as common life after the other's death and before the other's birth, *tradition as common life after death and before*.

Tradition exposes the ambiguity of a self that is in itself beyond itself, of a self out and without itself. That may explain why tradition is both an understanding that, understanding for everyone, no longer understands (alienation) and a non-understanding that opens for other understandings (emancipation); that is why it appears as source for both life and death. Heidegger saw this ambiguity clearly when he remarked in *Being and Time*: "the tradition that hereby gains dominance makes what it 'transmits' so little accessible that initially and for the most par it covers it over instead. What comes down to us hands over to obviousness; it bars access to those original 'wellsprings' out of which the traditional categories and concepts were in part genuinely drawn. Indeed, it makes us wholly incapable of even understanding that such a return is necessary".[11] As "what comes down to us", tradition is life; as what "gains dominance" and becomes master of life, delivering what has come down to us as obviousness, common, habitual, assured meaning, tradition is death. Ontological involvement, presented in tradition, is in fact the involvement in the play of life and death, the play of generations, the play between by-passing and passing on and along, in which the self discovers itself beyond and out of itself, in which existence becomes exposed to the paradox of a continuous transition.

Tradition unfolds its meaning in the play of generations. Generation means primarily to be generated, to be born. To be born means, however, to come from, and, more precisely, to come after others. Coming after, descendent is from where the belonging to the antecedent, to the previous and foregoing can be experienced. Only as coming-after, the before us can be seen as being both time be-fore and time fore-ward. The coming after of the born and generated comes not only after the "parents" but also after the death of all others. Tradition as transmission of what came down to us is a life after the death of others, an experience of life-after-death in this life. It is, in fact, neither life nor death but life-after-death, a life threatened by death and death that can discover a new life in its transmission. What Heidegger thought in terms of "being-toward-death" (*Sein-zum-Tode*) can be understood as the experience of nascent life after the death of others, thus, as Heidegger himself stated in *Being and Time*: "factual *Dasein* exists nascent (*gebürtig*)", and, nascent, it dies in the sense of being-toward-death.[12]

Assuming life-after-death in this very life as a basis for developing the hermeneutical meaning of tradition, how should we describe this life-after-death in life? In the nineteen-sixties, the Czech phenomenologist Jan Patočka wrote notes for the development of a phenomenology of life-after-death.[13] He departs from the view of death as a "close history" with "dead possibilities" that cannot reawaken in its proper originarity. As a life after the death of a near other, "my life", says Patočka, is a life experiencing emptiness and lack of reciprocity, a life that dies with the death of our others, rather than a life that experiences by analogy its own mortality when the other dies. To experience one's own existence as life after the death of our others means to experience one's own mortality as a way of being that constitutes itself in relation to others, a way of unmediatedly experiencing our being as a being with others, and thereby a self constituted intersubjectively. Patočka's phenomenological descriptions of a life after the death of others show how the death of the near other presents both the uniqueness of one's own existence and its co-existentiality. It shows both my existence and co-existence as constituting each other. In these unfinished pages, we can read an attempt to describe phenomenologically how factual existence is both reciprocity and interruption of reciprocity, how death disrupts the bounds of life and how life is bound of reciprocity. However, what Patočka never discusses is how factual existence is nascent, being born existence and, as born, an enigmatic discontinuity in the continuous flux of life. Thus, the born is both the continuity of all lives that came before and a discontinuity insofar as it is unique and, as such, impossible to reduce entirely to previous life. In this sense, those born are at once and at the same time united and separated from those foregoing, discovering reciprocity in non-reciprocity and non-reciprocity in reciprocity. Born, nascent life exposes, in fact, an in-betweeness, for it is at the same time a life after the death of others and a life before the birth of others. It is a life after death and life before birth, life of the unborn.

Born, nascent life is the perspective from which tradition shows itself as the movement of coming down to us, through us and beyond us. As such, tradition is life after death *and* life before birth, the movement of carrying further a loss of the world and a not yet transformed world. Transmission of tradition shows omitting or reveals concealing the *non-world* pulsating in the self-evidence and communicability of the world in tradition. In its system of familiarity and security, the system of self-evidence where everything fits well together and can be perfectly explicated, showing no need for *further* explanation or inquiry, the world is always passing on and thereby always exposed to a loss.

Traditional world appears indeed as too much world. Overwhelming and all-encompassing, tradition is abundance, giving itself as "too much", which can be experience both as suffocating feeding of the singular and as a "surging sea" to which the singular surrenders "in such way that it crests and breaks", as Walter Benjamin expressed it vividly.[14] Being suffocated when fed by tradition, or living from abundance as a wave surrendering to its movement so that it can crest and break, shows how the singular belongs to tradition as fragility. Fragility is the real bound to tradition insofar as, being within tradition, the singular emerges as the fragile turning-point between breaking down and breaking through. Comparing the fragile way the singular belongs to the 'too-much' of tradition with a wave surrendering to the abundance of a surging sea, Benjamin turns the question of tradition back on its "phenomenological" residue, so to speak, namely, to the experience of a world passing on and along, being therefore a world always losing itself and never having totally acquired itself as world. Seizing tradition as what emerges "precipitously like a wave from living abundance (...)", Benjamin dislocates tradition back to the pathos of its movement, the pathos of existing in fragility, that is, of existing in permanent loss, after the death of others and before the birth of others. As life after death and life before birth, tradition is life after a loss of the world and before the birth of the world.

In the text Derrida wrote as homage to Gadamer on the occasion of his death, he addresses the question of tradition as "carrying the world of the others" and, hence, as a question of how to live a life after the death of the other. He describes this carrying the world of the other as carrying "the world after the end of the world," and thus "death", he says, "is nothing less than an end of *the* world (...)."[15] Because the world is the world of each and everyone, being all, world and the world of all, each death is death of the whole world. But because Derrida sees only the work of tradition as life after death, as carrying the world after the end of the world, he considers that: "The survivor, then, remains alone. Beyond the world of the other, he is also some fashion beyond or before the world itself. In the world outside the world and deprived of the world."[16] The survivor, who carries the world after the end of the world – the generation, we could add – appears here as loneliness, because what is left of view is that survivor, the one who carries "the world after the end of the world" is nascent, insofar as he/she was born. What is forgotten here is that a life after death is at once and at the same time a life before birth, a life of the unborn. From this horizon, the "survivor", as who is born, can never be alone and that "no one carries alone the world" (*Denn keiner trägt das Leben allein*), recalling a verse by Hölderlin.[17]

To carry further the world after a loss of the world and before a transformed world defines tradition from its own movement. This description of tradition corresponds to the meaning of tradition in the experience of loss of traditions. Loss of traditions brings into to play this other meaning of tradition as life after death and life before birth. This becomes very clear in a life in exile. Exile can be considered an extreme experience of the hermeneutical meaning of tradition. The existential situation of exile is that of no longer having a world in the home-world and never arriving at an alien home, being alien at home and not at home in the alien. It is a situation of in-betweeness that has nothing to do with being between places or experiencing an interval between two times. It is a situation of being without return and without arrival. Here, one carries further the world after losing the world, bringing it to the waiting of a world to come rather than to a new world. Thus, in exile, one is always with the without the world, without the world before, the world that one once had and was and without the world after, the world that one does not have and is not. In exile, one is always with and without the world, is *with-out*, as it is possible to say in English with a single word, being with-out the world before and with-out the coming world. It is a situation of continuous being with others who were left behind in time and space, and therefore of being without them with them. And it is, on the other hand, a situation of being without others who have not yet existed, without the unborn, without potential births, being with this without, being without others with them. The loss of the world implicated in a life after death and the not yet of a world in a life before birth casts the world of tradition as the world of an in-between, a world without world that appears as a world of rest, a world resting in continuous transition.

Notes

1. Nelly Sachs. "Chor der Ungeborenen" in *Werke. Kommentierte Ausgabe Bd 1, Gedichte 1940–50* (Frankfurt am Main: Suhrkamp 2010), 42.

2. Friedrich Daniel Schleiermacher, *Hermeneutik und Kritik*, ed. Manfred Frank (Frankfurt am Main: Suhrkamp, 1977), 75.

3. Immanuel Kant, *Foundations of the Metaphysics of Morals, and What is Enlightenment?* (Upper Saddle River: Prentice-Hall, 1997).

4. Such arguments against hermeneutical claims for understanding and interpretation are important for Foucault, Habermas, Deleuze, Derrida, Sloterdijk, among many others.

5. On tradition as a strategy for dealing with the problems of the present, see Aleida Assmann, *Zeit und Tradition, Kulturelle Strategien der Dauer* (Köln, Weimar, Wien: Böhlau, 1999).

6. Bringing clarity to this wordly condition for philosophical understanding can be considered the greatest contribution of hermeneutical philosophy, from Schleiermacher to Heidegger and its developments by Gadamer, Ricoeur, and Derrida.

7. Edmund Husserl, "Die Frage nach dem Ursprung der Geometrie als intentional-historisches Problem," *Revue internationale de philosophie* (Bruxelles) 1 (1939), 203–225, and *Research in Phenomenology* 1 (1939), 203–25. Translation: "The Origin of Geometry," in *The Crisis of European Sciences and Transcendental Phenomenology. An Introduction to Phenomenology*, trans. David Carr (Evanston, IL: Northwestern University Press), 1970, 353–378.

8. Jean-Luc Nancy, *La communauté désoeuvrée* (Paris: Christian Bourgeois, 2004).

9. Maurice Blanchot, *La communauté inavouable* (Paris: Éditions de Minuit, 1983).

10. Ibidem.

11. Martin Heidegger. *Sein und Zeit*, GA2, (Tübingen: Max Niemeyer, 1967), 21; *Being and Time*, eng transl. J. Stambaugh, (Albany: State University of New York, 1996), 19

12. "Das faktische Dasein existiert gebürtig, und gebürtig stirbt es auch schon im Sinne des Seins zum Tode". Ibidem, GA 2, p. 374; J. Stambaughs's translation reads very differently: "Factical Da-sein exists as born, and, born, it is already dying in the sense of being-toward-death", ibidem, 343.

13. Jan Patočka. "Phénoménologie de la vie après la mort" in *Papiers phénoménologiques* (Grenoble: ed. Jerôme Millon, 1995), 145–156. See Erika Abrahms' notes on the manuscript on page 295. For a very inspiring comment on these manuscripts by Patočka, see Filip Karfik "Das Leben nach dem Tode und die Unsterblichkeit" in Unendlichwerden durch die Endlichkeit (Würzburg: Königshausen & Neumann, 2008), 90.

14. Walter Benjamin. Letter to Gerhard Scholem, Sept 1917, in *The Correspondence of Walter Benjamin* (Chicago/London: The University of Chicago Press, 1994), "Theory is like a surging sea, but the only thing that matters to the wave (under-

stood as metaphor for the person) is to surrender itself to its motion in such a way that it crests and breaks. This enormous freedom of the broken wave is education in its actual sense: instruction – tradition becoming visible and *free*, tradition emerging precipitously like a way from living abundance (...) To educate is to enrich theory (...)", 94

15. Jacques Derrida, "Rams. Uninterrupted Dialogue – Between Two Infinities, the Poem" in *Sovereignties in Question. The Poetics of Paul Celan* (Fordham University Press, 2005), 140.

16. Ibidem.

17. Friedrich Hölderlin, "Die Titaten" in *Sämtliche Werke. Stuttgarter Hölderlin-Ausgabe,* vol 2,1 (Stuttgart: W. Kohlhammer, 1951), 218.

Requirements of an Aesthetic Concept of the Canon

ANDERS OLSSON

The concept of a canon has a wide range of applications. Religion and the arts are not the only fields in which cultural memory has traditionally had a normative function. Every field of knowledge, implicitly or explicitly, is organized around its own canon of exemplary models. And yet the treatment of cultural memory as a canon is so widespread and pervasive that it serves in many respects as a bridge between discrete disciplinary modes of thinking. Moreover, the process of canon formation itself presents features and problems which are common to all these fields of knowledge. Even though this article primarily addresses the way the canon is viewed by scholars in the arts, particularly literary studies, it can hopefully illuminate the role of paradigmatic memory within the contemporary humanities more broadly.

I will begin by briefly considering the meaning and uses of *canon* as a concept in a historical perspective, before moving on to a discussion of the violent debates over the canon which have taken place in the last two decades. I will then outline my own view of what an updated, workable, and aesthetic concept of the canon might look like. I envisage a plausible concept of the canon as not only proceeding from the institutional valorizations of schools and universities but as having a connection to aesthetic valorizations in the fine arts. For this reason, the historical process of canon formation demands our attention. This backwards glance is additionally warranted by the fact that the concept of the canon in contemporary aesthetics debates diverges substantially from the term's etymology and older meaning. Finally, I will review the difficulties of canon formation in the current era of globalization when the world no longer has an undisputed cultural centre that can create unifying memories with canonical validity.

What do the word canon and the concept canonization mean?

Historically, the concept of the canon has had an essentially sacred function shaped by the establishment of the Bible as holy scripture and the hegemony of Christianity in the fourth century and after. Before gaining its normative force, the word *canon* had far less abstract, etymologically stable meaning of "pipe" or "rod". Manfred Fuhrmann, who has described the term's etymology and history, nonetheless observes that it did not need to travel far in order to acquire its current connotations of "measuring-stick," "rule," or "regulation".[1] Starting in the second century, the term "kanones" began to be used of ecclesiastical edicts on matters of faith, forming the basis for ecclesiastical or canon law. All of which brings us to its decisive evolution into the discriminatory and critical function that has proved so crucial for modern usage. In 367, we find the first enumeration of the 27 texts that today comprise the New Testament. Everything not included in this canon came to be designated "apocrypha" ("secret", "contraband", "inauthentic").[2]

This pre-modern, sacred usage has lent the concept a connotation which even now plays an important role in debates over the canon. For some, the canon is by its nature a concept whose roots in theology or metaphysics present an obstacle to secular uses of the term. These latter are generally seen as originating with Leyden philosopher David Ruhnken in 1768, who was the first to use "canon" as an umbrella term for exemplary yet secular authors.[3]

However, little purpose is served by over-analysis of the word "canon" when studying canonization as a historical phenomenon. As Ruhnken points out, the new secular usage of the word had a long lineage in which the same principles operated. There were simply different words or expressions for the morally elevating and the aesthetically distinguished. In pre-Christian classical literature, a distinction on formal grounds between "authentic" and "inauthentic" as well as between "exemplary" and "non-exemplary" had already been made as far back as the Hellenic Period in connection with ritual festivals in which a winner was chosen.[4] The Museion (Museum or Library) of Alexandria, which made an authoritative selection of texts according to categories such as "adopt", "permit", and "elect", had a special role in the canonization process. Scholars refer to three types of canonization in antiquity which did not involve the actual concept of a canon: transcription of an oral text, public declamation as an event, and collation in other texts.[5]

Canonization as historical process

Understanding canonization as a historical process thus requires a broader perspective than merely the history and semantics of the word itself. One way is to turn our attention to the orders of preference thrown up during the battle fought between advocates of old and new, famously dubbed the Quarrel of the Ancients and the Moderns (*la querelle des anciens et des modernes*). As Ernst Robert Curtius has shown, the conflict between old and new models is a recurrent feature of the West's cultural history, with "the Ancients" invariably denoting a canon of classical authors.[6] Imitation of these exemplary writers was a necessary stage in a canonization process being constantly renewed, where renewal not infrequently turned into revolt under the aforementioned banner. Just as Virgil before him had imitated Greek models, Dante cited Virgil and other Latin authors in order to bolster the authority of his Italian vernacular. The classics were essential for the new nation-states of the Renaissance, which needed to legitimize their own vernacular canons. While these new national processes of canonization often took place in parallel to those of classical authors, the latter was to become increasingly subordinate. During the eighteenth century it became common to speak of literary genres as having or lacking classical models.

This process involves not merely the use of textual exemplars in teaching but the productive creation of value by means a written word that has already been standardized. Primarily this occurs with the emergence of literature itself, which need not be copied slavishly but is able to incorporate quite heterogeneous and even unruly materials. We see this clearly in the modern era, where imitation is no longer the basis for transmission. By the time Joyce invokes Homer in *Ulysses*, revolt has become a part of the canonization process. Canonization in this respect is a matter not of a hierarchy, imposed from above and originating in institutional and political vested interests, but of an inner dynamic that is a prerequisite for the existence of literature and the arts.[7] There is no contradiction between this fundamental inner process and the crucial didactic function of canonization in school and university teaching. But the actual dynamic between canonization and de-canonization, usurpation and renewal, naturally enough becomes most tangible during the creative process. The standardizing exemplars of the classroom often stand in direct opposition to literature's own striving for innovativeness.

Yet this dynamic is not always apparent. The canonization process in the West is strikingly stable between the fifth and thirteenth centuries, during which period the same classical names recur on school syllabi: Cicero, Virgil, Horace, Ovid, or Juvenal. Curtius shows that the classical paradigms, though losing ground steadily, continue to reappear well into the seventeenth and eighteenth centuries, offering undeniable evidence of a relative continuity in the European system of canons.[8] But even before romanticism opens up a yawning chasm in the canon system, a series of battles are fought between old and new, starting in the Renaissance. Seen against the backdrop of these fierce and recurring battles, we can ask ourselves just how new and revolutionary the canon debate of our own era really is.

A modern secular canon: aesthetic autonomy and historicization

By the eighteenth century, when Ruhnken began using the concept of the canon in a profane sense, there had emerged three tendencies which were to shape the arts of the post-Romantic period: first, an aestheticization of the concept of the canon; second, a questioning of fixed orders of precedence, and, with it, an intrinsic uncertainty about the permanence of valorizations; third, the development of nationally-oriented canons, which flourished in the mid-nineteenth century, in striking contrast to the more universalist aspirations which had preceded them.

As regards the first tendency, the autonomy of the aesthetic in Pre-Romantic Germany has unquestionably been decisive. The successive disconnection of the arts from the state apparatus, the academies, and the schools during modernity has affected canon formation. Since the Enlightenment, Pierre Bourdieu has emphasized, liberation from the state apparatus and social economics has made the arts into an autonomous field.[9] This notion of autonomy has been developed by Theodore Adorno in aesthetically more sophisticated fashion under the heading of the negative dialectic. It should be added that this insistence upon autonomy contrasts with the dissolution of the boundaries between the arts on the one hand and the marketplace and society on the other, which has been a hallmark of the postmodern era.[10]

What this fragile and historically conditional autonomy means for the concept of the canon is far from evident. To be sure, it makes cultural phenomena far more susceptible to the pressures of the marketplace and mass culture. Culture becomes less dependent upon patronage, something that gives it freedom and a new critical function even while making it vulnerable. It has to compete on the terms of the market, where, as already noted, different consecratory entities compete against each other, and where canonized values have significance only if their credibility has media backing. The gradual dismantling of a critical public sphere also undermines the critic's role with respect to the notion of a new contemporary canon formation.

Aesthetic autonomy can thus be described as very much under threat from levelling and boundary-crossing tendencies in society, and it may be asked whether Bourdieu's sociology, for example, has engaged with this development.[11] The difficulty with forming a modern concept of the canon lies in preserving the aesthetic as a distinct sphere in a society whose value formations are so powerfully governed by the market.

The historicization alluded to earlier is closely linked to this autonomization of the concept of an aesthetic concept. Autonomy is in itself the expression of a historical process that dates from the beginning of modernity. As a project, the modern is defined by renewal, yet it can just as easily lead to regimented adaption to the market as to autonomy. Within the arts, however, it can be noted that modernism, led by the avant-garde, has been characterized by a radical settlement with a cultural heritage regarded as burdensome and even crippling.[12] For this reason, and to a far greater extent than preceding centuries, the twentieth century has been characterized by a series of rapidly changing canonizations and decanonizations. In this way a canon can be seen to manifest greatly diminished stability and longevity, compared with earlier.[13]

In any event, this indicates that the development of a contemporary aesthetic concept of the canon cannot avoid addressing the status of the arts as a threatened sphere in later modernity, nor the contested endurance of their value-formations.It is no coincidence, either, that Bloom, in *The Western Canon*, discusses his colleagues' flight from aesthetics to ideology as typical of the current climate.[14]

As regards the third tendency in the wake of Romanticism, national canon formation continues to flourish in the era of globalization. Yet we find ourselves today, in the wake of modernism's breakthrough, in a dynamic dialogue between national and transnational, and provincial and cosmopolitan, points of view. A wider global perspective is now essential, even though it cannot provide an overview of the whole.

The meaning of contemporary canon criticism

Contemporary canon criticism is divided between various revisions to a traditional canon and rejection of the concept of the canon *tout court*. In some instances, the critique has had consequences for the concept of literature.[15] Revisions have taken the form of a radical and comprehensive widening of the canon to include women's literature, children's and juvenile literature, non-European literature, and popular literature. In particular, the inclusion of popular culture in the canon has posed a challenge to the traditional notion of art. However, there also exists a form of canon criticism which addresses the very foundations and which calls into question the concept of a canon as such.[16]

It is easy to see that this entire multilayered canon critique is not a narrowly institutional phenomenon but has causes which lie beyond the university.[17] It was social and political processes, starting in the 1960s, that led to the feminism which now forms one of the most important components of this critique, but it also involves perspectives derived from popular literature and postcolonialism. Developments in media served to diffuse the formats, myths, and genres of mass culture, which obviously enhanced the status of popular culture. The effects of globalization are less easily parsed since these have partly broadened the narrowly Eurocentric space of culture, and partly strengthened its Americanized and Western-oriented aspects. But in both cases, they have resulted in a threat to the autonomous sphere in which European canon formation in its traditional sense might take place. It is difficult to prove that any one factor has undermined the faith in a common Western canon. What's important is the realization that this faith has been destroyed, with far-reaching consequences for our notions of literature, for the literature that is being and will be written, and for the institutional teaching of literature.

Nevertheless, the fact that the canon debate resulted from a mobilization of political opinion centred on the university has served to simplify it in a way that is problematic. The canon has been treated as an ideological expression of vested interests, a means of representing a particular cultural and historical perspective. In consequence, it has been argued, the Western canon is an exclusive, symbolic expression of the worldview of white Western men.[18] Similarly, Marxist, post-colonial and feminist criticism has been defined by the view that the canon merely mirrors or expresses a given power structure of class, race, or gender.[19]

Many other examples of this trope could be mentioned. There is no doubt that, with regard to ethnic identity, race, or gender, the Western canon traditionally has been intimately allied with the powers that be, and is unable to satisfy the demands for recognition made by these oppressed or marginalized groups. The problem lies in treating a canon as a simple representation of vested interests. The anti-canon of these critics risks becoming the inverted form of an order that is equally in thrall to vested interests. A pragmatic attitude replaces the inherited canon with a more "equitable" representation of those interests that one wishes to advocate. E. Dean Kolbas is thus surely right to argue that representation and pragmatic utility are aspects of the canon debate which ought to be criticized.[20] However, I wish to draw other conclusions than Kolbas does from these tendencies, and to propose that this pragmatic quality can also be found in those advocates of a more traditional canon formation.[21]

The problem with both these tendencies – representation and pragmatism – is that they are unable to account for canon formation as a historical process: how it occurs, how it is established, and how it acquires its enduring significance. It often takes a long time for a canon to evolve, taking place neither exclusively nor even primarily in schools or in the media but rather among the writers themselves. One of the strengths of Harold Bloom's work is that he has chosen to move discussion of the canon, beyond the sterile issue of blacklists in schools, into a creative dialogue with cultural memory.[22] Canon formation is not only tied to officially sanctioned schools and institutions, as, for example, the influential canon researcher Paul Guillory has argued, but, perhaps above all, creative production and reproduction in the arts.[23] What Bloom is trying to show through his own engaged proposal for a Western canon is how it must be understood as being in a state of constant revision, as an ongoing *querelle des anciens et des modernes* that is constitutive of our entire literature and cultural heritage.

Canon formation as a Wirkungsgeschichte (Effective-History)

If contemporary canon debate suffers from representational thinking and excessively narrow pragmatism, both factors ascribe institutions and individual vested interests far too prominent a role in canon formation. What legitimates new aesthetic canon formation if it is as governed by vested interests as that which it is meant to replace? In this way, a conflict is created between old and new, in which new blacklists are drawn up voluntarily, invoking an authority that is problematic from the start because it only responds to the immediate interests of the individual. Canon formation of this kind is not the result of a historical process, but of a broad and relatively durable value-formation. Which theoretical formulations could do the job better?

What should be borne in mind about Bloom's elegiac-heroic defence of the canon is its productive element, which regards canon formation as an inner, often violent, process within a comprehensive cultural memory. The weakness in his account is that it is extraordinarily individualistic, which makes it virtually impossible to use as an account of the material and discursive conditions of canon formation. In my view, better prospects for explaining what a canon historically has been are offered by the hermeneutics of German philosopher Hans-Georg Gadamer, specifically his concept of *Wirkungsgeschichte* (Effective-History),which makes it possible to consider the canon from both a productive (artistically creative) and a reproductive (critical/didactic) perspective. In the latter half of the twentieth century, Gadamer's ideas have been of tremendous importance for the way that scholars in the humanities understand their own work, yet without affecting critical debate over the concept of the canon.[24]

The advantage of the concept of *Wirkungsgeschichte* is that it cannot be reduced to political or ideological interests. As we have seen, canon formation takes place across large tracts of time, in which the same constellation of models exert their influence independently of changes in political power. But it is, perhaps above all, the important role of time in value-formation that needs to be highlighted. We know how difficult it is to judge rightly in the present, and that it takes time for negative prejudices to disappear and for sustainable values to gain a foothold. Almost unknown in their own day, Blake or Stagnelius are today indispensable to the literary canon. The same goes for Proust, Kafka, or Celan in the twentieth century. The notion of a history of effects has an inbuilt corrective that is never available to a pragmatism focussed on immediate utility. It involves eliciting a constellation of works and authors that is all the more durable for never being conclusive.[25]

Wirkungsgeschichte is a dynamic process that can be grasped in the act of writing as well as of reading. It can thus account for canonization as an inner linguistic process in ways a pragmatic approach cannot. But it has also shown itself to be a powerful theory when it comes to reception history and the critical response to literature.

Another valuable quality in the notion of *Wirkungsgeschichte* is the ability to account for both the continuity of canon formation, by means of the normative power of the works in question, and its changeability, by means of the unfinished and open character (in principle) of the work. According to Gadamer, a work is constitued only in the act of reading, encountering new, changeable horizons.[26] Since the end of the 1970s, scholars have talked about "opening the canon". But it should be noted that this openness is, in some sense, built into Gadamer's theory. Every work and every constellation of canonized works are in principle open to change, despite the binding power of canonization.

Gadamer himself did not develop a theory of canons. But I think that it might be developed relatively easily if one bears in mind his discussion of *Wirkungsgeschichte* as it relates to exemplary works such as the classic or, rather differently, what in a late essay he refers to as "an eminent text".[27] Understanding is always a productive act for Gadamer, and it means that all periods construct the work anew from their own premises. But such behaviour is never purely pragmatic, since we can understand only those things that our historically-conditioned understanding makes it possible for us to understand. This sets a limit to the possibilities for renewal.

As Aleida Assmann has observed, Gadamer's notion of the classic has been criticized, not least by reception-aesthetics theorists, for its substantialism – its faith in the work's intrinsic ability to survive independently of social frameworks. One solution might be the idea that greatness can only be achieved through a juxtaposition of two moments in time, that which produces the work and that which receives and legitimizes it. However, Assmann does defend Gadamer from the charge of having differentiated the classic as part of a timeless order. Reception theorists, notably Rainer Warning, actually tend to throw the baby out with the bathwater in their efforts to dispense with the substantial notion of tradition, in favour of historical processes in a state of continuous rupture. The central issue is how to explain how entities such as classics and canon formations occur. According to Assmann, the answer must lie in an "ongoing confirmation and renewal".[28] The concept of the canon that follows has been sketched out along these lines.

In actual fact, Gadamer views the history of the classics, and hence of canon formation, as running parallel to, and not entirely independent of, political history. He has paid insufficient attention to the unique rhythm of canon formation, which is created as much through recurrent confirmation as through sudden displacements and reversals.

The significance of repetition and transferral for canon formation

It ought to be possible, therefore, to use the role of repetition in transferral as a way to reformulate the concept of a canon as a qualified form of *Wirkungsgeschichte*. In which case, this becomes an act of confirmation and thus of preservation. A classic is a work whose continued topicality over time allows it to remain valid. This does not mean that it can be described as unchanging. On the contrary, it has undergone a continuous process of change as a result of the stream of interpretations being perpetually renewed in the effective-history.[29]

One condition of canonization, then, may be the power of a work to engender repetition and to engage with new readers. Rather than speaking of the intrinsic value of aesthetic phenomena, as Gadamer does, we might formulate this repeatability as an aesthetic criterion: a work can be said to have artistic value only if one can profitably return to it. As far as I can see, this kind of constructivist reading of Gadamer is enabled by the fundamental historicity of understanding in his hermeneutic. Canon formation, however, also has another, more passively confirmatory role in history, concerning a mode of cultural reproduction which is decisive in school teaching and which is of considerable social significance. In *Mansfield Park* (1814), one of Jane Austen's characters remarks: "Shakespeare one gets acquainted with without knowing how. It is a part of an Englishman's constitution".[30] Not every canonized author has the normative power of Shakespeare, of course, but the creation of norms can be felt on levels other than that addressed by current debates over the canon.

Repetition has at least three important functions in canon-formation: an aesthetic, a didactic, and a social. The last of these involves cultural reproduction and community, with citation serving to assert the value of familiarity; everyone has long been able to recite famous passages from Shakespeare's works, recycle their figures of speech and descriptions, and thereby recirculate them. Familiarity is a necessary component of canon formation.[31] Yet it may be asked whether familiarity and proximity play the same decisive role in canon formation in the era of Modernism, where the norm of quality in fact turns on "strangeness, irreducible distance, and heteronomous alterity."[32]

From the perspective of contemporary sociology, familiarity is also a double-edged value since in our society it is increasingly mediated, disseminated, and impacted by the market in the form of media and advertising. Recognition here has a value in itself, which replaces the qualitative values that originate from a relatively independent critical entity. In a system of this kind, repetition is far more likely to undermine aesthetic canon formation than to shape and strengthen it.

The various functions of repetition are not strictly separated, and presumably both didactic and aesthetic repetition are present in the social sphere evoked by Austen. But a reasonable hypothesis is that, from 1750, the aesthetic function acquires a special significance in the West for the establishment of canons during the inception and dedication of the arts. It is axiomatic that canon formation constitutes a qualified form of *Wirkungsgeschichte*, in which one has to differentiate between texts that are exemplary in varying degrees.

To this end, as has been noted, late Gadamer distinguishes a type of text called "the eminent text", what I prefer to call "the imminent text". This text is precisely characterized by its capacity to recall our attention and thereby to meet the requirements of aesthetic canonization. More than in *Wahrheit und Methode*, Gadamer here asserts the material attributes of the aesthetic work, as a result of which he moves beyond a hermeneutic narrowly focussed upon meaning. The work of art reveals a unity of meaning and a euphony which only "the inner ear" can distinguish. The text is here regarded as an autonomous image that wishes to be read and reinterpreted. He seems to imagine that there are texts which impose special demands on the comprehension of the recipient, quite independent of the latter's own role. He notes that the eminent work must be tested anew, a "Verweilen" of the recipient, before it can be understood fully. For Gadamer, as for Kant, this means that the aesthetic work cannot be absorbed into a concept.[33]

It may be objected that Gadamer's definition of this kind of text is exclusively directed towards the auditory sense, and excludes other senses from the realm of aesthetic experience. The key issue, however, is that he is interested in establishing a perspective on the aesthetic text that is more material than before, which makes his ideas more applicable to the canon debate in general.

Although Gadamer does not refer explicitly to it, there is arguably a canon problematic underlying repetition in both its forms – automatized and reproductive, and conscious and sophisticated. The former involves canonization that has become a self-evident, almost unconscious, part of one's being. The latter involves the grounds for a canonization which need not already have taken place, yet which may have. It is this condition of possibility which primarily concerns me here.

Inevitably, however, Gadamer's concept of the eminent text raises the same issue that came up earlier in the context of the concept of the classic. Doesn't the idea of the eminent text presuppose a higher, intrinsic value, precisely the thing we had decided to exclude from the discussion?

Well, maybe not. One might say that a text, in order to be included in a canon, must be able to demonstrate a confirmatory and durable repeatability, something which the imminent text does. *Verweilen*, the intransitive verb used by Gadamer, expresses the fact that we have been induced not only to return to the same work at various points in history, but also to remain *with* the work in the present by continually rereading individual parts and details.

Calling the canon into question: the possibility of intervention

As already noted, Gadamer has been criticized for advocating an unreflective and conservative concept of tradition.[34] His writing evinces a scepticism towards the possibility of a radical break with the cultural framework that defines the attributes of understanding. The whole purpose of his hermeneutic is to follow Heidegger in conceiving of understanding as a thoroughly historical phenomenon.

And yet we have already remarked upon the possibility of interpreting Gadamer more constructively by focussing on his openness in principle to the Other: a philosophical view of the work of art as only coming into existence through contact with the reader.[35]

For aesthetic canon formation, as we have seen, *Wirkungsgeschichte* is never entirely subordinate to the passage of political history, because aesthetic experience can establish a new relation to tradition and thereby reconstitute the process of canon formation. What does the intervention and creation of a new canon entail for a system that has already been established? Can we envisage an entirely new system, should this prove to be necessary, using the concepts currently at our disposal? And what does this mean for our view of inception and dedication, those two polar opposites which must be thought through together in order for a viable concept of the canon to become a possibility?

These questions are prompted by the fact that sudden discoveries are being made which deviate from tradition, and that powerful new canonizations of major artists and critics have been initiated successfully. While the possibility of intervention can change the system fundamentally, it has two implications. It can designate a discovery that is more or less contingent, being subsequently justified and integrated into the canon system, but it can also designate a historically new aesthetic reflection, with decisive consequences for norm-creation. The discovery in 1850 of the Sumerian epic *Gilgamesh*, lost for 2,000 years and then instantly incorporated into the Western canon, attests to the first possibility. The discovery of Longinus's tract *On the Sublime* after 1600 years is an example of the second, with the concept of the sublime having an immediate impact on aesthetic thinking, and entering the everyday speech of educated men and women in the salons of France and England during the eighteenth century.[36] To these can be added the ways in which the contributions of individual scholars such as Ernst Robert Curtius and Erich Auerbach have radically affected our view of our literary heritage.[37]

It is probable that only the notion of specificity in aesthetic phenomena can account for the possibility of intervention. How should a reasonable concept of the aesthetic canon be formulated today? Bourdieu can hardly come to the rescue here, given his lack of interest in aesthetic value beyond its sociologically determined context. Nor has Paul Guillory, who minted the concept of *cultural capital*, shown much interest in aesthetic value beyond its social function. Of far great interest are those efforts to cling to the notion of aesthetic value as its own historical process. Following Kant, these have often referred to the work of art's singularity as a way generating an array of ideas without becoming restricted to a general concept.[38]

AN AESTHETIC CONCEPT OF THE CANON

World literature and the destruction of the single exclusive tradition

The situation today, in which the rubric *world literature* has become the bearer of a widened concept of literature comprising numerous centres and traditions, has exploded the notion of a single, basically Eurocentric, normative canon. This concept of tradition, as represented by T.S. Eliot, for instance, has been fundamentally put into question.[39] The very concept of world literature requires the inclusion of strongly heterogeneous cultural traditions and memories. At the same time, no-one is capable of mastering the entire field of national and transnational canon formations currently in existence. We are being forced to live with numerous parallel and incomplete canon formations in a wide array of languages. For this reason, Mads Rosendahl Thomsen has proposed that contemporary discussion henceforth refer to canonized constellations of works which display a formal or thematic family likeness.[40] The problem with such a model, however, is that it insufficiently addresses the universalizing normative power of canon formations. Their formal and thematic attributes are insignificant in this respect. Another problem is that it does not pay enough attention to the factor of time in canon formation. Although Rosendahl Thomsen is aware that canons are always larger than individuals, it can never be freely constructed in accordance with current needs. In her pioneering study *The World Republic of Letters*, Pascale Casanova has shown how dependent literary value formation is upon long historical processes with ties to dominant cultural centres.[41] Today, no such obviously consecratory centres exist in the way that Paris long did, yet canonization has continued to exert the same binding force, one of whose inescapable premises is permanence. What is today needed, I believe, is thus a notion of a core canon that can continue to show its power to endure, allied to new candidates, in an unending constellation of works.

Realizing the importance of reading for this process, David Damrosch has shown how globalization, while admittedly broadening our view of the limits to canonization, has not forced the West to alter its classical value formations to any significant degree.[42] New names and canon formations have appeared in recent years without dislodging, for example, the "big six" of the English Romantic constellation (Blake,

Wordsworth, Coleridge, Keats, Shelley, Byron), who have shaped the canon of English literature for the past two centuries. What Damrosch instead sees happening is the proliferation of the Anglophone canon formation through the addition of new luminaries. He refers to the once-minor classics as a *shadow canon*, which has now been relocated to an out-of-the-way spot reserved for all but ignored authors. In return, another category, known as *counter-canon*, has emerged as a necessary effect of revisions to the canon. This belongs not to what was once "our" tradition but, rather, comprises a host of new writers who have only recently attracted our attention. Even imminence can be seen to have a surprisingly protracted temporal structure. It involves an extended, prosthetic memory which is always required to proceed from precise linguistic and cultural conditions yet which can never invoke its "own" tradition or some basis in dominant culture.

As regards those canonical works which were previously most celebrated, their position has become, if anything, even more central by having been played off against other works and literatures at a global level.

This redefinition of canon formation, to which we have today become party, nevertheless demands a completely new concept of reading and memory formation, one that is mobile and flexible. And yet, I submit, it must proceed even more strongly from an understanding of the act of reading as a productive event, if it is not to become lost among in a mass of ungraspable fragments. Without cultural belonging or linguistic immersion and expertise, we will also lose our ability to comprehend the aesthetic specificity of canon formation. And yet I have only been able to gesture here towards an approach to understanding canon formation today in the wake of world literature and the widening of the space of literature.

What should a modern concept of the aesthetic canon look like?

My intention has been to outline some criteria for a modern concept of the aesthetic canon. I have done so against the backdrop of the history of the concept of the canon and in light of the heated discussions of the concept of the canon which have taken place during the last two decades. My thought was that a viable concept of the canon should not only be usable in relation to the present moment but connect with how canon formation has taken place in history. Two weaknesses in the canon debate have been identified: a mode of representational thinking that ties canons to vested interests and institutions; and a pragmatic perspective based on immediate needs or so-called "use values". In contrast to these tendencies, I have, inspired by Hans-Georg Gadamer, developed the idea of the canon as a historical process and a view of the canonized work as "imminent". It calls to us time and again throughout history, thereby signalling its canonical status.

I have suggested that a viable concept of the canon should today proceed from two criteria: repetition both in the qualified, aesthetic sense, in which the work invites reconsideration, and in the reproductive sense, denoting greater familiarity; and the possibility of intervention, which we have experienced in the past, and with which we are today confronted as the canon system enters a phase of dramatic, boundary-crossing transformation. More than ever, we need a productive and reader-oriented perspective on the canon, since it is becoming increasingly difficult to argue for a single, culturally agreed-upon basis for canon formation.

During the last two decades, as we have seen, criticism of the concept of the canon has often proceeded from the view that the canon is an instrument of power wielded primarily in schools in the form of blacklists. It is natural, therefore, to connect the canon, not with pleasure, but with obligation and duty. For example, while Frank Kermode could speak of "pleasure and change" in canon formation in his 2001 Tanner Lectures, in the discussion afterwards John Guillory was only willing to acknowledge "needs" in the encounter with significant literature.[43]

This is a clash between two views of the canon, one productive and the other merely reproductive, and even if the latter element must be present in any viable theory of the canon, our starting-point should be the former. Gadamer's most important criticism of the Romantic hermeneutic was that it viewed understanding as the reproduction of an originary production. But there is no reproduction that does not also include a productive element, or, as Gadamer writes: "One understands differently insofar as one understands at all."[44] This also holds true of reading and – my argument here – of that which must underlie any new canon.

Notes

1. Manfred Fuhrmann, *Der europäische Bildungskanon* (Frankfurt am Main: Insel, 2004), 37.
2. Ibid. See also Jürgen Dummer, "Entwicklungen des Kanongedankens in der Antike", *Begründungen und Funktionen des Kanons. Beiträge aus der Literatur- und Kunstwissenschaft, Philosophie und Theologie* (Heidelberg: Winter, 2001), 9–20.
3. Fuhrmann, *Der europäische Bildungskanon,* 39; Dummer, *Begründungen und Funktionen des Kanons,* 9.
4. Fuhrmann, *Der europäische Bildungskanon,* 39; Dummer, *Begründungen und Funktionen des Kanons,* 16.
5. Dummer, *Begründungen und Funktionen des Kanons,* 13–14.
6. Ernst Robert Curtius, *Europäische Literatur und lateinisches Mittelalter* (Tübingen/Basel: Francke, 1993), 256–257.
7. For Gottfried Willems' defense of canon formation as an inner, constitutive process, see "Der Weg ins Offene als Sackgasse. Zur jüngsten Kanon-Debatte und zur Lage der Literaturwissenschaft," in *Begründungen und Funktionen des Kanons,* 217–268.
8. Curtius, *Europäische Literatur und lateinisches Mittelalter,* 169.
9. Pierre Bourdieu, *The Field of Cultural Production: Essays on Art and Literature* (Cambridge: Polity Press, 1993), 112.
10. See in particular Theodor Adorno, *Ästhetische Theorie* (Frankfurt am Main: Suhrkamp, 1970).
11. I refer the reader to E. Dean Kolbas's Adorno-inspired *Critical Theory and the Literary Canon* (Cambridge Westview Press, 2001).
12. Astradur Eysteinsson discusses Modernism's relation to tradition in "Modernism in Literary History," *The Concept of Modernism* (Ithaca/London: Cornell UP, 1990).
13. As Fuhrmann comments: "Here one could quite easily claim that the concept, while admittedly preserving its identity of 'an exemplary selection of what is available', has lost one of its other constitutive features, namely 'that which remains valid forever or at least for a very long time'". *Der europäische Bildungskanon,* 39.
14. Harold Bloom, *The Western Canon. The Books and School of the Ages* (New York: Harcourt Brace & Company, 1994), 17.
15. In the aforementioned essay, "Der Weg ins Offene als Sackgasse. Zur jüngsten Kanon-Debatte und zur Lage der Literaturwissenschaft," Gottfried Willems has proposed three forms of criticism: revision of the existing canon, revision of the concept of literature, and rejection of all canon formation.

16. Thus Geoffrey Jay calls for the abolition of the concept of the canon on explicitly pragmatic grounds, so that "use value" can lead to a situation in which "we may stop thinking in terms of canons altogether". *American Literature and Cultural Wars* (New York: Cornell UP, 1997), 56 and p.176.

17. See Willems, *Begründungen und Funktionen des Kanons*, 222.

18. See Henry Louis Gates, Jr., *Loose Canons: Notes on the Culture Wars* (Oxford: Oxford UP, 1992), 35.

19. See, for example, Hilde Hein, "Refining Feminist Theory", in *Aesthetics in Feminine Perspective*, ed. Hein/Korsmeyer (Bloomington: Indiana UP, 1993), 14.

20. See E. Dean Kolbas, *Critical Theory and Literary Canon*, chapter 2.

21. See Richard Rorty, *Contingency, Irony, and Solidarity* (Cambridge: Cambridge, 1989), 80-81, or Charles Altieri, "An Idea and Ideal of a Literary Canon", in *Canons*, ed. Robert von Hallberg (Chicago: University of Chicago Press, 1984), 44.

22. Bloom, *The Western Canon*, 17.

23. See, for example, Guillory's statement: "authors learn whom to read and how to judge in the schools" and "[...] confront a monumentalized textual tradition already immersed as speakers and writers in the social condition of linguistic stratification." *Cultural Capital: The Problem of Literary Canon Formation* (Chicago: The University of Chicago Press, 1993), 355, 63.

24. On the concept of a history of effects, see the chapter "Das Prinzip der Wirkungsgeschichte" in Hans-Georg Gadamer, *Wahrheit und Methode*. 4th edition (Tübingen: Mohr, 1975), 284-290. Gadamer's name does not appear in the otherwise valuable discussion of the canon in Mads Rosendahl Thomsen, *Mapping World Literature. International Canonization and Transnational Literatures* (London/New York: Continuum, 2008).

25. On time as a corrective and temporal distance as a productive factor in understanding, see Gadamer, *Wahrheit und Methode*, 281.

26. Gadamer, *Gesammelte Werke 8, Ästhetik und Poetik I* (Tübingen: Mohr, 1993), 291.

27. Gadamer, "Der eminente Text und seine Wahrheit" (1986) in *Gesammelte Werke 8*.

28. See Aleida Assmann, *Tid och tradition. Varaktighetens kulturella strategier*, trans. Peter Jackson (Nora: Nya Doxa, 2004), 142, which contains both her critique of Gadamer's concept of the classic and a proposed solution to its inherent problem.

29. On the notion of the classic, see the chapter titled "Das Beispiel des Klassischen" in Gadamer, *Wahrheit und Methode*, 269-275.

30. *Mansfield Park* (London: Collector's Library, 2004), 409-410.

31. In this connection, see Pierre Bourdieu, *The Rules of Art. Genesis and Structure of the Literary Field* (Stanford: Stanford UP, 1996), 159.

32. Assmann, *Tid och tradition. Varaktighetens kulturella strategier*, 161.

33. Gadamer, *Gesammelte Werke 8*, 289.

34. See, for example, Jürgen Habermas, "Der Universalitätsanspruch der

Hermeneutik", *Hermeneutik und Ideologiekritik*. (Frankfurt am Main: Suhrkamp, 1971).

35. Gadamer, *Wahrheit und Methode*, 343.

36. Curtius examines Longinus's equally spectacular and capricious history of effects in *Europäische Literatur und lateinisches Mittelalter*, 402–404.

37. See Ulrich Schulz-Burschhaus, "Curtius und Auerbach als Kanonbildner" in the aforementioned *Begründungen und Funktionen des Kanons*, 155-172.

38. See, for example, Timothy Clark, *The Poetics of Singularity. The Counter-Culturalist Turn in Heidegger, Derrida, Blanchot and the Later Gadamer*. (Edinburgh: Edinburgh UP, 2005).

39. A famous statement of Eurocentric canon formation based on Virgil's *Aeneid* is Eliot's essay "What is a Classic?", *On Poetry and Poets*. London: Faber and Faber, 1971 (1957). In *Das kulturelle Gedächtnis* (München, 1997), Jan Assmann replaces the concept of tradition with "memoria" or "memory".

40. See Rosendahl Thomsen, *Mapping World Literature*.

41. Pascale Casanova, *The World Republic of Letters* (Cambridge: Harvard University Press, 2004).

42. David Damrosch, "World Literature in a Postcanonical, Hypercanonical Age", in *Comparative Literature in an Age of Globalization,* ed. Haun Saussie (Baltimore: Johns Hopkins UP, 2004).

43. Frank Kermode's introductory lecture in *Pleasure and Change, The Aesthetics of Canon. With Geoffrey Hartman, John Guillory and Carey Perloff*, ed. Robert Alter. (Oxford: Oxford UP, 2004).

44. Gadamer, *Wahrheit und Methode*, 280.

2. Monuments of Time

Social Dreams of History: Museum, Utopia, Mythology

JOHAN REDIN

> The true world – unattainable, indemonstrable, unpromisable; but the very thought of it – a consolation, an obligation, an imperative.
>
> *Friedrich Nietzsche*
> How the 'True World' Finally
> Became a Fable

The Crypt of Civilization

In August and September 1977, the United States space agency NASA launched its Voyager program by sending two unmanned probes, Voyager I and Voyager II, on an expedition to study Jupiter and Saturn. The probes were also designed to continue their journey through the outer solar system without a final destination. Like the previous shuttles Pioneer 10 and Pioneer 11 (containing the famous metal plaque representing man and woman in a "state of innocence"), the Voyager probes included a sophisticatedly designed artifact: a gold-plated copper disc comprising a phonographic record engraved with symbols explaining how it should be played. The "Voyager Golden Record" contains 115 analog-encoded images, together with audio tracks of greetings in different languages, beginning with ancient Akkadian and ending with a modern Chinese dialect. Also enclosed are ninety minutes of music, including Mozart and Bach as well as Chuck Berry and various samples of ethnographic recordings. The intention, according to NASA, is "to communicate a story of our world to extraterrestrials".[1]

It will take at least 40,000 years before the Voyager probes enter another planetary system, a timeframe that defies rational speculation.

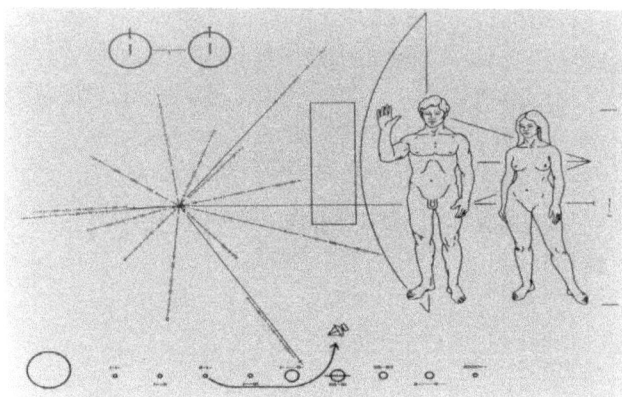

Fig 1. Metal Plaque. Pioneer 10 and 11 missions, 1972–1973. Courtsey NASA/JPL Caltech.

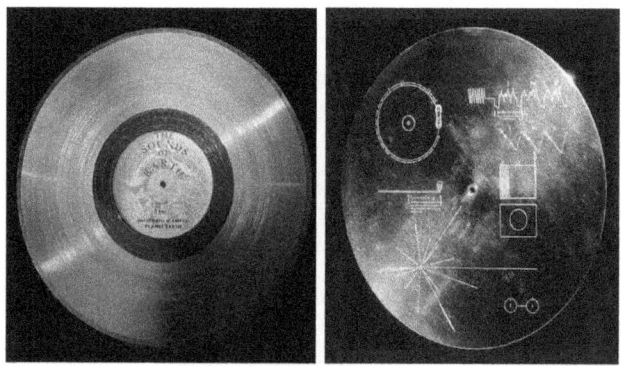

Fig 2–3. Voyager Golden Record. Voyager I and II missions, 1977. Courtsey NASA/JPL Caltech.

Fig 4. The Crypt of Civilization. Oglethorpe © Oglethorpe University, 1936.

Currently, a non-profit French organization is preparing the satellite KEO, an interstellar time capsule packed with thousands of individual spoken messages and images representing daily life on earth. This vessel will also contain human blood (selected at random) and samples of air, water, and earth. It is scheduled for launch in 2012, and will return to earth in about 50,000 years.[2]

In the year 8113, Oglethorpe University (if it still exists) will unlock its time capsule "The Crypt of Civilization", an airtight chamber which was sealed inside university grounds in 1936. The crypt is an 18 m^2 room resting on granite bedrock, located in a converted swimming pool with a heavy stone roof. It houses a variety of artifacts and treasures, mainly donated (some of them by King Gustav V of Sweden), including the university's massive archive of sustainable microfilms, more than 800 classical works of literature (approx. 640,000 pages), and voice and sound recordings ranging from Popeye to Adolf Hitler, Joseph Stalin and Franklin D. Roosevelt. "Done on an epic scale never before conceived," the Crypt of Civilization is regarded as "the first successful attempt to bury a record for any future inhabitants."[3]

Extraterrestrials and future humans: at a first glance, this would seem to be a question of the future. Nonetheless, this is all about how we represent the past. These are just three examples drawn from an astonishing number of projects that have taken a quite radical approach to history. Far from being communications with a distant future, these are attempts to preserve the present.

If it's true that the emergence of national museums was a consequence of the French Revolution and the "new" Europe's "will to identity" (a story that still continues), then it is just as true that this will was born from a revolutionary impulse. The museum was a response to vandalism. The outcome of the revolution (and the many revolutions to follow) created new social reforms, not only for the society as such, it also laid ground for an obsession with the past and the creative elements of cultural memory. In the present essay, I will reflect upon three simultaneous revivals that were initiated during this period and perhaps still are with us: the cult of preservation, the utopian repossession of history, and the prospect of a new mythology.

JOHAN REDIN

Semiophores (Museum)

It is easy to ridicule this kind of future archaeological projects or "intergalactic collections" as being fundamentally naïve in nature; even if their almost desperate attempts to situate history outside of history itself can be quite moving. Launching something into space or burying it deep underground cannot, of course, bring it outside of history as such. Rather, it is an attempt to make it inaccessible and thus outside the horizon of experience, whereupon it enters the realm of desire. Just like the problem of radioactive nuclear waste, burying and hiding something means forgetting it, even if we remain paradoxically aware that it will in no way disappear.

But neither the Voyagers, nor the KEO-satellite, nor the capsule at Oglethorpe University contain any waste of this kind, at least not in a normative sense. It is, rather, the waste of cultural memory: objects. Whatever the physical and degenerative aspects, an object concealed for fifty thousand years has undoubtedly changed ontologically by the time it is recovered. And you don't even have to wait that long. Our closets, garages, and attics contain boxes of memories of different parts of our lives, items *by which* you want to be remembered when you are gone, or items you wish kept because they are connected to those now gone.[4] This desire for connection, the urge to memorialize, offers access to the past by actually obscuring the original object. The object acts as a go-between that mediates between past experiences and the present, and not only on a subjective level: our institutionalized ways of collecting originate in this very desire to make visible the invisible dimension of the in-between. Objects are withdrawn from the world and re-enter it with a new set of meanings; the object is there because of its extra-material qualities and therefore always an object of the present, regardless of its date of origin. As Krzysztof Pomian notes, objects convert into what he calls "semiophores" which reach a metafunctional level where existence depends upon the production of meaning.[5]

In this way, the Oglethorpe crypt corresponds directly to the institutionalized forms of our museums and archives. Consider briefly the following items from its inventory: a typewriter, dental floss, a radio, some plastic toys, an original Hollywood manuscript, a bottle of Budweiser...[6] All objects lose their function once the crypt is sealed, in much the same way as a medieval spoon, by the time it winds up in a museum, is no longer a spoon. The relation between history and representation enters this economy of mediation. Preservation becomes an act of production. This is the kernel of the complex relationship between man and objects, and perhaps the reason why we keep generating them by the billion and, eventually, trying to preserve them by the billion.

The emergence of public museums during the nineteenth century is often considered in immediate relation to the formation of the national state and reformist tendencies throughout Europe.[7] The rise of history and archaeology as disciplines contributed considerably to the formation of 'national identity', as did of course art and architecture. Modernity, or the birth of the new by negotiating the old, needed its collective memories of partly fabricated past experiences and partly fabricated ruins. The staging of history in a public sphere of shared knowledge was a seminal way of achieving this. Thanks to new technologies, it became possible to resurrect the baroque idea of reassembling the world in one single place and lending it the appearance of a whole by means of carefully selected fragments and exemplars. However, baroque allegory was converted into realism only by erecting the historical within an imaginative space – a space open to the density of a textual narrative as well as the synthesizing strategy of using the interval (the gap) between objects.[8]

As an institution, the museum is a time capsule in itself, one that mixes static time with dynamic in analogy with the relation between memory and forgetting. It is at the same time inclusive and exclusive. What you see are exhibitions or public collections: scenes arranged or reconstructed from its often considerable inventory. The heart of the museum is not its exhibitions but its depository, often located underground in climate controlled rooms where artifacts serve as representatives of different historical concerns. It is a belated version of the crypt, not only in the usual sense of catacombs and relics in Romanesque churches, but as the architectural internalization of its own ideological energy.[9] There is nothing mysterious about this "energy"; it's like fossil fuel, the accumulation of matter, age-old resources that serve the production of the new. What comes into play is a construc-

Fig. 5. Detail of inventories.
© Oglethorpe University.

Fig 6. Door to the Crypt.
© Oglethorpe University.

tive tension between the objects "at rest" (in suspension, or repository dwelling) and those on display. The rationality of the disposition is as strange and uncanny as the cemetery: the being *there* of all that is no longer *here*.[10] Yet the museum is not necessarily a cemetery of artifacts being exhibited on *lit de parade*; quite the reverse, it is consumed in the auratic gleam of fetishized mediators. By entering, you may feel "closer to history"; but history is not available for revisiting: it is encrypted and reinstalled in an imaginative space.

Other Spaces (Utopia)

Imaginative space is a modeling element that combines the prospective ideas of culture with the material performativity turned into semantics (i.e. archaeological remains, textual propositions, comparative semiophores, etc.). It is this mode of imagination that generates a social dream of history.

The word "dream" should not be taken as the antonym of reality: it is the possibility of making *present* a world that is *other* to the world in which it takes place, and to do so without contradiction. History could therefore be viewed as a co-creation of chronologies where the actual is conditioned by the possible.[11] By entering the realm of aesthetics, and integrating history with epistemic representations, the imaginative space submits to the political imagination. This plasticity of ideology, turning conclusions into inceptions, is also recognized in the utopian force of creative imagination as a will to history that stresses the will to future.

The concept of utopia has a long tradition that binds together fiction, history, and philosophy into proposal aspects of imagination. Since Thomas More's 1516 novel, utopia has primarily been discussed as a literary genre that underwent a sudden inflation in the nineteenth century.[12] Utopian representations are the desire for the world to be *otherwise*, but also to control it, to create a miniature kingdom so as to escape or to reform. Like the museum, it can make universal claims by using a delimited space in opposition to the outside. However, despite having a literary form, utopia could equally well be considered an individual mode of thought that reaches for the very essence of an imaginary reconstruction of society.[13] It is not exclusively about the ideal state, the *eutopia* or vision of the best of all worlds. The necessity is the *space* that is not yet historical, not yet actual, but that borrows their conceptual forms.

The utopian as political modeling opens up the space between the actual and the possible while often mistaking it for the neutral. What is common to all varieties of utopian thinking is the placing of a new historical situation within a given one, beyond maps and constitutions (the remote island, the state) or by exceeding temporality (once upon a time…). This is the condition that makes utopias future-oriented by essentially remodeling the present, in other words subjected to a historical condition but contesting it by creating a *non-topos*, a *no-where*, presented as a *now-here*.

The no-where of the has-been – in other words, history in its most uncorrupted and melancholy sense – is nothing but the other of the present, navigating our concerns and handling our repressions. Moreover, the idea of 'a world' as such is always a product of the imagination; you are *in* the world, you grasp it with your senses, yet you own it only as a montage of memories. The utopian is an attempt to overcome this, and more or less in the same way as the museum has to pretend to be outside history looking in. This pseudo-position, reached by intentionally forgetting the initial stance, replaces 'a world' with a non-topos in order to make it operative; otherwise, it's just any fiction. Thus all the benefits from reaching this position have to be judged according to the unavoidable weakness that haunts all utopian thinking: whatever the intention, it is forced to be totalizing, since it could never be open-ended; all is there for a reason, and there are no coincidences, no history, no future, only the perpetual present of the ideal.

The Oldest Program (Mythology)

German Romanticism knew about this, which is perhaps why they did not settle for constructing utopias in the classical sense. Christian utopianism and messianic speculation about *futurus* and *adventus* is readily observable in the work of Friedrich von Hardenberg (Novalis) and Friedrich Schlegel, where it is repeatedly theorized within an aesthetic-theological context.[14]

While the French Revolution was a revolution of the people, idealism and romanticism were a "revolution of the spirit"; a statement made loud and clear with Hegel's philosophy of the absolute. Initially, however, there were politically radical attempts to confront essential institutions such as the university, the church, the monarchy and the state; a "poetic revolution" which regarded society as needing to move towards a shared imaginary center, "just like mythology was for the classical age".[15] In a text from 1800, Schlegel suggests a "new mythology" that will remove all distinctions between the productive imagination and the historical, philosophical fact of being in the world. The world is grasped aesthetically, i.e. creatively, yet identified only when broken down into discursive knowledge. But the world is itself a productive and originary force that acts in response to the co-producing power of the subject. Historical time is fundamentally a tension between past and future, and it is the imagination, not reason, that holds the two together. Between past and future, romanticism wanted to leave the door open.

Although Schlegel did not know of its existence, similar ideas were elaborated in an anonymous document of 1796/97 that was more or less written collectively by Friedrich Hölderlin, Friedrich Schelling, and G.W.F Hegel. The document, much later given the title *The Oldest Systematic Program of German Idealism*, suggests that the "monotheism of reason" must be combined with the "polytheism of art and imagination".[16] That the past is recalled by memory and imagination does not mean that it remains past; it is not a virtual container of stagnant impressions or physical remnants in depositories and libraries. It is there endlessly for our desires of recreation. They call for a "new mythology", a new imaginary center, which should not be mistaken for a demand for a new religion or archetypal narratives in the style of Herodotus or Ovid. Even if romanticism is known for its obsession with antiquity it is not a *return* of the classical mythology they anticipate.[17] Mythology provided an opportunity to imagine a new society in which all conditioned principles would be superfluous, and to bring the imagined community into a community of imagination.

Today the idea of a new mythology may seem preposterous and 'romantic' in the pejorative sense of the word.[18] Nonetheless, some of its central ideas were implemented in administrative forms, and later, under the spell of science, eventually acquiring institutionalized and even repressive functions. In complete contradiction, history held society hostage and this in terms of an official authority of its *heritage*. In other words, the very phenomenon of the museum is equally preposterous, not to mention the NASA version of its representation of the distant future. In their pursuit of collecting, classifying, restoring, and narrating, cultural memory and historical representation have perhaps lost track of their common denominator: the imagination and the very ability to *make up the past*. What if the past is not (and never will be) "there" as something irreversible and finished, but something yet unfinished.

Notes

1. <http://voyager.jpl.nasa.gov/spacecraft/goldenrec.html.> The project was managed by Carl Sagan.

2. See www.keo.org. The project is an initiative by the French artist-scientist Jean-Marc Philippe.

3. <http://www.oglethorpe.edu/about_us/crypt_of_civilization/history_of_the_crypt.asp.> Project initiated by Thornwell Jacobs (1877–1956) and now run by a special committee at Oglethorpe University. Jacobs describes his program in "Today–Tomorrow: Archeology in A.D. 8113", *Scientific American* (November 1936). See also William E. Jarvis, *Time Capsules: A Cultural History* (McFarland 2003).

4. For a sensitive study of this immaterial distribution of the material, see Elizabeth Hallam and Jenny Hockey, *Death, Memory & Material Culture* (Oxford: Berg, 2001). On "der Akt der Belebung" and the continuation of living by means of things, see Jan Assmann, *Das kulturelle Gedächtnis* (München: Beck, 1999), 33 f.

5. Krzysztof Pomian, *Der Ursprung des Museums: Vom Sammeln*, trans. Gustav Rossler (Berlin: Wagenbach, 1998), 49 ff. For the argument that making the past present is in fact a detachment from the past, see Michel de Certeau, "The Historiographical Operation", in *The Writing of History* (New York: Columbia University Press, 1988), 56–112.

6. < http://www.georgiaencyclopedia.org/nge/Article.jsp?id=h-864>

7. Tony Bennett, *The Birth of the Museum* (London: Routledge, 1995) and Benedict Anderson, *Imagined Communities: Reflections on the Origin and Spread of Nationalism*, rev. 2nd ed. (London: Verso, 2006).

8. For different features of these premises, see Jonathan Crary's *Suspensions of Perception: Attention, Spectacle and Modern Culture* (Cambridge: MIT Press, 1999) and Barbara M. Stafford's *Visual Analogy: Consciousness as the Art of Connecting* (Cambridge: MIT Press, 1999).

9. Johan Redin and Peter Jackson, "The Crypt: The Obscure Administration of Cultural Memory", *Temenos: Nordic Journal of Comparative Religion*, (Helsinki 2011), forthcoming.

10. Michel Foucault, "Of Other Spaces", *Diacritics* 16 (Spring 1986), 22–27. See also Johan Redin, "Inför fornminneslagen", *Glänta* 1.11 (Gothenburg 2011), 106–109.

11. I am thinking of the coexistence of the *two* Romes in what would later be termed Renaissance (rebirth). The resurrection of antiquity *within* early modernity was also the birth of archaeology itself; see Leonard Barkan, *Unearthing the Past: Archaeology and Aesthetics in the Making of Renaissance Culture* (New Haven: Yale University Press, 1999); cf. the chapter "Creative Anachronism" in David Loewenthal's *The Past is a Foreign Country* (Cambridge: Cambridge University Press, 1985), 390 ff. On imagination as extra-temporal ordering, see Johan Redin and Gabor Bora, "Fossils and Terrestrial Philosophy: Leibniz' *Protogea* and Aesthetics", in *Cardanus: Jahrbuch für Wissenschaftsgeschichte*, Vol. 6 (Heidelberg: Palatina, 2006), 75–86.

12. See Lyman Tower Sargent, "The Three Faces of Utopianism Revisited", *Utopian Studies* 5:1 (1994), 1–37, and Phillip E. Wegner, *Imaginary Communities: Utopia, The Nation and the Spatial Histories of Modernity* (Berkeley: University of California Press, 2002).

13. The rehabilitation started with Ernst Bloch and has been continued by the British sociologist Ruth Levitas. See her *The Concept of Utopia* (Hertfordshire: Syracuse University Press, 1990). For utopia across aesthetic borders, see the anthologies edited by Jörn Rüsen and Michael Fehr, *Thinking Utopia: Steps into Other Worlds* (Berghahn 2007) and *Die Unruhe der Kultur: Potentiale des Utopischen* (Velbrück 2004).

14. For a thorough consideration of romantic utopian modes and historical consciousness, see Hans-Joachim Mähl, *Die Idee des goldenen Zeitalters im Werk des Novalis. Studien zur Wesensbestimmung der frühromantischen Utopie und zu ihren ideengeschichtlichen Voraussetzungen* (Heidelberg: Winter, 1965). On *futurs* and *adventus*, see Alice A. Kuzinar, *Delayed Endings: Nonclosure in Novalis and Hölderlin* (Athens: University of Georgia Press, 1987), 29–40.

15. Friedrich Schlegel, "Rede über die Mythologie", in *Werke in einem Band*, ed. Wolfdietrich Rasch (München: Hanser, 1982), 496–503.

16. For a translation, see *The Early Political Writings of the German Romantics*, ed. Fredrick Beiser (Cambridge University Press, 1996), 1–6. The fragment was found by Franz Rosenzweig and first published in 1917. On the long controversy over its authorship and content, see Peter Hansen, *Das älteste Systemprogramm des deutschen Idealismus: Interpretationen und Rezeptionsgeschichte* (Berlin: de Gruyter, 1989). The title is confusing since it does not in fact represent a systematic approach at all but, rather, outlines prototypical ideas that return in the very different systems of Schelling and Hegel as well as in the mythopoetic notes of Hölderlin.

17. Dieter Sturma, "Politics and the New Mythology: The turn to Late Romanticism", in *The Cambridge Companion to German Idealism*, ed. Karl Ameriks (Cambridge University Press, 2000), 219–238.

18. Not to say even frightening in the perspective of the German "longing for a new kingdom" during the era of National Socialism. This lineage is inviting in terms of political rhetoric and has been stressed in several ways; yet it is far more complex than creating equilibrium between these documents and the ridiculous ideas of Alfred Rosenberg. For a thorough analysis of the historical implications, see Manfred Frank, *Der kommende Gott: Vorlesungen über die Neue Mythologie* (Frankfurt: Suhrkamp, 1982) and *Gott im Exil: Vorlesungen über die Neue Mythologie II* (Frankfurt: Suhrkamp, 1988).

Walking Through History: Archaeology and Ethnography in Museum Narration

JOHAN HEGARDT

Introduction

In 1866, a new National Museum (*Nationalmuseum*) opened opposite the Royal Palace in the centre of Stockholm. Its purpose was to show Swedish history, from the beginning to the present, through prehistoric and medieval sections on the ground floor and art history on the second and third floors. The museum's prehistoric and medieval collection was named the Museum of National Antiquities (MNA), and carried on a separate existence inside the National Museum.

In 1940, after many years of chaos resulting from space shortages at the National Museum, MNA was transferred to a new building in the district of Östermalm. This also meant that the National Museum became a more conventional art history museum. One important reason for the relocation was proximity to the Nordic Museum, which had been founded together with the folk heritage park Skansen by Artur Hazelius (1833–1901) in the late nineteenth century, with holdings going back to the sixteenth century, or, more precisely, 1523. According to established Swedish history, Sweden became an independent state when Gustavus I (1496–1560) was crowned King of Sweden on 6 June 1523, and visitors to the Nordic Museum are greeted by a monumental statue of Gustavus I. MNA, on the other hand, assumed responsibility for prehistoric objects and religious art from the Catholic period (1050–1523). Together, the two museums created a straight chronological line from prehistory to the present.

In May 2010, an exhibition of Swedish history opened at MNA. This was the first time since 1940 that the museum had hosted a permanent exhibition, which crossed the historic threshold of 1523 that had conventionally demarcated the two museums' areas of interest. With the exhibition "The History of Sweden", the MNA now covers the history of Swedish society from prehistory to the present and beyond in chronological order.

In this essay I will address the chronologically-based historical narrative that has been and is today in use in museum displays at the MNA. My argument will be that this narrative only makes sense through analogy with ethnography, and that museum displays organised chronologically play a part in the implicit structures of time/space oppression and racism. I will try to show this through some examples from the history of archaeology and anthropology and from the MNA.[1]

A world of ethnographic objects

During the late eighteenth century Europe was flooded with ethnographic objects. These objects became important for philosophy, history, and the social and natural sciences, as well as for shaping a progressive, teleological narrative of cultural development. Numerous studies have addressed this topic.[2] However, I will here take my lead from Emmanuel Eze's study *Achieving Our Humanity*.[3] Eze points out that "Once God has been reconceptualized as a 'clock maker' rather than as unknowable dice thrower, the human science – and philosophy in its suit – found new modes of existence and new frames of reference".[4] Moreover, according to Eze, we need to explore further the extent to which "modern philosophical thought has contributed to the formation and maintenance of ideologies of racialism and, indirectly, racism – in academic discourse as in general culture".[5] Eze's point is that philosophy is indebted to ethnography and anthropology, and he asks: "How did the origins of modern philosophy and the science of anthropology provide the theoretical grounds for the formation of race as a modern idea?"[6] To answer this question, Eze returns to Kant, Descartes, and Hume, among others.

What Eze's work shows is that ethnography helped eighteenth-century philosophers, social scientists, and historians to structure the world chronologically and, in the process, to contribute to the formation of racist ideologies. This is my point of departure and I will try to show how important ethnography was for the formation of modern archaeology during the nineteenth century, and how archaeology in turn supplied ethnography with a historical and chronological perspective on ethnographic material. The relationship between these two disciplines also lies at the heart of chronologically-based museum narratives, which means that we are dealing with a perspective where ethnography plays a crucial part in creating meaning, with respect not only to the past but also to latterday racism. Yet it was not, and is not, possible for ethnography to do this alone. It needed a universal history, time, and chronology. Together, these perspectives created an idea of cultural progression and evolution that have been on display in museums since at least the late-nineteenth century.

Geology, anthropology and archaeology

Prior to the early nineteenth century, European history was silent beyond the written sources. Fossil finds and catastrophic changes that could be studied in the layers of the Earth were explained through reference to The Old Testament.[7] However, these explanations were challenged during the first half of the nineteenth century by archaeologists and geologists, and as was the Biblical dating of the Earth to 4004 B.C. and the idea that Adam was the first human being. Instead, a time/space paradigm and evolution were gradually accepted.[8]

The Swedish zoologist, geologist, and archaeologist Sven Nilsson (1787–1883) was one of the first Europeans to use the word "prehistory" in a scientific context,[9] which opened the way for a new approach to history and time. In the 1820s, Christian Jürgensen Thomsen (1788–1865) was appointed secretary of the Antiquities Commission in Copenhagen, where he presented his famous three-age system in 1836: the Stone Age, the Bronze Age, and the Iron Age.[10] Prehistory had now a chronology.

During the early nineteenth century, nationalist narratives became increasingly important, along with natural science and a strictly empirical epistemology.[11] Thomsen worked closely with Adam W. Hauch (1755–1838), a natural scientist and an important figure at the Royal Court in Copenhagen, who argued in his writings for a strictly empirical science.[12] Hauch demanded that all museum collections in Copenhagen be ordered by chronology and, through his influence, Thomsen became one of the most important European museum curators of the first half of the nineteenth century.[13]

Chronology is not enough, however, for the creation of significant cultural-historical narratives in museum displays. As has been stated, Europe was during the second half of the eighteenth century flooded with ethnographic objects, which Thomsen and Nilsson later used in their comparative studies and museum displays to assign social and human functions to archaeological artefacts. Nilsson's and Thomsen's work was to influence colonial anthropology during the late nineteenth century and early twentieth century.

Lewis Henry Morgan (1818–1881), Edward B. Tylor (1832–1917), and James George Frazer (1854–1941) were the towering figures of colonial anthropology during the late nineteenth century. They viewed Scandinavian archaeology as important. Tylor wrote: "It was with a true appreciation of the bearings of this science that one of its founders, the venerable Professor Sven Nilsson, declared in 1843 in the Introduction to his 'Primitive Inhabitants of Scandinavia', that we are 'unable properly to understand the significance of the antiquities of any individual country without at the same time clearly realizing the idea that they are the fragments of a progressive series of civilization, and that the human race has always been, and still is, steadily advancing in civilization.'"[14]

Tylor's three stages of development – Savages, Barbarians, and Civilisation – first appeared in *Primitive Culture*, a book published three years after the English translation of Nilsson's *Primitive Inhabitants of Scandinavia* (Swedish edition, 1843).[15] In it, Nilsson stressed that the human race had progressed through the Savage, Nomadic, and Peasant Stages, in order reach nineteenth-century civilisation.

According to Morgan: "The terms 'Age of Stone', 'of Bronze' and 'of Iron', introduced by Danish archaeologists, have been extremely useful for certain purposes, and will remain so for the classification of objects of ancient art; but the progress of knowledge has rendered other and different subdivisions necessary."[16] Social and cultural evolution was powered by economic change, and every culture depended on the historical complexity of technology and economy.[17]

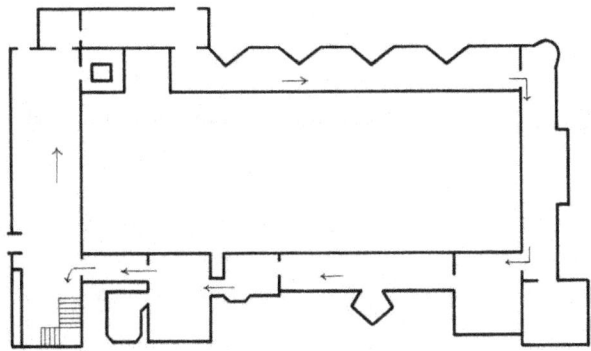

Fig. 1. Walking through history. MNA, 1943. First arrow: Entrance hall. Thereafter: Stone Age, Bronze Age and Iron Age. Last arrow points to the medieval sections of the museum. Courtesy of Riksantikvarieämbetet. Image © Riksantikvarieämbetet.

Frazer was well aware of Scandinavian archaeology when he constructed his three-stage system based on the successive movement from magic through religion to science.[18] He used references to Sven Nilsson, directly and indirectly, drawing on Llewellyn Lloyd (1792–1876) and other sources.[19] He asked: "– just as on the material side of human culture there has everywhere been an Age of Stone, so on the intellectual side there has everywhere been an Age of Magic? There are reasons for answering this question in the affirmative."[20]

Through geology, archaeology, and other similar sciences, the time/space paradigm was invented, and the world ordered and collected accordingly. We are dealing with a rather wide and complex "text" that the agents both shaped and were shaped by. This text still exists and is on display in many cultural-historical museums such as the MNA in Stockholm. Since the beginning of the nineteenth century, and throughout the twentieth century, these museums have communicated a narrative of cultural-historical evolution. Like chronology, this narrative – that European humanity and societies, mentally and technologically, have developed from primitive societies to increasingly advanced societies according to the evolutionary logic of race and culture – made sense, and still makes sense, to the public. This perspective is strengthened and explained through ethnographic references.

JOHAN HEGARDT

*The History of Sweden
and Prehistory number one*

The Swedish government decided to build a National Museum as far back as 1845. At that time Bror Emil Hildebrand (1806–1884) was responsible for the nation's antiquities. He responded immediately, writing a memorandum in which he explained in detail how the new museum should be organized. He emphasized that the museum must be based on Thomsen's chronologically-structured museums in Copenhagen. By structuring the museum in this way, the museum would guide its public through history in the right order. But there were also other rooms in his museum. One of these contained ethnographic objects, from many parts of the world, which were important for professional archaeologists working with chronological comparison.

When in the 1930s it had been decided that MNA should move to new buildings, Axel Bagge (1894–1953) wrote a memorandum stressing the importance of using ethnographic films of what he called "recent" people in exhibits about life in prehistoric societies. It should be noted that during the 1930s ethnographic films became increasingly important around the world.[21]

These two examples show how the idea of ethnographic comparison has been, and continues to be, central to the museum. The MNA today presents the historical development of society from a remote past into an unknown future. This is effected by means of various exhibitions, two of which I will discuss here: "The History of Sweden" and "Prehistory number one". It is my intention, not to criticize museum staff, but to show how chronologically-structured museum displays, implicitly and in relation to a "broader text", contribute to the formation and maintenance of implicitly racist ideologies.

The first things we see when entering "Prehistory number one" are two large ice-blue pillars, illustrating the Ice Age. A text explains that the exhibit focuses on people by means of questions such as "What are human beings?" or "Who am I?" The museum also writes: "We know how people lived and died, but it is more difficult to know their feelings and thoughts: What did they like, what did they believe in, and what were they afraid of?"

Why ask these questions? The exhibit addresses historical subjects

Fig. 2. Timeline in the exhibit "The History of Sweden".
Photo: Johan Hegardt

who, since the early nineteenth century, have been considered ethnographically. The museum still relies on the idea of a progressive series of cultural stages culminating in the European Enlightenment. By means of this "broader text" the museum implies that these historical subjects could not have asked themselves, "What can I know? What can I do? What can I dream of?" – that is, the questions famously posed by Kant in his essay "Answer to the Question: What is Enlightenment?" The difference between Kant's questions and those asked by the museum are significant. They seem to presuppose that primitive Stone Age people, and more "developed" Bronze Age or Iron Age people living in a world of magic or religion, did not and could not ask the same questions that have been asked by educated people since the Enlightenment.

That this is an example of the distinction between the modern versions of *humanitas* and *anthropos* – us and the object, or time and the other – is underscored by another statement in the exhibition: "They all lived long ago. Much is strange, but there are similarities with our time and us. It could have been you living then." If we had lived then, however, we would not have been the same as we are. Through the logic of the time/space paradigm, historical subjects, like ethnographic subjects, are humans but at the same time something less.

The timeline in "The History of Sweden" races through history, touching on historical events and objects about which the museum thinks we ought to know something, before disappearing into the future. The tendency is that the ethnographic analogy follows history until the sixteenth century. Twelfth century rulers, for instance, are described as a kind of "mafiosi" related to God, implying an ethnographic parallel with tribal societies in contemporary Afghanistan, for example. After the sixteenth century, however, history becomes transparent and there is no need for ethnographic analogy. Europe has become Europe, reason is taking shape, and the continent is moving in its own historical direction. For Sweden, as the exhibition underscores, the crucial date is 1523.

The museum's walk through history is made possible by the time/space paradigm and a "broader text" that has been shaped by many different sciences since the mid-nineteenth century. Neither this paradigm nor the scientific perspectives existed before the end of the eighteenth century. Yet in museum displays time is often still viewed as something universal and neutral, structured vertically and chronologically. Walking through history is a walk through space that has been mapped out spatially. Time is evolution and evolution is time. In this paradigm the Other is also mapped out and confined within a system of coordinates that covers not only the surface of the planet but also its layers of soil. The technical and instrumental structures of the time/space paradigm come to life through ethnographic analogy. The remains of historical culture X are defined in terms of contemporary or "recent" culture Y, and the other way around. This takes place, as we have seen, on the basis of technology, for example, stone tools. But it also has social, moral, and intellectual implications, as has been underlined in philosophy, ethnography and archaeology, since the late eighteenth century. It is here that the ethnographic analogy comes to the fore in the walk through history. Without it, we would neither understand the narrative nor find it significant. Described in this fashion, the time/space paradigm becomes a tool in the ongoing marginalization of those that have lived and who continue to live outside time or outside the present, as Emmanuel Eze has shown. And museum displays organised chronologically and in combination with ethnographic comparison continue to play an implicit part in cognitive structures of racism.

The question is, would we care about this chronologically-structured story if it were not for its distancing of the Other and mirroring of the self through questions about who we are and what it means to be human? According to Eze, Enlightenment philosophers, together with ethnographers, archaeologists and many others, answered these questions with ethnocentric flair and racial chauvinism.[22] There was a time when this narrative made sense but in today's world of cosmopolitan transmission, difference, and new obligations, which Kwame Anthony Appiah and others have analysed, it is time for us to move on to other narratives.[23]

Notes

1. This essay emerges from "A Historical Museum and How it Shaped Sweden", a three-year project launched in January 2009 and financed by "The Royal Swedish Academy of Letters, History and Antiquities", "The Swedish Arts Council", and "The Museum of National Antiquities" (from 2010 known as "The National Historical Museum"), and is affiliated with the research program "Time, Memory and Representation". The focus of the project is to determine how the production of meaning by museums has influenced Swedish society.

2. For example, Johannes Fabian, *Time and the Other: How Anthropology Makes its Object,* foreword by Matti Bunzi, (New York: Columbia University Press, 2002). Patricia Lorenzoni, *Att färdas under dödens tecken: Frazer, imperiet och den försvinnande vilden,* Logos/Pathos nr 10. (Glänta production, 2008).

3. Emmanuel Chukwudi Eze, *Achieving Our Humanity: The Idea of the Postracial Future* (New York & London: Routledge, 2001).

4. Eze, *Achieving Our Humanity.*

5. Eze, *Achieving Our Humanity,* ix

6. Eze, *Achieving Our Humanity,* 3

7. Gerhard Regnéll, "Zoologen och arkeologen som var geolog," in *Sven Nilsson: En lärd i 1800-talets Lund,* ed. Gerhard Regnéll (Lund: Studier utgivna av Kungl. fysiografiska sällskapet i Lund, 1983), 26.

8. Glynn Daniel, *A Hundred and Fifty Years of Archaeology* (Duckwoth, 1978).

9. Daniel, *A Hundred and Fifty Years of Archaeology.*

10. Christian Jürgensen Thomsen, "Kortfattet Udsigt over Mindesmærker og Oldsager fra Nordens Fortid," in *Ledetraad til Nordisk Oldkyndighed.* (Kjöbenhavn: Udgiven af det Kongelige Nordiske Oldskrift-Selskab, 1836), 27–90.

11. Ernest Renan, "What is a Nation?", trans. and annotated by Martin Thom, in *Nation and Narration* ed. Homi K. Bhabha (London and New York: Routledge, 2006), 8–23.

12. Adam Wilhelm Hauch, *Inledning till naturkunnigheten. Öfversatt ifrån andra danska upplagan af C.G. Sjösten.* (Stockholm, 1800/1808, 1st edition 1795).

13. Jørgen Jensen, *Thomsens museum: Historien om Nationalmuseet* (Copenhagen: Gyldendalska Boghandel Nordisk Forlag A/S), 1992.

14. Edward B. Tylor, *Primitive Culture: Researches into the Development of Mythology, Philosophy, Religion, Language, Art, and Custom.* 2 vols. Vol. I (London 1871), 55–56.

15. Sven Nilsson, *The Primitive Inhabitants of Scandinavia: An Essay on Comparative Ethnography, and a Contribution to the History of the Development of Mankind: Containing a Description of the Implements, Dwellings, Tombs, and Mode of Living of the Savages in the North of Europe during the Stone Age.* Third new edition and with an introduction by J. Lubbock (London, 1868).

16. Lewis H. Morgan, *Ancient Society or Researches in the Lines of Human Progress from Savagery through Barbarism to Civilization* (Harvard University Press, 1964), 15.

17. Morgan, *Ancient Society,* 15

18. James G. Frazer, *Den gyllene grenen: Studier i magi och religion* (Stockholm: Bokförlaget Natur och Kultur, 1925), 828–829.

19. Llewellyn Lloyd, *Peasant Life in Sweden* (London: Tinsley Brothers, 1870). Frazer, *Den gyllene grenen,* 832, 834, 835, 836.

20. Frazer, *Den gyllene grenen,* 74.

21. Beate Engelbrecht, ed., *Memories of the Origin of Ethnographic Film* (Frankfurt am Main: Peter Lang, 2007).

22. Eze, *Achieving Our Humanity,* 16.

23. Kwame Anthony Appiah, *Cosmopolitanism: Ethics in a World of Strangers* (London: Penguin Books, 2006).

Creative Confusion: Modern Ruins and the Archaeology of the Present

MATS BURSTRÖM

Archaeology isn't what it used to be. It used to limit itself to studying relics of the distant past, its very narrative of being seemingly premised on the lack of any sources of knowledge beyond ancient artefacts and remains. In the absence of texts, one had to make do with things. Over time, however, archaeology has broadened its field of enquiry to include periods with written documentation. Today, archaeology even concerns itself with the recent past that lies within the experience and memory of living people.

Since most people still associate archaeology with the study of ancient history, an archaeology of the present can sound like a contradiction in terms. The concept can seem confusing and fanciful. Many people are surprised to learn that the material of their own lives has become a topic of interest for archaeology, a discovery that forces them to reflect on the passage of time and on their own place in history. This is not always a pleasant process; the limited duration of one's own existence suddenly becomes more visible than before. The individual is reminded that there was a time before his or her own life, and that there will also be a time after. One's lifetime is put into a larger context in which different periods of time converge and overlap in the present moment.

The emergence of an archaeology of the present means that archaeology as a field can no longer be defined in terms of chronological criteria. It's also clear from the thoughts and emotions triggered by the study of contemporary objects that material traces are important as more than just sources of knowledge. Archaeology of the present has begun revealing to us the outlines of a research field that refuses to be constrained by Modernism's rigid distinction between then and now, reason and emotion. This boundary-crossing is becoming particularly apparent in the investigation of Modernism's own material remains.

Modern ruins

There is a striking preoccupation with modern ruins these days, which finds expression *inter alia* in the fine arts, film, internet photo galleries, literature, and popular ruin sites. Moreover, there has been a vogue for books filled with aesthetic photographs of abandoned twentieth-century locations in varying stages of decay. Not infrequently, the photographs are seen as speaking for themselves.

In Sweden, Jan Jörnmark's books about abandoned places (*Övergivna platser*[1]) are the best known and most successful examples of this genre. His website[2] is also popular, and his pictures have formed the basis of photography exhibitions as well as radio and TV programmes. Working with pictures and text, Jörnmark, who is an economic historian, has shown convincingly how "big" history and "small" history are related, and how global business cycles have consequences for an individual local community and its inhabitants. Such dependent relationships are familiar enough as a general phenomenon, but Jörnmark's images of its material impact convey a powerfully physical dimension of reality. The Swedish radio show *Kulturradion* aptly described Jörnmark's first book as "a fascinating archaeological study of things suddenly consigned to the past – factories, housing estates, amusement parks".[3]

Internationally, too, one finds numerous examples of books addressed to a general readership that use suggestive photographs to convey an image of modernity in ruins. These books are often lavishly produced and bear evocative titles such as *Abandoned Places*,[4] *Beauty in Decay*,[5] *Dead Tech: A Guide to the Archaeology of Tomorrow*,[6] *Deathtopia*,[7] *Derelict London*,[8] *Forbidden Places: Exploring our Abandoned Heritage*,[9] *Paradiesruinen*,[10] *Ruins*,[11] *Ruins of Detroit*,[12] and *Unquiet Ruin: A Photographic Excavation*.[13] Some deal with a single building, city, or country, while others range across national boundaries and between different continents. As the titles indicate, their authors are keen to promote such investigations as a process of archaeological excavation.

Academic research also shows a strong interest in twentieth-century ruins, using photographs to convey their particular atmosphere. In Britain, for example, cultural geographer Tim Edensor started a debate with his mapping of industrial spaces in *Industrial Ruins: Space, Aesthetics and Materiality*.[14] Another example is the thought-provoking study of the remains of Pyramiden, a Soviet mining town in the High Arctic, by Norwegian photographer Elin Andreassen and archaeologists Hein B. Bjerk and Bjørnar Olsen in their book *Persistent Memories*.[15] Olsen is also leading the international research project "Ruin Memories: Materiality, Aesthetics, and the Archaeology of the Recent Past".[16]

The question is, how should we understand this strong interest in modern ruins? Is it merely an expression of the classical romanticizing of ruins, now projected onto more recent remains simply because these have had time to fall into ruin? Or is there something else at work here?

The meaning of time

Archaeologists have a unique understanding of how time and its passage take material form in the world of living people, yet archaeology's relation to ruins is far from uncomplicated. The Finno-Swedish author Göran Schildt writes:

> Now, it's a fact that archaeologists and ruins are in a sense enemies. The archaeologist sees in the ruin only what it was before it became a ruin; he wants to investigate the building's practical purpose and he does what he can to *conserve* whatever he comes across, lifting those severely timeworn remains out of time so that they are not spoiled further.[17]

While acknowledging some sympathy for this attitude from the point of view of historical research, Schildt adopts another perspective:

> From this perspective, which might be termed poetic or ontological, all conservation is a loss because it deprives the ruin of its essential quality: its relation to time. Can anything give us a more vivid understanding

of time's exceptional dimension, and of our own place in this context, than such flotsam and jetsam ... ?

As Schildt suggests, when dealing with remains of this kind from ancient Greece or Rome, most of us regard their ruin as a normal state. Time's arrow has flown its course, leaving behind collapsed temples and fallen columns. Our own experience does not allow us to feel the original shape of the building structure, and, were they suddenly to reappear in all their former glory, it is far from certain that they would correspond to our classical ideals. Perhaps we would be disappointed at their garish colour and lack of open spaces.

Matters are otherwise with modern ruins. Even if we have no personal experience of many present-day spaces, we are nonetheless very familiar with their general form. We know the approximate physical form of twentieth-century factories, residential districts, or amusement parks, and we have a basic understanding of how they have been used. This recognition creates a feeling of intimacy. When we then encounter these spaces in a state of ruin or gradual decay, they affect us in another, more personal way than ancient ruins.

This is the effect used in the famous final scene in the film *Planet of the Apes* (1968). As the last surviving astronaut rides along the beach, he suddenly sees the remains of a familiar statue – the Statue of Liberty – sticking out of the sand and pointing towards the horizon. He is devastated by the painful realization that his long journey in space has led him precisely back to Earth, which has been laid waste by a nuclear war during his absence.

To our eyes, modern ruins give another, often more brutal impression than classical ruins. This was also the starting-point for Albert Speer's famous "Theory of Ruin Value".[18] In 1934, his first major commission as architect for Hitler was to design a permanent stone replacement for the temporary grandstand beside the Zeppelin Field in the rallying grounds at Nuremberg. In order to make room, it was necessary to pull down some buildings used for vehicles. Passing by the demolished piles, Speer was appalled by their hideousness; rusty iron reinforcing rods protruded in every direction, lying higgledy-piggledy among shapeless lumps of concrete and other detritus. Speer proceeded to formulate a theory of ruins, whose central idea is that buildings should be constructed in such a way that they offer a majestic and imposing spectacle even in a state of ruin after hundred or thousands of years. Speer illustrated his theory with the help of a romantic drawing that showed what the Zeppelin Field's new grandstand would look like as a ruin, with fallen columns and ivy growing over its partly collapsed walls. Hitler was persuaded, and gave orders that henceforth all important buildings in the Third Reich should be constructed in accordance with Speer's theory of ruins. Most of these buildings had not been completed, however, by the time the thousand-year Reich was itself consigned to the dustbin of history.

Speer's theory has become a headache for Nuremberg's municipal authorities. How to deal with the thorny cultural legacy presented by the rallying ground and its colossal buildings? On the one hand, to restore these buildings risks recreating the imposing and ideologically freighted symbol which the Nazi regime intended. On the other hand, to allow their remains to become derelict instead would seem to be in accordance with Speer's theory of ruins. The solution adopted by the authorities has been to leave the buildings in a state of semi-disrepair; they are to look neglected and can be used only for so-called "banal" purposes.[19]

The lure of decay

Heritage managers have run into difficulties when dealing with modern ruins and other present-day remains whose most significant feature is that they are a state of continuing decay. An old car wrecking yard in a bog outside Tingsryd in southern Sweden offers an illustrative example.[20] Each year the wrecking yard draws several thousand visitors, who come to look at the hundred or so cars, dating from the 1930s to the 1970s, which sit there in varying stages of decomposition. In an age of environmental awareness and recycling, car wrecks like these have become a rarity. Visitors naturally include a number of nostalgic car enthusiasts, who expertly record the various makes and models. But what attracts most visitors to make what is virtually a pilgrimage to this site, is the ongoing decay.

The fact that many visitors can themselves recall a time when these models were new, or at least still in circulation on the roads, increases

Nature reclaims that which until recently was most modern.
Photo: Mats Burström.

their fascination with the cars' current condition. Once well-kept status objects, these means of rapid conveyance now rest in silence as they are reclaimed by nature. The car cemetery provides something akin to a spiritual experience. Rusted through, with headlight sockets gaping and trees forcing their way through the chassis, these wrecked cars awake memories and thoughts. It is as if the fate of things forces us to contemplate our own.

The gap between what until recently was new and modern, and what is now slowly decaying before our eyes, is also the theme of a calendar, *Abandoned Autos*, published annually in the United States. In it, aesthetic photographs of rusty car wrecks in bucolic settings sit alongside advertising images from when the models were new. This juxtaposition of advertisements exuding optimism about the future with the physical remains of the present, is compelling. How things have changed in only a few years! The motif of "before and after" reminds us that the here and now, too, will become the past. How will we look back then on what is now? What will seem important and what will have been revealed as insignificant? Thinking about this can affect our life-choices and thereby alter the future.

In the late 1990s, the old car wrecks outside Tingsryd became the focus of a conflict of principles. Should the wrecks be considered a polluting of the countryside and thus taken away for scrap, or should they be allowed to remain in place and enjoy protection as items of cultural heritage? In an interview, the county council's chief archaeologist declared:

> Our task is to stop the process of decay, to prevent the site from degrading. Obviously, if you want to preserve the wrecks, you have to arrest the process of decay.[21]

This proposal for protecting the car wrecks would thus have stopped the very process of unhindered decay which gives the site its character and fascinates its many visitors. One is reminded of Schildt's words on the enmity between archaeologists and ruins as well as of his notion of conservation as stripping things of their relationship to time. The chief archaeologist's position reveals a kind of perspective on eternity that is not unusual in heritage management; temporal flow and material degradation are to be kept invisible while we strive to keep artefacts in a state of preservation by arresting time.[22] Naturally, all such attempts are doomed to failure.

The issue of the car wrecks' future was finally resolved after the local authorities agreed to lease the land for a nominal fee for the purposes of a "veteran car installation" (*veterankarossanläggning*). Apparently, the matter could only be resolved by the dubious expedient of creating a new word in Swedish.

Shadings of the modern

Like the concept of an archaeology of the present, modernity in ruins presents a kind of contradiction in terms. By definition, the modern is expected to represent what is new and forward-looking, not what is dated and already decayed. Nothing becomes un-modern more rapidly than that which is most modern, of course, but we usually imagine this stage as being very far from collapse and ruin. Perhaps we do not yet have the right words to describe a modernity in this condition, and perhaps it is for this reason that photographs have assumed so central a place in the contemporary fascination with ruins. With its presumed authenticity, the photograph takes up where the written word has to leave off.

For the German philosopher Edmund Husserl, the essence of a thing can only be understood by consideration from an array of perspectives, in different lights, and from various distances. The thing will then stand out in relief against what Husserl calls its "shading" (*Ger.* Abschattungen). Perhaps our preoccupation with modern ruins stems from their mediation of another image – another "shading" – of modernity itself. In contrast to the ruins of antiquity, we do not expect to encounter built spaces from our own lifetime that have fallen into ruin, certainly not unless they have been subjected to war, catastrophe, or, at the very least, severe neglect. For us, the modern ruin has the appearance of an anomaly. Beholding with our own eyes the full extent of ruination sends fissures though our image of modernity.

In a ruin, the material remains of modernity join the other relics of history. These traces of the recent past not infrequently feel strangely timeless. In many cases they might just as well belong to an ancient civilisation. Chronologically structured history is not the only way, and, perhaps, not even the most suitable way, to investigate our relation to this composite anteriority.

Archaeology of the present crosses disciplinary boundaries and calls into question modernity's categorical distinction between the past and the present. Under the gaze of archaeology, familiar everyday objects are transformed into archaeological artefacts. This intriguing journey from intimacy to distance can be confusing but also illuminating. How did something that just a moment ago was modern become both a ruin and an object of archaeological study? And what does this say about us, who have experienced both contexts? Do we belong to that which was, or to that which is? Or both?

The many questions raised by modern ruins give an insight into how the differences between then and now are not absolute. The mild confusion, experienced by many people, that comes with the knowledge that our own lives are now the object of archaeological investigation may turn out to be a creative force in our quest for new ways to understand history.

Notes

1. Jan Jörnmark, *Övergivna platser* (Lund: Historiska Media, 2007) and Jan Jörnmark, *Övergivna platser två* (Lund: Historiska Media, 2008). See also Katarina Wikars and Jan Jörnmark, *Atomtorg, porrharar & Hitlerslussar: 160 genom Baltikum* (Lund: Historiska Media, 2009).
2. "Övergivna platser", http://www.jornmark.se.
3. Katarina Wikars cited in"Historiska Media", http://www.historiskamedia.se/bok/overgivna-platser.
4. Henk van Rensbergen, *Abandoned Places* (Tielt: Lannoo, 2007), and Henk van Rensbergen, *Abandoned Places 2* (Tielt: Lannoo, 2010).
5. W.G. Romany, *Beauty in Decay* (Durham: Carpet Bombing Culture, 2010).
6. Manfred Hamm and Rolf Steinberg, *Dead Tech: A Guide to the Archaeology of Tomorrow* (Santa Monica: Hennessey + Ingalls, 2000). First published as *Tote Technik: Ein Wegweiser zu den antiken Statten von Morgen* (Berlin: Nicolaische Verlagsbuchhanlung, 1981).
7. Shinichiro Kobayashi, *Deathtopia* (Tokyo: Media Factory, 2000).
8. Paul Talling, *Derelict London* (London: Random House, 2008).
9. Sylvain Margaine and David Margaine, *Forbidden Places: Exploring Our Abandoned Heritage* (Versailles: Jonglez, 2009).
10. Jürgen Rostock and Franz Zadniček, *Paradiesruinen: Das Kdf-Seebad der Zwanzigtausend auf Rügen* (Berlin: Links, 2001).
11. Shinichiro Kobayashi, *Ruins* (Tokyo: Magazine House, 2001).
12. Yves Marchand and Romain Meffre, *The Ruins of Detroit* (Göttingen: Steidl, 2010).
13. Annie O'Neill, *Unquiet Ruin: a photographic excavation* (Pittsburgh: The Mattress Factory, 2001).
14. Tim Edensor. *Industrial Ruins: Spaces, Aesthetics and Materiality* (Oxford and New York: Berg, 2005).
15. Elin Andreassen, Hein B. Bjerck, and Bjørnar Olsen, *Persistent Memories: Pyramiden – a Soviet mining town in the High Arctic* (Trondheim: Tapir Academic Press, 2010).

16. "Ruin Memories", http://ruinmemories.org.//
17. Göran Schildt, *Ikaros' hav* (Stockholm: Wahlström & Widstrand, 1957).
18. Albert Speer, *Inside the Third Reich* (New York: Macmillan, 1970).
19. Sharon Macdonald, *Difficult Heritage: Negotiating the Nazi Past in Nuremberg and Beyond* (London and New York: Routledge, 2009).
20. Mats Burström, "Garbage or Heritage: The Existential Dimension of a Car Cemetery," in *Contemporary Archaeologies: Excavating Now*, ed. Cornelius Holtorf and Angela Piccini (Frankfurt am Main: Peter Lang, 2009), 131–143.
21. Fredrik Bergman, "Tillbaka till naturen," *Tidevarv* 1/99 (1999): 8–11.
22. Compare Michael Shanks, "The Life of an Artifact in an Interpretive Archaeology," *Fennoscandia archaeologica XV* (1998), 15–30.

Claiming Makunaima: Colonisation, Nation, and History in the Northern Amazon[1]

PATRICIA LORENZONI

Introduction

In the centre of Boa Vista, capital of the state of Roraima in the northern Brazilian Amazon, a large stone relief celebrates the state's pioneer spirit. Created in 1995 by local artist Luiz Canará, *Monumento aos Pioneiros* depicts an encounter between a group of pioneers, who enter the scene from the left, and a group of indigenous people whose number includes Makunaima, the founding hero of several ethnic groups from this area. Makunaima stands out by his size and by virtue of being the only figure identifiable by name.

In this article, I take *Monumento aos Pioneiros* as the starting-point for a discussion of competing historical narratives in a situation of settler colonialism. While the monument as a whole is a celebration of colonial pioneerism, the figure of Makunaima serves to bring conflicting historical narratives foreward. Through Mario de Andrade's *Macunaíma* (1928), regarded as one of the great Brazilian modernist novels, this founding hero was inscribed at the heart of the formation of the Brazilian people. Today, Makunaima's native land Roraima is often imagined as a final frontier. The most sparsely populated of Brazil's states, it has through migration waves during the last half century experienced a demographic explosion. It is riven by bitter conflicts between indigenous groups and settlers in which local politicians frequently depict indigenous claims to land as an obstacle to development. Despite being the state with the highest percentage of *índios*[2], Roraima is described by indigenous leaders as an "anti-indigenous" state. Tensions came to a head in 2009 when the Supreme

Federal Court voted in favour of demarcating *Raposa Serra do Sol* as indigenous land, an area of 1.7 million hectares that includes Makunaima's resting place at Monte Roraima.[3]

Makunaima's presence in the *Monumento aos Pioneiros* is an example of how indigenous names and symbols are invoked by those laying claims on Roraima. Within the broader issue of the struggle between different historical narratives, I am particularly interested in how the creation of continuities and discontinuities in history functions to mark the limits of the nation in a colonial context.

Colonising the Rio Branco

Roraima is one of Brazil's youngest states, created as such by the Federal Constitution of 1988 (CF88). Its capital had been planned at the time when Roraima was detached from the state of Amazonas and converted into a "federal territory" in the 1940s. Boa Vista was planned as a new and modern city with a fan-shaped centre modelled on Place Charles de Gaulle in Paris, and a huge golden statue of a *garimpeiro*, a gold panner, occupying the position of the Arc de Triomphe. *Monumento aos Pioneiros* is a few blocks away, in the historical centre of the old municipality, by the Rio Branco shore.

In thematising migrations, both monuments give material expression to the collective memories of settler colonialism. Other colonial histories predate these settler histories, however. In the eighteenth century, the Portuguese made several attempts to take control of the Rio Branco area. Their strategy included an effort to concentrate (*aldear*) the *índios* in mission stations and villages, placed strategically in order to demarcate the area. The claim that indigenous peoples were Portuguese subjects was crucial for Portugal's expansion into areas in which the Dutch and the British also had interests.[4]

By the latter part of the nineteenth century, non-*índio* settlers in somewhat larger numbers had started to move to the Rio Branco from other parts of what was now independent Brazil. Drought and land conflicts in the arid northeast contributed to this movement, which intensified during the twentieth century. Beginning in the late nineteenth century, large-scale cattle ranching was established, and the picture was further complicated in the twentieth century by the arrival of agro-industrial investors mainly from the Brazilian South. Since the 1970s industrial rice farming has grown considerably.[5]

Like the Amazon area in general, Roraima has functioned as a relief space for regional conflicts which have been "solved" by encouraging migration by poor rural workers as well as large-scale ranchers and farmers. The Amazon has been depicted as empty space, rich in land, gold, and opportunity.[6]

Since the eighteenth century, then, *índios* in Roraima have negotiated with and offered resistance to the Portuguese Crown, missionaries, the Brazilian federal state, the government of the Federal territory, the state government, private rural investors, poor rural workers, and gold panners. For the Portuguese, the *índio* was a necessary condition for the formation of a colonial population in the northern Amazon. Indigenous communities were initially a source of help and know-how for settlers in a new environment. During a second phase, however, they have been either a source of cheap labour or an obstacle to settlement.

Demographic data gives a hint of how *unsettling* a process colonisation has been for indigenous populations.[7] According to the *Centro de Informação Diocese de Roraima* (CIDR), the state's population in 1982 consisted of around 80,000 people, half of them indigenous. According to the 2000 national census, 28,000 people in Roraima identified themselves as indigenous. The centre *Nós esxistimos!*[8] currently offers a higher number, roughly 53,000 *índios*, in relation to a total population figure of about 450,000 in the 2010 census. Despite these statistical discrepancies, it is clear that *índios* within a very short space of time have become a minority in the state.

A dream called Roraima

The narrative presented by *Monumento aos Pioneiros* is indeed a colonial narrative. However, the history it privileges is one of settlement, which serves to obscure previous colonial projects. Its relief depicts a number of people – children, women and men – moving from left to right: four on foot, three in a canoe, and one on horseback. Those walking carry a baby, a manual of pharmaceutics, and a small flag. The canoe is named *Pioneiro*, and the man on horseback points the way forward, his hand almost touching the heads of the first of the six *índios* who occupy the extreme right of the scene. In the midst of the *índios*, who are strikingly naked alongside the fully-clothed pioneers, a huge bust of Makunaima holding a flower to his chest dominates the scene. While the sun rises above the pioneers, the *índios* are shown occupying a dense wilderness of plants and animals. Beside the monument, a stone plaque signed by Teresa Jucá, the city's mayor in 1995, reads:

> Tribute from the City of Boa Vista to the Pioneers who, with courage and hope, initiated the realisation of a Dream called Roraima.

The first thing we can note is the name itself. The name of the dream is taken from Monte Roraima, a mountain plateau on the border of Brazil, Guyana, and Venezuela. The birthplace and final resting place of Makunaima, it is a sacred site. While from a national perspective Monte Roraima marks the limits of Brazil, from Makuxi, Ingarikó, and Taurepang perspective it is situated at the centre.

In the very act of naming, something is appropriated. From settler perspective, Roraima is a place with a short history, which, being a history of colonial expansion, is interwoven with geography. This is apparent in the revival of the colonial genre of geographical-historical chronicle, such as Aimberê Freitas' *Geografia e história de Roraima* (1997).[9] Modest in size yet ambitious in scope, Freitas' book outlines geographic and demographic conditions, describes the past and present of colonial expansion, makes an inventory of natural resources, and indicates some directions for future development of the state. "Discovered" only 250 years ago, long after the "discovery of Brazil", Roraima is portrayed as a region with a need to catch up.[10] Its peripheral position is presented as both a lack and a source of pioneer pride.

It might be useful to read the monument and the book together. Freitas' text deals ambiguously with the role played by indigenous peoples in Roraima's history. On the one hand, the text recognises the *índio*'s participation in and resistance to colonial projects.[11] On the other hand, the *índio* is only part of Roraima's history as as either an instrument for, or an obstacle to colonisation. For Freitas, Roraima's history *is* colonisation.

Returning to the *Monumento aos Pioneiros,* a trilingual information sign states the following:

> It represents the union of the natives with their ways and customs, receiving the pioneers and *tamers* who arrived here. It is an homage to the *first people who were willing to populate and develop* this part of Brazil *until then never explored*. The display points to the Rio Branco River, focusing on the image of *Macunaíma, the first inhabitant* of the Rio Branco fields [... sic, Italics mine].[12]

Once again, we enounter an ambiguity relating to Roraima's history and the *índios*. While names and symbols, as in many parts of Brazil, are almost all indigenous – marking the land as having been inhabited by *índios*, at least at one point in time – non-*índio* settlers are described as "tamers" of a wild land, the "first people" willing to populate what was until then "unexplored". The use of the term "tamers" (*desbravadores*) marks the pioneers as spiritual descendants of the *bandeirantes* who explored the *sertões* (backlands) in colonial times looking for indigenous slaves and natural riches. The boy carrying a flag also alludes to the *bandeirantes*, who were named after the flags (*bandeiras*) they carried. As Antônio Carlos Robert Moraes remarks of the *bandeirante* myth, its narrative implicitly presents the pioneers as a driving force such that spatial domination comes to seem like the result of pioneer activity rather than its motivation.[13] Thanks to flags of demarcation and printed medical knowledge, the wilderness is tamed.

The description of Makunaima as the first inhabitant should not be seen as undermining this pioneer narrative. Rather, the evocation of Makunaima serves to expel the *índio* from the realm of history into that of mythology – seemingly an effect of the pioneers' arrival. The very replacement of the *índio* by the pioneer is also colloquially expressed in the slang term for Roraima-born people as "Makuxi", taking the name from one of the ethnic groups that traces its ancestry to Makunaima.

The índio as mythical ancestor

Non-indigenous Roraima society can be seen to make a double claim, to a pioneer identity and to an indigenous identity. The national-romantic notion of the *índio* as origin to the Brazilian nation here assumes a Roraimense form. A recurrent strategy by Roraima politicians opposed to the demarcation of indigenous land has been to claim to have *índio* blood in their veins, thereby invoking an *índio* of the past to hold up against the *índio* of the present.[14]

Alcida Ramos sees a paradox in the fact that Brazil's indigenous populations comprise so small a fraction of the population (less than 1%) while the *índio* occupies a central position in the national imaginary. For Ramos, "indigenism" (denoting a set of ideas and ideals concerning the *índio* and his/her relation to the nation) serves a similar function for Brazil as orientalism does for the West. There is, however, an important difference in the way that indigenous peoples themselves participate in the construction of indigenism: *Índios* and Brazilians live in temporal and spatial contiguity within a single nation-state.[15]

I would like to add another difference. While the Orient, for the West, has been an exotic and barbarous other, the *índio* is not merely the other but an intimate part of the construction of Brazil's national self. The *índio* occupies an ambiguous position of other/sameness that is deployed in the defence of, as well as in the resistance to, indigenous rights.

In late-eighteenth- and nineteenth-century nationalism, the *índio* was a bloodline that distinguished the Brazilian nation from Portuguese colonisers. Typically, this *índio* as symbol of the nation belonged to the early period of conquest and the eve of Brazilian history, and he fulfilled his destiny through self-sacrifice. This is how the *índio* appears in nineteenth-century literature (such as José de Alencar's *O Guarani* [1857] and *Iracema* [1865]) and art (such as Rodolfo Amoedo's *O último Tamoio* [1883]). As Antônio Paulo Graça has pointed out, the *índio* dies so that the nation may live.[16]

Graça discusses this imaginary in terms of a "poetics of genocide" that operates as a device to look away from a violent present for which one wishes not to be held responsible. Graça can be read alongside Benedict Anderson's reading of Renan. In *Qu'est-ce qu'une nation?*, Renan remarks of the violent past that, in order to form a nation, "we" must forget precisely so that we can be reminded that we have forgotten. Such "forgetting" is thus a sort of agreement by which we collectively ensure that certain pasts are all forgotten. Past atrocities take on the function of "reassuring fratricides". Renan mentions the Saint Bartholomew's Day Massacre of 1572, distant enough in time to have already acquired the status of a mythical memory. It is no coincidence, remarks Anderson, that Renan is silent about more recent massacres such as the Paris Commune of 1871; this still "real" memory is much too painful to be "reassuring".[17] What of the *índio*, then? As Graça shows, nationalist obsession with the self-sacrifice of the *índio* creates a discontinuity with ongoing genocidal violence. The *índio* is at the heart of national formation only insofar as no continuity is admitted to exist between this *índio* and contemporary violence.

Creating new continuities

Having suffered dramatic population loss in the recent past, many surviving indigenous groups are today in a stage of gradual recovery – demographic, cultural, and political. The conditions for recovery, as most indigenous groups and NGOs working on indigenous rights agree, are intimately linked to land rights. The CF88 represents a break in that it recognizes the "originary right" of *índios* to their traditional lands. In the process, it has profoundly changed the conditions for demarcation of indigenous lands. What is recognised is a right that predates the foundation of the Brazilian state and that is therefore not subject to negotiations with state or private interests. Another crucial change is the granting of full citizenship to *índios*, meaning that exercising civil rights no longer jeopardizes the collective rights of *índios*.[18]

In the strong reactions provoked by these changes, demarcation of indigenous land has frequently been described as a threat to national sovereignty. The *índio* who refuses assimilation and instead insists on separateness is represented as an obstacle to a needed Brazilian unity. This line of argument is especially strong in the case of border areas, as the case of *Raposa Serra do Sol* illustrates. One of the most active critics in this respect has been Aldo Rebelo, a parliamentarian from São Paulo who collected a number of articles on the subject in his 2010 book *Raposa-Serra do Sol: O índio e a questão nacional*. Let us briefly examine it.

Significantly, Rebelo begins his discussion by establishing the *índio*'s crucial role in Brazilian notions of the nation. Brazilians, he remarks, search for a distant indigenous ancestry, almost as if blood ties could confer authentic Brazilianness. Rebelo discusses this idea as if from the outside, even as it works through his own text. On the front cover the *índio* is represented by Albert Eckhout's seventeenth-century painting, *The Dance of the Tapuias*; an exotic motif from the eve of conquest. Rebelo reminds readers of the *índio*'s role in making the nation, and invokes heroic resisters of colonisation who chose death over captivity.[19] The text operates by means of a discontinuity between these historical heroes and contemporary indigenous struggles, in which the former are nation-makers and therefore part of Rebelo's own ancestry, and the lattter stand in opposition to the nation. Contemporary indigenous mobilisation is figured as a threat to the *índio* of Rebelo's front cover, the exotic fetish of Brazilian nationalism.

The violent ends met by the *índio* heroes of Brazilian nation-making can be read as Renan's "forgotten" atrocities. Recreating historical conflicts between *índios* and colonisers as "reassuring fratricides" presupposes a sharp discontinuity with contemporary indigenous struggles. One of the most frequent strategies is the questioning of the authenticity of those claiming to be *índios*. The speaking of Portuguese, the wearing of clothes, the use of cellphones, computers, or cars – all of these are presented as delegitimising.

In the indigenous mobilisation, on the other hand, the issue is not only that memories of past (and, it should be added, present) atrocities are far too painfully alive to be reassuring, but also in *what way* to speak these memories as part of history. In indigenous political articulations, we see an attempt not only to give voice to that which has been silenced but also to reclaim the fetishized *índio* and, with it, the right to speak in the name of the nation.

The *Conselho Indígena de Roraima* (CIR) is one organisation that works very consciously with these concepts. Growing out of a collaboration between indigenous community leaders and Catholic missionaries, CIR was created in the 1980s as a way to coordinate the struggles of Roraima indigenous communities. The majority of communities in *Raposa Serra do Sol* are linked to CIR. From a nationalist point of view, as very frequently articulated in the Roraimense press, the organisation is criticised for supposedly being separatist, funded by foreign interests and not even "real *índios*".

At the same time as working inside the movement to raise historical awareness and establish genealogies of resistance,[20] CIR's public response has increasingly taken the form of reinscribing contemporary indigenous resistance within a national-historical narrative. Nationalist rhetoric has been countered by claims that *índios* are those in whom "the blood of the true Brazilian people flows". In an open letter on the *Raposa Serra do Sol* published in 2008, CIR reminded readers that the Portuguese colony was only able to demarcate its northern borders with the assistance of the indigenous subjects who formed the population of Rio Branco. CIR's historical references are the same as those of Freitas but reversing the perspective: the *índios* are here the active agents. It was *índios*, not whites, who served as the "walls of the backlands" (*muralhas dos sertões*) by protecting sovereignty in this part of Brazil.[21] With their national affiliation and their authenticity as *índios* being questioned, CIR reconstruct themselves as the original Brazilians, traditional guarantors of Brazilian sovereignty both in the past and for the foreseeable future.

This letter can be read as an attempt to reclaim the mythical *índio* forefather as well as the right to define his significance in the present. While the *índio* forefather is disconnected from non-*índio* nationalist rhetoric, he is re-connected to the nation. Following Žižek, we see how CIR, by insisting on the nation, is rearticulating the conditions of belonging, thereby depriving non-indigenous Brazil of the right to define its own tradition.[22] By reclaiming Makunaima precisely as part of the nation, those whose loyalties are put in question opens a space from where they can be the ones to question the landed elite.

Notes

1. Research for this article has been carried out with the financial support of Riksbankens Jubileumsfond and The Royal Society for Arts and Sciences in Gothenburg.

2. I have opted not to translate the Portuguese term *índio*, which is used by indigenous groups as a self-designation.

3. Paulo Santilli, *Pemongon Patá: Território Macuxi, rotas de conflito* (São Paulo: Editora Unesp. 2000), 93–127; Carolina Mota and Bianca Galafassi, "A demar-

cação da Terra Indígena Raposa Serra do Sol: processo administrative e conflitos judiciais" in *Makunaima grita! Terra indígena Raposa Serra do Sol e os direitos constitucionais no Brasil*, ed. Julia Trujillo Miras et al. (Rio de Janeiro: Beco do Azougue Editorial, 2009).

4. Nádia Farage, *As muralhas dos sertões: os povos indígenas no Rio Branco e a colonização* (Rio de Janeiro: Paz e Terra, 1991); CIDR, *Índios e brancos em Roraima*, Coleção histórico-antropológico no 2 (Boa Vista: CIDR, 1990), 15.

5. CIDR, 7.

6. Santilli, 10-11, 61; Alcida Ramos, *Indigenism: Ethnic Politics in Brazil* (Madison: University of Wisconsin Press, 1998), 222, 226.

7. Antônio Carlos Robert Moraes, *Território e história no Brasil*, (São Paulo: Annablume, 2008), 138; Santilli, 38-39, 82.

8. *Nós Existimos* is a collaboration between various indigenous and civil rights NGOs, unions, and Catholic organisations (www.nosexistimos.org).

9. For another work in this genre, see Adair J. Santos, *Roraima:História geral* (Boa Vista: Editora UFRR, 2010).

10. Aimberê Freitas, *Geografia e história de Roraima*, (Manaus: Gráfica Belvedere, 1997), 92-93.

11. Freitas, 102, 116-117.

12. I have modified the English text slightly, so as to make it consistent with the Portuguese version.

13. Moraes, 86.

14. Ramos, 110, 178.

15. Ramos, 4-7.

16. Antônio Paulo Graça, *Uma poética do genocídio*, (Rio de Janeiro: Topbooks, 1998), 146.

17. Benedict Anderson, *Imagined Communities: Reflections on the Origin and Spread of Nationalism* (London & New York: Verso, 1991), 200-201.

18. On pre-88 indigenist policy, see Antônio Carlos de Souza Lima, *Um grande cerco de paz: Poder tutelar, indianidade e formação do Estado no Brasil*. (Petrópolis: Vozes, 1995).

19. Aldo Rebelo, *Raposa-Serra do Sol: O índio e a questão nacional* (Brasília: Thesaurus 2010), 25-29.

20. CIR, *Filhos de Makunaimî: vida, história, luta* (São Paulo: Ediçoes Loyola, 2004).

21. CIR, "Carta das comunidades indígenas" (April 28, 2008), accessed April 10, 2010, http://www.cir.br/portal/files/images/manifesto_da_rss.doc.

22. Slavoj Žižek, *Först som tragedi, sedan som fars* (Hägersten: Tankekraft, 2010), 124.

The Times of Television: Representing, Anticipating, Forgetting the Cold War

STAFFAN ERICSON

There seems to be quite a lot of history on television these days. This observation might be made in the most mundane of settings, in front of the TV on an average night while skipping through the channels (realizing that some version of WW2 is never far away). It might be confirmed systematically by studying the schedules of an average week (realizing how the better part of your prime-time viewing could easily be spent looking backwards, through fiction, documentaries, docudramas). It might find endorsement in the vogue for history in high-profile TV series such as *Rome* or *Mad Men*, which has been hailed as "the new rock 'n roll"[1] of the business. And it would resonate with a widespread consensus about the transformation of the medium in recent decades[2], during which the relative scarcity of centralized broadcasting has mutated into an abundance of "narrowcast" channels and time slots. One obvious way to fill all these slots: the relentless recycling of stored material.

This is not what television was supposed to be all about. Since its arrival, the essence of the medium has been identified with a paradigmatic form of transmission: the live broadcast. Thus television is claimed to be "relentlessly in the present, immediate, simultaneous, and continuous".[3] Its preferred temporal dimension is that of an "insistent presentness – a *'This is going on*" rather than a *'That has been'*"[4]. Consequently, it will fail in representing the past: "[T]elevision produces forgetfulness, not memory, flow, not history."[5] "Its grammar, so to say, permits no access to the past."[6]

To be sure, we might still question whether the past we see on the television screen actually *is* history. For Fredric Jameson, we are looking at "images, simulacra, and pastiches of the past", mere surrogates for our "historical amnesia".[7] For French historian Pierre Nora, we are riding on that "tidal wave of memorial concerns",[8] which actually reflects a double loss: that of memory as a spontaneous, social practice; and that of history as a professional, critical task.

Then again, we cannot be sure that the history we see on television actually *is* from the past. *The Live Broadcasting of History* was the provocative subtitle of Daniel Dayan's and Elihu Katz's seminal 1992 book on "media events"[9], which defined a long-running genre: the live, ceremonial coverage on television of moon landings, Olympic games, royal weddings, and presidential elections. As far back as the early 1970s, Nora had proposed that historians must come to terms with "the return of the event"[10]: "From now on, the mass media has a monopoly on history". What counted as a historical event could no longer be separated from the time of the "media system", i.e. the "perpetual" or "chronic" present. We have by now become acquainted with 24-hour news channels such as CNN, which scour the present for moments of "instant history": the terrorist attacks of 9/11, the election of a black American president, or revolution in an Egyptian square.

Today, it seems clear that television can be a site of both simultaneity and storage, can raise claims of "historical" significance *before*, *during* and *after* events take place. When live coverage and historicity converge, we enter unstable epistemological territory, potentially mined with "category mistakes" and/or secondary, derivative forms. (Is history really "witnessed" on television?[11] Do audio-visual archives really store "memories"?[12]). On the whole, television theory has had obvious problems in converting its categories into legitimate forms of knowledge. Film has its montage (transformed into historical experience by Walter Benjamin and Godard), the novel has its narrative (reused by historians, according to Hayden White). Television has its "flow".[13] Which not only lacks a "work", it seems to avoid representation as such. "Televisual images", writes Richard Dienst, "do not represent things so much as they take up time."[14] But what sort of time *is* that? Images on TV screens emerge from a scanning process that seems to recognize no "before" or "after", the time of every image – live or recorded – ultimately referring to the time of its production (i.e. "real time").[15]

THE TIMES OF TELEVISION

"The Times of Television" is a project[16] that attempts to describe three temporal forms used by television for historical representation: *the time of the chronicle*, in which television organizes successive flows of time through documentaries, drama series, annual chronicles, etc; *the time of catastrophe*, as in live broadcasts of traumatic events where history is represented as catastrophe, crisis, disaster, that is, as breaks in the flow of successive time; *the time of ritual*, as in the televised, preplanned ceremonial events (Olympic games, presidential inaugurations: inviting audiences to witness history in the making). Its main hypothesis is that these three forms and their interrelations are fundamental for understanding how current television represents history.

Representing the Cold War

In the chronicle format, television seems to claim the role of a "proper" historian: *re-presenting* what actually happened, using well-established conventions. These have been summarized by one experienced producer as "the breaking up of historical events into smaller, accessible story-lines that can be well told using archive film and interviews with eye-witnesses".[17] This producer is referring to CNN's documentary series *Cold War* (1998) (hereafter *CW*). This project was initiated by Ted Turner, CNN's founder, and offered to Sir Jeremy Isaacs, producer of the classic series *The World at War* (1970). *CW* was supervised by a team of international historians representing both superpowers. Its original research included recording over 500 interviews with eye-witnesses and scanning over 8000 films in international archives. It generated a number of by-products, including a website with over a thousand pages, an instructor's guide for classroom applications, coffee-table books, and pocket versions. The project core, however, was 24 hours of television broadcast by CNN and the BBC in 1998, which explicitly claimed to relate "the central story of our times".[18]

In what ways, then, does such a representation of history reuse, intervene in, or transform traditional categories of historiography?

For Paul Ricoeur, historical knowledge always has a tripod basis: "trace, document, question".[19] These categories seem easily compatible with the components mentioned above: interviews (with firsthand witnesses of history), authentic images from the past (from the archives), and the narrative of an invisible voice-over (providing explanation and understanding). Moreover, Ricoeur has described the historian's task as being the establishing of a "third" time[20] – "historical time" – mediating between notions of time that are, on the one hand, universal (objective, in succession), and, on the other, existential (subjective, experienced, lived). *CW* is clearly aiming at historical transformations that have impact on our "ordinary lives", through modes of experience that television does well: the ephemeral, the everyday, the intimate, and the situated (this sense of the past radically fades when *CW* is translated into book format).

Even so, and perhaps for these reasons, CNN's series generated significant controversy. Commentators on the left and the right, political pundits as well as professional historians, found enough emissions and distortions to fill a book.[21] Responding to those critics, John Lewis Gaddis, a leading historian of the Cold War and a senior consultant on the series, tried to explain the specifics of representing history on television. There were time constraints, of course, and limits to processes taking place in front of a camera. But the main mistake made by critics, according to Gaddis, was to expect *any* kind of "single interpretative framework".[22] In *CW*, there were only the "multiple voices" of witnesses and the narrator of scripts that were authored by a different writers for each episode. Viewers of *CW* were thus given neither historical orthodoxy nor moral equivalency:

> What they do get is an exposure to historical complexity: a sense of how things looked at the time, an awareness of how people who did not know the future attempted to anticipate it, perhaps even the ability to imagine themselves in their place and to ask the tough question: What would I, in similar circumstances, have done? In short, they gain historical maturity.[23]

While some critics had clearly missed a more specific settling of accounts ("Who won? Who were the good guys and the bad guys?"), their frustration at the lack of *any* "moralizing impulse"[24] may signal a difference between television history and "history proper", at least of the sort practiced by professional historians since the late nineteenth century. For, according to Hayden White (in turn, invoking Hegel), there is only one way in which the narrative of a chain of *real* events *could* possibly conclude: in a summing-up of their "meaning" for "the purpose of moralizing judgments".[25] The lack of such an impulse may not be unique to history on television, of course. For White, this lack is precisely what distinguishes proper history from medieval history writing, i.e. from chronicles:

> More specifically, the chronicle is usually marked by a failure to achieve narrative closure. It does not so much conclude as simply terminate. It starts off to tell a story but breaks off *in medias res*, in the chronicler's own present.[26]

"Into the middle of things" is, in *CW*'s case, into the present of television. In what ways, then, is history in *CW* organized according to the specific codes of televisual time? It is related in twenty-four hour-long episodes[27], i.e. units of clock time, or, with Ricoeur, "universal" time. This is, of course, also the unit of television scheduling, the primary context for any broadcasted program (more so than the "outside world"), and in itself a mediation of "universal" and "lived time" insofar as it proposes to synchronize the time of "watching television" with the experience of work, leisure, holidays, family time, etc.

Furthermore, like most of television, it is serialized: every episode displays some kind of independent, finite nature, while simultaneously serving as one unit in a serial chain that is presumably infinite.[28] When looking closer for a beginning and end of the whole chronicle, the viewer can identify familiar temporal categories. The first seconds of the first episode: a mechanical voice counting down – "5, 4, 3, 2, 1" – followed by images and the sound of a huge atomic explosion: time itself must come to a halt in order for this particular story to begin. The final seconds of the final episode: President George Bush, Sr. looks straight into the camera and declares that "the Cold War has now ended": an excerpt from the President's annual Christmas speech to the American people, i.e. a speech by the protagonist of a media event. In other words, the "time of this chronicle" is begun by "the time of catastrophe" and stopped by "the time of the ritual".

Most discussion of television and representation sooner or later identifies a moment at which media and reality are about to implode, as if the answer to what television represents is: television itself. As if the self-identification of a witness to a third party – "believe me, I was there" – is not only being raised by interviewees but *by the medium itself*. As if only television, like the State and its legal system in Hegel's version of history, can supply proper subject matter. As if a "cold" war could not *take place* (Baudrillard) anywhere else, in accordance with that logic of "deterrence", excluding any transition from the virtual to the actual.[29]

With *CW*, this option may seem particularly tempting. After all, the history of the Cold War is more or less contemporaneous with the history of television[30] and the emergence of a spectator position, frequently illustrated in the series, for which historical events were already, initially, watched on television (the Kennedy assassination, the Beatles performing on The Ed Sullivan Show). We are perhaps given fair warning in the opening twenty-second credit sequence, the only staged sequence of the series, that introduces each episode: the eye of the camera is situated in the depths of a very dark hall. At the other end, we see silhouettes of a group of men – soldiers? – opening a door, letting in daylight, peeking into the dark with flashlights. This hall looks like an underground cave but its walls are screens, covered with a flurry of moving images – authentic scenes from the history of the Cold War, projected over one another. We barely have time to see that these are chronologically organized as the camera is moving from the depths of that dark/past towards the blinding light of the door/present which serves as a backdrop to the title, "Cold War": Plato's cave relocated in a bunker.

Even if this war did not "take place", then, it certainly did *take time* (as suggested by the movement of that camera). And to the extent that television suggests that this time be experienced as "historical", it certainly also implies that represented events "actually happened", *outside* the world of television (much in the way that television wants us to assume that live media events are broadcasted, not created, "on location").

For Ricoeur, the search for referentiality is ultimately what differentiates history from fiction. (A distinction that, according to Ricoeur, is not sufficiently recognized by White.) This search remains the task of the historian and is to be executed by the (often highly complex) linkage of trace, document, and question.[31] On television, and particularly in *CW*, the apparent equivalent of such "linkage" is executed through the *editing* – the mixing and switching[32] – of archival footage, witnesses, and narrative. More precisely, the "search for referentiality" in *CW* unfolds as an attempt to compensate for or supplement not merely television's own self-referentiality but the lack of veracity inherent in each component presented: archival footage, witnessing, and narrative.

To illustrate: The film clips come with a potential "reality effect": an indexical guarantee that "this past was present" (and *CW* maintains a strict distinction with the imaginary, allowing no clips of fiction or reenactments). As unrelated instants, however, these clips may fall short as historical representations (much like real events in their singularity) to the extent that, as White puts it, they "do not offer themselves as stories".[33] In *CW*, the narrator immediately steps in to provide linkage and coherence. In one sense, then, the voice-over legitimizes the authenticity of those images, at least for White, who claims that our "desire for the Real" is imposed upon historical events precisely through the coherence of stories. In another sense, the images legitimize the authenticity of the narrator's account, since the idea that "real events are properly represented when they can be shown to display the formal coherency of a Story"[34] constitutes an "embarrassment"[35] - as this property is shared with fictional or imaginary events. Any storyteller of actual events is thus under pressure not to mix the orders of imaginary and real, a pressure that may be relieved by narrating them over indexical images.

Still, whether separately or in combination, neither narrator nor indexical image has the credentials for the type of authority most treasured by television, that of "being there". The invisible narrator will make no such claims, and the camera may have once registered the past as present, but those (causal) relations are no longer in effect. There is, of course, a risk of retroactive manipulation. Prior to that, however, the camera falls short in another sense: while the act of mechanical recording may guarantee objectivity, the camera cannot give testimony.[36] But, then again, *CW* will present its own long line of witnesses. In fact, the only talking heads allowed on screen are people who "saw it with their own eyes" (i.e. not history experts, location guides, or interviewers). This again furthers the distance from imaginary orders (fictions, after all, are not "witnessed"). To be sure, those witnesses will introduce the frailty of human memory (forgetting, misrepresenting), and the risk of subjective interests (committing perjury). But, again, these pitfalls may be instantly countered by the objective recording of the camera or the coherency of the narrative.

Hayden White suggests that the "realness" of any historical discourse consists, not only in events having occurred, but in their being remembered and placed in chronological sequence. If so, then *CW* holds a full deck of cards. Taken separately, historical footage, witness, and narrator are surely disparate, possibly contradictory, regimes of authenticity and truth (as are the related discourses on "media", "memory" and "history").[37] But when merged as in *CW*, the effect might be, to use another distinction by White, a history that is not so much "narrated" as "narrativized", a history in which "events seem to tell themselves".[38] To exemplify: We see historical images of Soviet tanks surrounded by protesting Czechs in the streets of Prague in 1968, the voice of the narrator stating the time, location, and circumstances. His voice is suddenly interrupted by a Czech woman describing the pain of her knee being crushed under a tank. In the footage, we now see the face of a young woman in agony under one of the tanks, and, within seconds, her face, thirty years later, bearing witness. We can now forget what the narrator was saying (he was setting up that switch) since events are "telling themselves", media, memory and history all contributing to cover any potential shortcoming in each another (yes, those images were authentic; yes, the memory of that women can be trusted; yes, those events in Prague belong to a chronological sequence; yes, the work of time can be registered: it is already marked in that woman's face).

Anticipating the Cold War

Watching witnesses on television has temporal as well as epistemological implications. While those witnesses may reiterate the past, they are also well suited to the "insistent presentness" of television, talking to us as if in real time, in neutral studio settings, never accompanied by music or sound effects (unlike the narrator or the voices from the archives). In fact, in the way that their faces and voices return to fill the screen, they resemble news anchormen: points of convergence in the present for any story that might come out of the past. And to witness someone bearing witness, as viewers of *CW* do, is already in a sense to be engaged in time travel. For Dori Laub, who videorecorded Holocaust survivors for the Yale Project, it means accepting "an event that has not yet come into existence, in spite of the overwhelming nature of the reality of its existence". And, moreover, that this event "in effect, *does not end*".[39] Just like the medieval chronicler who, according to White, represents historical reality "as if real events appeared to human consciousness in the form of unfinished stories".[40]

In other words, the time of witnessing may be well adapted to the time of television, which may be well adapted to the time of the chronicle. If John Gaddis is to be believed, it might all end up in "historical maturity": the "awareness of how people who did not know the future attempted to anticipate it". Anticipation is, no doubt, the attitude to time that *CW* wants to promote in its viewers: "For forty-five years", declares the slogan to the series, "the world held its breath".[41] On television, the "story of our times" is a story waiting for its event – nuclear Armageddon – to happen. Which, as we well *know* by now, it did *not*. So how are we to engage with *that* story?

In the prologue to the first episode, after the atomic blast but before the opening credits, the narrator speaks for the first time:

> A cloud hides the sky. A nuclear shadows falls across the human future. Midway through the twentieth century, two superpowers prepared for a conflict which might have ended life on the planet.
>
> *Switch from atomic explosion to images from the present: the exteriors of a luxurious hotel.*
>
> Spring flowers, the warm light of day. The pleasures of life. But under this American hotel there was a hidden gate. It led to an underworld.
>
> *Switch to underground facilities: empty screening rooms, plenary halls, bedrooms, showers, weapon supplies. The narrator is now our guide to a real Cold War bunker.*
>
> This was the shelter for members of the Unites States Congress in the event of nuclear war. Down here, the politicians would represent the dead and the dying in the world overhead. For a handful of human beings, there was all they needed to wait out the nuclear winter. But nerves might snap, then order would be kept by force. The lost world

> above the shelter would become only a memory, a myth. The living would come to envy the dead.

Not what "has happened", nor what "is happening", but "what would come to happen". The projection of a (hypothetical) future into a past yet to be determined. The equivalent of projecting a (hypothetical) past into the future, i.e. the "future anterior" or future perfect (what "will have happened"). This was the tense that leapt out at Roland Barthes in his readings of historical photographs: the prisoner about to be executed in a nineteenth-century American jail "*that* is dead and *that* is going to die".[42] Also the tense of Walter Benjamin's Arcades Project in which Benjamin, according to Peter Szondi, "could see future events only in those instances where they already had moved into the past."[43] In the opening sequences of *CW*, we see a past activated through anticipation of (extreme) future trauma. When this happens, a televised event is no longer securely attached to the past. For Thomas Elsaesser, this may be what ultimately distinguishes the mediated past from the past of the historian:

> By this I mean that a past event, passed on in media images, is both un-dead and not-alive. It is always exceeding, in whatever small and insignificant way, the place and time, the status and hierarchy a historian might assign to it. This makes the discourse of media memory constitutively traumatic: always ready to return, always capable of jumping at us, fundamentally uncanny, never to be forgotten, but also never quite remembered, because interfered with, blurred, or overlaid by other images, other memories. [44]

Forgetting the Cold War

Except that, sometimes, some images *are* forgotten. Surprisingly, despite the lively debate and vast resources expended, this is the fate of the *CW* series, a decade after its initial screening. It was never made available on DVD, and is nowhere to be found in that multichannel process of recycling. The homepage which CNN created to accompany the series was "retired" in 2009. To see *CW* today requires the mobilizing of old communication media: tracking down eight used VHS-cassettes, having them delivered to your door, and locating a VHS player that still works.

"Why is this series buried?"[45] asks a frustrated online commentator after failing to find more episodes. "Is it too long? Has America/the world moved on?" CNN has stated that its copyright for much of the archival footage only lasted for ten years. If so, the "story of our times" not only lacked closure but was destined to self-destruct in the legal system of immaterial rights. Online commentators are more inclined to believe that America did indeed "move on" and that the narrative of its past took a drastic turn after 9/11. If so, we may be registering the effect of what Aleide Assman has termed an "impact event"[46] – one that must be remembered but that exceeds the form of existing cultural patterns.

Could the events of 9/11 be told in a televised chronicle like *CW*? Does this form belong to the past? Watching the series today, one notes something, well, outdated about not only its content (the Cold War world) but also its technology (those VHS tapes). This certainly need not imply the end of television, nor of history. But maybe it offers an opening for historical analysis, at least for someone like Walter Benjamin, who found that newly obsolete objects were peculiarly charged with historical energy. In this case, the object left behind would be the "story of our times" as described above: situated in between liveness and historicity, using the future anterior tense, and employing multiple registers of referentiality and authenticity – witnessing, narrative, documentary footage – all supplementing each another as if historical events can "tell themselves". A full deck of cards to illustrate, in Elsaesser's terms again, the potential of the three discourses of "history", "memory" and "media", though often in dispute, to function as each other's guardians. Has this potential been lost? If so, are we better or worse off?

Notes

1. Taylor Downing, "Bringing the Past to the Small Screen", (in) David Cannadine (ed.) *History and the Media* (New York: Palgrave Macmillan, 2004), 7.

2. Cf. Milly Buonanno, *The Age of Television: Experiences and Theories*, (Bristol: Intellect Books, 2008), and John Ellis, *Seeing Things: Television in the Age of Uncertainty* (London: I.B. Tauris, 2000).

3. Marita Sturken, *Tangled Memories* (Berkeley: University of California Press, 1997), 24.

4. Mary Ann Doane, "Information, Crisis, Catastrophe", (in) Patricia Mellen-

camp (ed.) *Logics of Television* (Bloomington, Ind.: Indiana University Press, 1990), 222.

5. Stephen Heath, "Representing Television" (in) Patricia Mellencamp (ed.) 1990, 279.

6. Neil Postman, *Amusing Ourselves to Death*, (London: Penguin, 1986), 136.

7. Anders Stephanson and Fredric Jameson, "Regarding Postmodernism: A Conversation with Fredric Jameson", *Social Text*, No. 21 (1989), 18.

8. Pierre Nora, "Reasons For the Current Upsurge in Memory", *Transit/Eurozine*, 2002, http://www.eurozine.com/articles/2002-04-19-nora-en.html

9. Daniel Dayan and Elihu Katz: *Media Events. The Live Broadcasting of History*, (Cambridge, Mass.: Harvard University Press, 1992).

10. Pierre Nora, "L'événement monstre", *Communications* 18, 1972, and "Le retour de l'événement", in *Faire de l'histoire vol 1* (Paris: Gallimard, 1974).

11. John Durham Peters claims it can't, in "Witnessing", (in) Paul Frosh & Amit Pinchevski, *Media Witnessing: Testimony in the Age of Mass Communication*, London: Palgrave Macmillan, 2009), 35.

12. For Pierre Nora, such memories are "prosthetic": "Between Memory and History: Les Lieux de Mémoire", *Representations* 26 (Spring 1989).

13. The main concept of television theory, first established in Raymond Williams, *Television: Technology and Cultural Form* (London: Routledge, 1974/1997).

14. Richard Dienst, *Still Life in Real Time: Theory After Television* (Durham: Duke University Press, 1994), 64.

15. Cf. Andrzej Gwózdz, "Aspects of Television Temporality", *Kinema, A Journal of Film and Audiovisual Media*, 2008. http://www.kinema.uwaterloo.ca/article.php?id=205&feature

16. Supported by the Royal Bank of Sweden Tercentenary Foundation, headed by the author, including Amanda Lagerkvist, Södertörn University, and Paul Achter, University of Richmond.

17. Taylor Downing (one of the co-writers of *Cold War*): "History on Television: The Making of *Cold War*, 1998" (in) Marcia Landy (ed.), *The Historical Film: History and Memory in Media* (New Brunswick, N.J.: Rutgers University Press, 2001). Downing connects the establishing of this format to Jeremy Isaacs' 1970s television series on WW2, *The World at War*. In terms of the six historical modes of documentary film defined in Bill Nichols, *Introduction to Documentary* (Bloomington, Ind: University of Indiana Press, 2001), it resembles the "expository mode" – using an objective, "Voice of God", voice-over for narration, explanation and argument, with footage added to strengthen the narrative. This mode was established in documentaries of the 1920s and 1930s, and became influential in newsreel reporting during WW2.

18. Jeremy Isaacs and Taylor Downing, *Cold War* (London: Abacus, 1998/2008), ix.

19. Paul Ricoeur, *Minne, historia, glömska* (*La mémoire, l'histoire, l'oubli*, 2000, Göteborg: Daidalos, 2005), 234.

20. Paul Ricoeur, *Time and Narrative* vol. 3 (Chicago: The University of Chicago Press, 1988).

21. Arnold Beichman (ed.), *CNN's Cold War Documentary: Issues and Controversy* (Stanford, Ca.; Hoover Institution Press, 2000).

22. John Lewis Gaddis, "The Cold War, Television, and the Approximation of Truth", (in) Arnold Beichman (ed.) 2000.

23. Gaddis 2000, 43.

24. Hayden White, *The Content of the Form: Narrative Discourse and Historical Representation* (Baltimore: Johns Hopkins University Press, 1990), 24.

25. White, 1990, 24.

26. White, 1990, 5.

27. In fact, closer to 50 minutes, the equivalent of an hour prescribed by the international standards of television, in expectance of the "natural breaks" of commercials.

28. Cf. Buonnano 2008.

29. Jean Baudrillard, *The Gulf War Did Not Take Place* (Bloomington, Ind.: Indiana University Press, 1995).

30. Cf. James Schwoch, *Global TV: New Media and the Cold War, 1946–1969* (Urbana, Ill.: University of Illinois Press, 2009).

31. Ricoeur, 2005, 324.

32. An extended version of this paper, in preparation, uses Dienst's (1994) distinction between "still time" and "automatic time" to elaborate on television's "mixing and switching".

33. White, 1990, 4.

34. White, 1990, 4.

35. White, 1990, 21.

36. Cf. Guido Isekenmeier, "Technical Testimony: (Audio-)Visual Media as Witness", in Ulrik Ekman and Frederik Tygstrup (eds.), *Witness: Memory, Representation, and the Media in Question* (Copenhagen: Museum Tusculanum Press, 2008), and Jacques Derrida and Bernard Stiegler, "The Archive Market: Truth, Testimony, Evidence", in *Echographies of Television* (Cambridge: Polity, 2002).

37. Thomas Elsaesser, "History, Media, and Memory - Three Discourses in Dispute", in Ulrik Ekman and Frederik Tygstrup (eds.), *Witness: Memory, Representation, and the Media in Question* (Copenhagen: Museum Tusculanum Press, 2008).

38. Benveniste quoted in White, 1990, 3.

39. Dori Laub, "Bearing Witness or the Vicissitudes of Listening", in Shoshana Felman and Dori Laub, *Testimony* (New York: Routledge, 1992), 57.

40. White, 1990, 5.

41. Isaacs & Downing, 1998/2008, cover.

42. Roland Barthes, *Camera Lucida: Reflections on Photography* (London: Vintage/Random House, 2000), 96.

43. Peter Szondi, "Hope in the Past: On Walter Benjamin", *Critical Inquiry* Spring 1978, Vol.4:3, 501

44. Elsaesser, 2008, 409.
45. http://topdocumentaryfilms.com/cold-war/
46. Aleida Assman, "Resonance and Impact – The Role of Emotions in Cultural Memory", notes from lecture at Södertörn University, 18/5 2001, (in preparation for publication as Södertörn Lectures 6).

3. Politics of Time

Year Zero:
The Temporality of Revolution Studied Through the Example of the Khmer Rouge

ANDRUS ERS

The notion of Year Zero – the claim to be making a radical break with history – is central to modernity. The most famous instances of this trope are the instituting of a new calendar in 1792 during the French Revolution, and the proclamation of Cambodia's Year Zero by the Khmer Rouge in April 1975. In this essay, I will begin by outlining the historical background to this nexus of ideas as they relate to the French Revolution, before proceeding to analyse it in greater detail using the example of the Khmer Rouge.

The French and Cambodian revolutions are both events that provide strong evidence of the connection between time and power, and of time's usefulness as a resource both for political action and as creator of meaning. More specifically, we appear to be confronted here by two examples of what might be termed *revolutionary temporality*, a form of temporality centred on the claim to be making a radical break with the past. My investigation thereby joins a broader field of research situated at the intersection between philosophy, history, and political science, and pioneered by thinkers such as Reinhart Koselleck and Quentin Skinner.

Year Zero / The End of History

By way of introduction, it should be noted that modernity also incorporates a range of variations upon this theme in its wider sense. In both military science and medicine, the adoption of a kind of zero point is central. For example, it can denote the point of impact for bombing, the point in time at which a military operation goes from the planning stage to execution, or index cases in the spread of an epidemic. In its current form, contemporary history is organized around a number of such zero points. To name just some of the most significant examples: the end of WWII in 1945 became Germany's *Stunde Null*; the bombings of Hiroshima and Nagasaki were described as zero points, and the site of the 11 September attacks was dubbed "Ground Zero". In the realm of epidemiology HIV/AIDS research has its own historical narrative. As early as 1987, a research group claimed to have identified a Canadian air steward, Gaëtan Dugas, as the epidemic's Patient Zero. Presumed to be the original source of transmission for the global epidemic, he was thought to be in a position to provide vital clues for solving the riddle of this disease. Although later studies rejected these findings by advancing alternative theories of transmission, Dugas quickly became a key figure in the mythology and historiography of the disease.[1]

Conversely, modernity has been characterized by a continual search for the end of history, a point at which we can be said to have arrived, to be complete or redeemed, a point at which the truth of humankind and society has been revealed once and for all. When the Marquis de Condorcet predicted the future development of humanity in *Outlines of an Historical View of the Progress of the Human Mind* (1795), he seemed to be speaking from a vantage point in time and space – post-revolutionary Enlightenment France – from which the truth of humanity's history and future prospects could finally be apprehended. Condorcet believed himself to be on the verge of taking the final, decisive step. Were it to be taken, humanity would be redeemed – free, equal, and rational – and continue its journey upon even ground. Subsequently, the trope has taken a variety of forms, for example, in the writings of G. W. F. Hegel, Karl Marx, Auguste Comte, and Francis Fukuyama. With the fall of the Berlin Wall in autumn 1989, Fukuyama's article "The End of History", which had been published that spring, came to seem like a prophesy fulfilled. The collapse of the communist bloc in the East appeared to mark the end of history in a Hegelian-Kojèvian sense, a point at which the precepts of liberalism had acquired a universal character as defining the ultimate goals of humanity, ostensibly rendering obsolete every alternative path to human liberation and redemption.²

The mythology of the American Revolution, too, is premised upon the idea of a zero point, an intellectual trope which received its most striking formulation in Thomas Paine's oft-cited statement in *Common Sense* (published in 1776, the year of revolution): "We have it in our power to begin the world over again. A situation, similar to the present, hath not happened since the days of Noah until now. The birthday of a new world is at hand."³ This mythology also includes the notion of a specifically American historical task – "Manifest Destiny" – according to which America is the bearer of a set of universal ideas and ideals which it has been charged with disseminating to the rest of humanity. It is a conviction that has guided and legitimated American expansionism under the administrations of James Polk, Woodrow Wilson, and George W. Bush, among others.⁴

The French Revolution's Year Zero – the instituting in 1792 of the French revolutionary calendar and metric chronology – is probably the single most famous instance of this trope. Instituting a new chronology fitted well with several central aspects of the Revolution and the idea of the Republic. It paralleled an array of other reforms jointly premised on the notion of basing the social order on *nature*, rather than on heritage, history, or tradition. Reforms such as the creation of the Republic, the declaration of the Rights of Man, and the metrical measurement of space and material objects, were seen as the counterparts of a system ordered by Nature in which humanity was no longer bound by the tyranny of the past.⁵

As historian Michael Meinzer has shown, the introduction of the revolutionary calendar came to mark the birth of the Republic, rather than the moment of the Revolution. Immediately following 14 July 1789, official documents and pamphlets began referring to 1789 as "l'an de –" or "l'ère de la Liberté". After the proclamation of the Republic in September 1792, however, it was decided that the new chronology should begin retrospectively on 2 January 1792, which thereby marked the official instituting of the "era of liberty". After 1792, the calendar was variously described as "the French Revolutionary Calendar" ("Le calendrier révolutionnaire française") and "the Republican Calendar" ("Le calendrier républicain"). The revolutionary calendar divided the year into twelve months, named after the seasons (e.g. Brumaire, from the French word *brume*, meaning fog; Thermidor, from the Greek word *thermon*, meaning heat). Each month was divided into three weeks of ten days, the tenth of which was a day of rest ("décadi"). Meinzer has also argued that instituting a new chronology had strong implications as an act of *realpolitik*: it erased in a single gesture all the religious references that had structured Christian chronology, replacing them with a system grounded in Nature. As such, it directly indicated a conflict that was fundamental to the Revolution: the struggle against the Church as a political institution.[6] Alongside this powerful symbolic connotation was the fact that its introduction coincided with the most brutal phases in the progress of the Revolution – the Terror of 1793–94 – which presumably is an important reason why the idea of Year Zero has acquired a sinister aura.

As Reinhart Koselleck has observed, each of these zero points echoes Christianity's own Year Zero.[7] A significant difference should be noted, however: at least until the American and French revolutions, the Year Zero of Christianity was static in nature. It was a pre-existing reference point from which Western chronology had subsequently been developed.[8] What distinguishes the modern phenomenon, my particular concern here, is its dynamic character. It involves a series of zero points – albeit often claiming to be absolute and definitive – which recur time and again, in various guises, as it were, being successively revised as developments unfold.

The Khmer Rouge and the historical threshold

This is not the place to investigate the entire intellectual history of this very broad topic. In what follows I shall restrict myself – in order to foreground and discuss a number of topics which I regard as central to this problematic – to one of the more extreme instances of the use of this concept: the Khmer Rouge's Year Zero in Cambodia in 1975. It makes an interesting case study on several counts: partly by virtue of its radicalness, but also because it is linked in various ways to the French example outlined above.

It is, moreover, an interesting example of Koselleck's thesis, that modernity in the final instance must be understood as a particular mode of experiencing time. A number of Koselleckian themes can be briefly adduced in this regard: the specifically modern sensation of living in a period of continual rupture; the eschatological aspect of temporal experience; the demand for absolute and definitive change, and a view of the present as a moment for conclusive historical-political action. And, most fundamental of all: the ceaseless acceleration, the battle against the clock, the idea that all previous developments must be surpassed in order to achieve victory.[9]

The Khmer Rouge's project can be likened to a continually accelerating tornado of events in which classical Marxism-Leninism was mixed with Maoism, traditional Khmer-Buddhist mythology, and a distinctly racist variety of nationalism. It was nostalgically backward-looking and utopian, hyper-emancipatory in its claims and unique in its brutality. The ideology of the Khmer Rouge has often been represented as anti-modern, a characterization with which I will take issue in this essay.[10] As I will elaborate, my own view is that Cambodia's Year Zero must be understood as an extreme example of a quintessentially modern phenomenon.

Recalling the French example alluded to above, it should be mentioned that Cambodia was a protectorate of French Indo-China between 1863 and 1953, making it part of France's empire. After 1953, the country became an independent constitutional monarchy under Prince Norodom Shianouk. The deposing of Shianouk in 1970 in an US-backed coup accelerated the guerrilla war which the Khmer Rouge had begun in the nineteen-sixties.

With the exception of Pol Pot, every member of the group which emerged as the Khmer Rouge leadership (Noun Chea, Ieng Sary, Son Sen, and Khieu Sampân) had studied at a prestigious seat of learning in Paris in the fifties, including the elite Institut d'Études Politiques de Paris and the Sorbonne. Sary and Samphân had written doctoral dissertations on Cambodian agriculture and economics. Pol Pot had studied electronics at a vocational institute of higher education albeit without completing his degree. He was well known as a talented organizer and quickly assumed a leadership position within the group. Although Pol Pot and Ieng Sary had joined the French Communist Party in 1951, the group chose to organize itself into the secret Cercle Marxiste, which operated under the mantle of the Khmer students' organization in France. When they came into contact with representatives of Viet Minh at a youth festival in East Berlin in 1951, the idea of a guerrilla war was born. Pol Pot's biographer Philip Short has described the group's fascination with French culture in general (the Enlightenment, Rousseau, Hugo, Montesquieu, etc) and, above all, the French Revolution; Peter Kropotkin's *The Great French Revolution 1789–1793* was an ever-present point of reference for the group.[11]

It makes sense, then, that Ieng Sary should have initiated a discussion within the Cercle Marxiste on the topic of the French Revolution and its teachings. For Sary, the Revolution offered a number of suggestive parallels. Prince Shianouk was felt to be another Louis XVI; it seemed possible to forge an alliance between peasants and bourgeois intellectuals against an absolute monarchy. The problem, according to Sary, was that the French Revolution had not gone far enough. The revolutionaries had stopped short rather than pursue it to its ultimate conclusion. Sary and his comrades held Robespierre in particularly high esteem. Suong Sikoeun, later one of Sary's closest collaborators, maintained that Robespierre's incorruptibility, radicalism, and consistency were exemplary. "If you do something, you must do it right through to the end. You can't make compromises. You must always be on the side of the absolute – no middle way, no compromise."[12]

If the Paris years were defined by schooling in classical Marxism-Leninism, then the guerrilla warfare years in Cambodia were to a large extent defined by Maoism. Crucially, Maoism also provided the Khmer Rouge with an activist perspective on history, something that sheds considerable light upon their own Year Zero. This activist perspective – as opposed to the orthodox Marxist representation of history as a rational process of necessary advances – emphasized human will and the triumph of determination over material conditions. Put differently: not so much *learning* from history as *overcoming* it, diverting history in the right direction, as it were, by means of superior will and resolution.[13]

The French Revolution, as already noted, had met with failure by stopping halfway. Yet even Mao, argued Khieu Samphân, the movement's chief theoretician, had not been radical enough to overcome history by definitively abolishing private property, the family, received knowledge, and traditional teaching. For Samphân, the task of making communism a reality entailed an ideological zero point: "zero for him and zero for you – that is true equality." Moreover, the task would be derailed by any deviation from this formula.[14]

It is evident that the Khmer Rouge, in deliberate and skilful fashion, drew on history for political ends. Their leadership made repeated reference to the importance of "grasping the wheel of history", and how history would crush those who stood in the way of development. In 1976, as part of Pol Pot's consolidation of personal power, official party historiography was revised with an eye to the older Indo-Chinese guerrilla fractions within the movement, by moving the date of the party's founding forward from 1951 (the First Indo-Chinese War) to 1960 (Pol Pot's election to the Central Committee). At a meeting of the Central Committee in March 1976, it was noted with regard to historiography that "we must rearrange the history of the Party into something clean and perfect [---] Do not use 1951 – make a clean break."[15]

Although the French Revolution was a continual point of reference, the party presented its own project as *sui generis* and unprecedented, one that would eventually serve as a model for future revolutions. The entire project was suffused with a sense of urgency: unless they got there before Vietnam, their militarily superior neighbours would swallow them up. The internal Marxist analysis indicated that Cambodia had to proceed directly from feudalism to communism – and within four years, at that – in a so-called "Super Great Leap Forward".[16]

Cambodia Year Zero

The Khmer Rouge was surrounded by an aura of anonymity and secrecy that gave the organization the character of a zero point around which events in time and space turned. Until 1977, it referred to itself simply as Angkar ("the Organization"). Its leadership assumed anonymous *noms de guerre*. Unlike Ho Chi Minh ("Enlightened One") or Stalin ("Man of Steel"), for example, Pol Pot (born Saloth Sar) is a common Khmer peasant name. Their true identities only became known after the fall of the regime in 1979. The organization's love of numbers is strongly reminiscent of the French Revolution (S-21 [the headquarters of the security police], B-1 [the Foreign Ministry], etc). The leadership typically used names like "Brother Number One" (Pol

Pot), "Brother Number Two" (Noun Chea), etc. In official documents, the number of potential traitors of the people was given as an exact percentage; the number of Vietnamese whom every Khmer had to kill in order to secure victory was set at thirty, and so forth.[17]

Unlike the French Revolution, Cambodia (from 1975, Democratic Kampuchea) never officially proclaimed a new chronology, nor did it ever introduce a new calendar. On the contrary, the few official documents which survive from the period 1975–1979 refer repeatedly to the standard Christian, Western chronology: throughout, documents allude to "the glorious 17 April 1975", to "the First Four Year Plan of 1976–79", and to "1960" as the moment of the party's official founding and the starting-point of the revolutionary struggle.[18]

In Cambodia, the concept "Year Zero" had a narrower meaning, as the Khmer Rouge's term for the emptying of the cities that immediately followed their victory against Lon Nol's US-backed regime on 17 April 1975.[19] Even so, much in the Khmer Rouge's ideology and concrete political actions supports the image of their seizure of power as a historical zero point.[20] A series of parallels with the revolutionary temporality of the French Revolution can be adduced in this regard: the demand for an absolute transformation, including, among other things, the claim to be making a decisive break with the past. Some of the official documents that have been preserved from Pol Pot's regime make repeated reference to the Cambodian Revolution as unique and unprecedented. In these documents, Cambodia's past – together with the experiences of other countries– is dismissed, time and again, as irrelevant.[21]

The uniquely radical claims of the Cambodian revolution have long been well-known. They encompassed a wide array of reforms directed towards the institutions of traditional bourgeois society. Money, markets, and private property, schools, institutes of higher education, newspapers, and religious institutions – all were immediately abolished after the seizure of power. Early eyewitness accounts relate how the hospital in Phnom Penh was emptied of patients, how the National Bank was set on fire, money burned in the streets. Immediately after the victory proclamation, book-burnings were orchestrated in front of the National Library and the Lycée français René Déscartes.[22] The country's borders were closed immediately and the "cleansing of the country from foreign influences" begun by deporting foreigners and domestic minorities such as Vietnamese, Muslim Khmer, Chinese Khmer, Thais, and Europeans.[23] It was also officially announced that "the individual" would be abolished. The traditional family would be replaced by the movement. In order to create a completely conflict-free society, revolutionaries were officially instructed not to have a personality. "The individual" was continually counterposed to "the people", with the former representing division, factionalism, inequality, bourgeois values, and foreign influence. "The people", meanwhile, embodied its polar opposite, something entirely pure: redemption; the extermination of particularity and contingency; and the realization of absolute freedom, equality, and fraternity through complete absorption into Angkar.[24]

The emptying of the cities that came to be designated Year Zero – probably the single greatest cause of the mass starvation and killings which convulsed the country between 1976 and 1979 – has often been portrayed as the expression of a reaction against modernity.[25] I regard this as an overly simplistic interpretation of events. Superficially, the idea of restoring the urban population to a form of imagined "home villages" seems like an anti-modern project, especially since it was combined with traditional Khmer-Buddhist mythology of an originary golden age that had been terminated by humanity's baleful desire for private ownership.[26]

And yet this entire mythology was structured according to a temporality far more complex than any simple notion of turning the clock back. Rather, the desire for a pre modern origin, a longing "to return to nature", is an essentially modern phenomenon. In a pre modern society, it would make no sense whatsoever. In the case of the Khmer Rouge, the issue was really a spatial movement from the cities out into the countryside, that simultaneously symbolized a journey back in time *and* a final step into an imagined future. To this was added some racist nationalism, a fascination with the French Revolution, conscious manipulation of their own historiography, a fixation with numbers, anonymity, and central planning, claims to be creating a new Man and transforming society absolutely, and a desire to divert history in the right direction.

In light of all these features, the Khmer Rouge's Year Zero stands revealed as a paradigmatically modern phenomenon that would be unthinkable in a pre modern society. As I have tried to show, proclamation of a new Year Zero – beyond its overt claim to be cutting ties with history – involves an opposite movement: a fixation on history. As such, it shares a fundamental premise of all modern attempts, from Condorcet to Fukuyama, to identify the end of history. These ostensibly contradictory impulses – the desire, variously, to end history and to institute a year zero – are in fact united by an underlying common desire to master history by bringing it to a definitive conclusion. What they share is a profound conviction that humanity stands on the brink of a final act after which it will continue its journey upon a level field. And yet it is as much the failure of these efforts – history, after all, just seems to keep on going – as the absoluteness of their claims that makes them so modern.

Notes

1. See for example Randy Shilts, *And the Band Played On: Politics, People, and the AIDS Epidemic* (New York: St. Martin's Press 1987).

2. For a systematic investigation of this theme in Hegel, Marx, and Kojève, see Perry Anderson, "The Ends of History" in *A Zone of Engagement* (London: Verso 1992).

3. Quoted in Jack Fruchtman, *The Political Philosophy of Thomas Paine* (Baltimore: Johns Hopkins University Press 2009), 58–59.

4. Anders Stephanson, *Manifest Destiny: American Expansionism and the Empire of Right* (New York: Hill & Wang 1995), 46, 111–121, 127–128.

5. Lynn Hunt, *Politics, Culture, and Class in the French Revolution* ([1984] London, Berkeley, Los Angeles: University of California Press 2004), 1ff, 70ff.

6. Michael Meinzer, *Der französische Revolutionskalender (1792-1805): Planung, Durchfürung und Scheitern einder politischen Zeitrechnung / Ancien Régime, Aufklärung und Revolution Band 20* (München: Oldenbourg 1992), 295–306. Cf. Reinhart Koselleck, "Remarks on the Revolutionary Calendar and Neue Zeit" in *The Practice of Conceptual History : Timing History, Spacing Concepts*, trans. Todd S. Presner et al, foreword by Hayden White (Stanford, Calif: Stanford University Press 2002), 148–153.

7. Koselleck, "Remarks on the Revolutionary Calendar and Neue Zeit", 151.

8. During the Middle Ages as well as the early modern period, the dating of Christ's birth, and the introduction of the Gregorian calendar, were the objects of a series of revisions and power struggles. That Christ's birth should be year zero was, however, uncontested. The concept was in this sense static by nature, even

though the methods of counting and periodizing were themselves subject to controversy.

9. Reinhart Koselleck, "Historical Criteria of the Modern Concept of Revolution", "'Neuzeit': Remarks on the Semantics of Modern Concepts of Movement", and "'Space of Experience' and 'Horizon of Expectation': Two Historical Categories", in *Futures Past : On the Semantics of Historical Time*, trans. Keith Tribe (New York: Columbia University Press 2004)

10. Se for example Ben Kiernan, *The Pol Pot Regime: Race Power and Genocide in Cambodia under the Khmer Rouge 1975-79*, (New Haven & London: Yale University Press 1996), 27, and Gina Chon & Sambath Thet, *Behind the Killing Fields. A Khmer Rouge Leader and one of His Victims* (Philadelphia: University of Pennsylvania Press 2010), 62.

11. Philip Short, *Pol Pot: The History of a Nightmare* (London: John Murray Publishers 2004), 73-74.

12. Short, *Pol Pot*, 73-74.

13. Kiernan, *The Pol Pot Regime*, 27.

14. Short, *Pol Pot*, 317.

15. David P. Chandler, *Brother Number One: A Political Biography of Pol Pot* (Oxford & Boulder, Colorado: Westview Press), 122; *Pol Pot Plans the Future. Confidential Leadership Documents from Democratic Kampuchea, 1976–1977*, eds. David P. Chandler, Ben Kiernan, Chantou Boua (New Haven: Yale Southeast Asia Studies 1988), 4, 121-126.

16. *Pol Pot Plans the Future*, 36, 120–123, 126, 171; Chandler, *Brother Number One*, 107.

17. Chandler, *Brother Number One*, 7-8.

18. *Pol Pot Plans the Future*, 213-227.

19. Chon & Thet, *Behind the Killing Fields*, 121–125.

20. Chandler, *Brother Number One*, 105, 227n.

21. *Pol Pot Plans the Future*, 123.

22. François Ponchaud, *Cambodia Year Zero*, trans. Nancy Amphoux (London : Allen Lane 1978) 17-38, 214-215; Chon & Thet, *Behind the Killing Fields,* 39.

23. Kiernan, *The Pol Pot Regime*, 33-40.

24. Short, *Pol Pot*, 318.

25. Se for example Kiernan, *The Pol Pot Regime*, 27 and Chon & Thet, *Behind the Killing Fields,* 62.

26. Short, *Pol Pot*, 317.

Ways of Warmaking

JENS BARTELSON

I

Does the concept of war have a history? Judging from the ways in which the concept of war is understood in the social sciences today, the answer is no. For many philosophers and social scientists, war is a timeless and immutable concept whose main function is to render changing practices of warfare intelligible. On this view, writing the history of the concept of war is a rather pointless exercise, since it would yield nothing but an endless reaffirmation of those timeless connotations.[1]

Despite this contention, the concept of war seems recently to have lost some of its principal connotations, a development that makes writing its history an urgent priority. While the concept of war has long been used to denote violent conflict either between or within distinct political communities, it is now widely used to describe a series of practices that defy such easy compartmentalization. Many commentators agree that the modern concept of war has lost most of its analytical purchase in a world in which sovereign states are now no longer the only belligerents, and in which the distinction between international and domestic conflicts has ceased to make much sense. Consequently, it is now possible to speak of war without implying the existence of any specific kind of agent or any definite level of hostilities; formerly metaphorical uses of the concept have become literal. Largely simultaneously, the distinction between peace and war has become more fluid. When they once defined two states that necessarily could not coexist temporally or geographically, war and peace now occupy the end points of a continuum comprising many intervening shades of grey.[2] Far from being timeless and immutable, then, the concept of war does indeed seem capable of change. But how have these conceptual changes affected contemporary practices of warfare? Do they simply reflect a desire to make sense of changing practices of warfare, or is there reason to believe that they have been instrumental in bringing about changes in actual practices of warfare?

To pose and frame this problem is the task of the present text. From my point of view, rather than being mere repositories of representations, concepts are actively involved in shaping the socio-political world. Since this world is only accessible to understanding and intervention by means of concepts, a focus on conceptual change becomes an important way of understanding political change. Beyond making some rather vague or superficial observations, however, most histories of political concepts have had little to say about how conceptual change affects political practices and institutions.[3] Rather than regarding war as a timeless and immutable concept whose sole task is to subsume and render intelligible the changing practices of warfare, I therefore wish to argue that the concept of war has indeed undergone significant change insofar as its meaning has varied across different historical and cultural contexts, and that these changes, in turn, have conditioned further changes in the practice of warfare across these same contexts.

Although social scientists and historians have devoted a great deal of intellectual labor to the causes of and justifications for warfare, the changing meaning and function of the concept of war have not yet been subjected to systematic treatment. This neglect is curious, since the concept of war has been foundational in modern political thought. Many of its transformations have had a profound impact on the practices of warfare as well as on the rest of the socio-political world by shaping the identities of agents and the boundaries separating them. In this project, I seek to amend this situation by inquiring into the changes which this concept has undergone between the sixteenth century and the present day. I will argue that these changes have been constitutive of the modern European system of states and its relationship to the world beyond Europe by virtue of having informed different practices of warfare among European states as well as between the Western and non-Western worlds. At the risk of simplifying matters, it can be argued that warfare was the very tool with which those boundaries were drawn.

But if concepts of war do not just merely render practices of warfare intelligible but also condition them, how are concepts and practices connected? I will suggest that a focus on *justification* can provide a mediating link between abstract conceptualizations and concrete practices. By studying justifications for warfare in some detail, we can gain important insights into the changing meaning and function of the concept of war in the history of political and legal thought as well as into the practices of warfare themselves. If justifications are understood as speech acts whose point is to command the approval of a given audience, then they are necessary to turn what might otherwise have been a merely random outburst of violence into a more organized form. By constituting war as a meaningful and legitimate activity, justifications for war shape not only the understanding of this activity among agents, but also the identities and interests of those involved. Hence the practice of justification is integral to the possibility of warfare since it provides a mediating link between abstract conceptions of war and the actual practices of warfare. I will use the term *warmaking* to describe the way in which these transitions from abstract conceptions of war to actual practices of warfare are effected rhetorical and political practice. This choice of terminology reflects my conviction that war – like any other social and political concept – is intelligible only by virtue of studying its actual usage in different contexts. As Peter Winch once pointed out, 'to give an account of the meaning of a word is to describe how it is used; and to describe how it is used is to describe the social intercourse into which it enters.'[4] As I see it, therefore, wars are made when conceptions of war are translated into practices of warfare.

The use of political concepts is enabled but also constrained by linguistic conventions, as is the range of justifications that can be performed by means of them. This requires us to pay close attention to the definitions of war and the classifications of different forms of warfare, since, as Nelson Goodman has put it, 'we are confined to ways of describing whatever is described'.[5] Since our attempts to explain actual occurrences of war presuppose a prior conceptualization of the activity to be explained, it is reasonable to ask whether such attempts to make sense of war are involved in shaping their object of inquiry. Existing explanations of why war occurs should thus not be taken at face value but, rather, carefully contextualized in order to understand how they furnish the conceptual resources for justifications for warfare. Studying the philosophical and scientific usages of the concept of war is thus essential to understanding modern practices of warfare, since 'human acts come into being hand in hand with our invention of the ways to name them'.[6]

Justifications of war typically draw on wider moral and legal frameworks that tell us under what circumstances recourse to force is necessary or legitimate, and when it is not. As Butler has argued, however contingent their form and content, definitions of war are never simply innocent semantic exercises. From our definitions of war follow normative principles, and from those follow rules making it possible to promote or restrict the violent practices thus defined. As a result, our moral responses to warfare are always conditioned by prior acts of definition and classification.[7] Since acts of war are frequently justified by reference to exceptional circumstances, the act of naming and classifying certain forms of violence as war, pure and simple, implies their removal from the realm of ordinary moral judgment and transposition to a domain ruled by necessity and contingency. A linked and equally important matter is the question of which violent practices are excluded by any particular definition of war. Restricting the range of applicability of the concept of war in such a way that certain forms of organized violence are excluded, means removing them from the purview of international legal and moral standards, thereby indirectly licensing violent practices that would otherwise seem highly objectionable.

If we want to understand how and why wars are waged, therefore, we should pay more attention to how justifications for war have conditioned actual practices of warfare, and how different justifications are made possible by different conceptions of war. All justifications for warfare must be understood against the backdrop of wider conceptual frameworks that render practices of warfare meaningful to the agents in question. These frameworks make certain justifications for war possible and others difficult, if not impossible. They do this by telling us who is entitled to wage war, under which circumstances the relevant audiences are likely to recognize the recourse to violence as legitimate, who those audiences are and why they are likely to accept certain justifications while rejecting others. In this project, I will refer to those wider conceptual frameworks as the *conditions of justifiability*.

II

As indicated at the outset, one important rationale for undertaking the present study are those changes that the concept of war has undergone during the last decades, pushing the meaning of this concept far beyond its modern connotations. The waning of these traditional meanings is reflected in the intellectual and moral disorientation we experience when we try to come to terms with current practices of warfare using old concepts. Since the modern concept of war has been used to refer to violent conflict either between or within political communities, the burden of rendering the concept of war meaningful and intelligible has fallen upon those seemingly innocent terms, 'between' and 'within.'

But how can we talk coherently about war in the absence of centralized authority and fixed boundaries? What happens to the applicability of the concept of war when actual wars are neither exclusively international nor civil, but rather both simultaneously? As Augustine once pointed out, 'war can only be waged by or within persons who are in some sense natural beings: beings who could not exist at all if peace of some kind did not exist within them.'[8] Whether something that looks like a war should be classified as international or civil in nature seems mostly to be a matter of the spatio-temporal extension of sovereign authority and the nature of the boundaries separating the belligerents. If sovereign authority cannot be properly localized, and the boundaries between belligerents cannot be properly drawn, then the agents involved cannot be properly identified, either. And if the agents involved cannot be properly identified, it becomes hard to make sense of that war since there is no-one to whom we can attribute motives. Hence, in the absence of sovereign authority and fixed boundaries, the distinction between international and civil war collapses, undermining our ability to explain and understand the incidence of warfare through reference to the interests and identities of easily identifiable agents. Since the distinction between war and peace is contingent upon the presence of both sovereign authority and firm boundaries between political agents involved in hostilities, it also becomes difficult to maintain in the absence of these requirements.[9] In short, when we are unsure what is 'between' and what is 'within', the concept of war seems to lose many of its modern connotations. It seems clear that some of these new conceptions of war go a long way towards justifying new practices of warfare simply by nullifying moral and legal restrictions on the use of violence that were coeval with the modern distinction between civil and international wars.[10]

Yet a full understanding of this transition necessitates a systematic historical treatment of the concept of war and its relationship to practice. Such an account is lacking, despite the crucial role performed by the concept of war in modern political thought. While the ideologies that legitimized imperialism and colonialism have received extensive treatment in recent years, the ways in which the use of force was justified in the processes of imperial expansion and colonial exploitation have attracted little attention from historians of political thought.[11] Curiously, even otherwise historically sensitive accounts of the rights of war seem to assume, perhaps in order to facilitate cross-comparison, that the concept's meaning and function have remained relatively stable over time and across different contexts.[12]

III

The changing legal norms of warfare, however, have attracted attention from legal historians. According to Carl Schmitt, war among European states gradually became subject to legal and moral restraints from the early-modern period onwards. This regulation was based on the idea that war was an activity between formal equals within an international system based on those entities' mutual recognition. Yet, for Schmitt, this limited form of war was made possible by European expansion and the appropriation of land on other continents. Beyond the lines of demarcation separating the European system from the rest of the world, no such restraints were considered valid or applicable. As Schmitt argued, beyond these lines was a zone 'in which, for want of any legal limits to war, only the law of the stronger applied... this freedom meant that the line set aside an area where force could be used freely and ruthlessly... everything that occurred beyond the line remained outside the legal, moral and political values recognized on this side of the line.'[13] As he went on to explain, 'the designation of a zone of ruthless conflict was a logical consequence of the fact that there was neither a recognized principle nor a common arbitrational authority to govern the division and allocation of lands.' But, simultaneously, 'a rationalization, humanization, and legalization – a bracketing – of war was achieved against this background of global lines.'[14] For Schmitt and many of his followers, then, the regulation of warfare between European states during the early-modern period coincided with, and was partially conditioned by, the unleashing of unprecedented violence against non-European peoples.

Consolidation of the modern system of European states merely meant that distinctions of faith were replaced by other methods of justifying discrimination and violence against non-Europeans. The thrust of Schmitt's argument is that the European state system and the global realm were historically co-constituted, and that European state formation and imperial expansion thus represent two sides of the same coin. During the emergence of the states system, European expansion was a safety valve for territorial rivalries between emergent states, even as the practices of expansion contributed some of the resources for state-building at home.[15] In this alien context, the concept of war and its cognates took on very different meanings. Not only was it easier to justify war against peoples deemed barbarous, uncivilized, or savage, but their alleged barbarism and savagery made it possible to justify methods that were gradually becoming unacceptable in warfare between Europeans. War against barbarians thus justified recourse to barbaric methods. Many of the violent practices that drove European expansion on other continents were not classified as wars at all, often because they neither involved relations between sovereign states, nor were based on prior recognition of an opponent's legal rights. Starting with Grotius, many of these practices were not considered instances of war, strictly speaking, and therefore lay beyond the scope of those legal theories that sought to impose restraints on warfare between sovereign agents in Europe.[16] Instead, many of these violent practices were defined as private wars, campaigns or punitive expeditions that needed no special justification under international law. And, since many of these campaigns and expeditions tended to involve private agents such as the East India Company, they did not need to be justified in relation to public law, either.

Other historians of international law have described how this duality was reproduced well into the twentieth century. As Koskenniemi has shown, during the nineteenth century, the principles of international law were only applicable to civilized peoples, while "uncivilized" peoples were subject to civilizing missions and attempts by European powers to impose sovereignty.[17] Moreover, as Anghie has argued, early modern international law and its notion of sovereignty evolved precisely out of a violent encounter with peoples on other continents. At the time of the *conquista*, Spaniards and American Indians were not subject to a universal legal code. Since the Spanish never recognized the Indians as holders of rights, 'war is the means by which the Indians and their territory are converted into Spaniards and Spanish territory, the agency by which the Indians thus achieve their full human potential.'[18] While naturalist jurisprudence had regarded non-European societies as belonging to a universal society of all mankind, and hence equally subject to the principles of natural law, the rise of legal positivism in the nineteenth century turned the focus towards the requirements of sovereignty and the distinction between civilized and non-civilized societies. Non-European societies could then be denied membership in the "Family of Nations" on the grounds that they lacked sovereignty and were uncivilized, which meant that they lacked effective means for asserting their rights and gaining international recognition. This exclusion paved the way, in turn, for their annexation by European powers and admission into international society on unequal terms, or forced these states to conform to Western standards of civilization in the interest of obtaining legal protection under international law. Colonialism was thus greatly facilitated by legal positivism, while the global spread of international law served to impose Western standards of civilization upon the rest of the world, in complete disregard for other cultural identities and legal standards. By the end of the nineteenth century, the hierarchy between civilized and uncivilized societies that had provided European expansion with much of its moral acceptability and political legitimacy had been firmly institutionalized and entrenched in legal practice.[19]

Other legal theorists have taken this analysis a step further by demonstrating how the distinction between civilized and uncivilized peoples also affected the laws of war and their application (or non-application) outside Europe. As Mégret has argued, nineteenth-century efforts to regulate the use of violence between European powers coincided with an unleashing of unprecedented violence against non-European peoples under the pretext of defending civilization from barbarism. The rules of war obtaining to warfare between European peoples did not apply to savages and barbarians outside Europe. Geographical and cultural distance made discrimination between civilized and non-civilized peoples intuitively appealing. The barbarous nature of the latter could then be used to justify acts of extraordinary brutality, their exclusion being justified by reference to anthropological assumptions about innate brutishness. Since these peoples did not distinguish between combatants and non-combatants, and since they waged war in ways that were more cruel and lawless that those of civilized nations, they could not be subject to the laws of war. In Mégret's summary of a key contemporary assumption: "savages" do not wage "civilized war", therefore "civilized warfare" cannot be waged against them".[20] For Mégret, the laws of war are "an integral part of the crystallization of the world into a world of states, part and parcel of the very constitution of that world." As such, the laws of war are "also and unmistakably a project of Western expansion and even imperialism, one that carries its own violence even as it seeks to regulate violence".[21] By these means, the spread of Western, 'civilized' methods of warmaking to the rest of the world was justified by reference to the 'uncivilized' methods of warmaking that prevailed among "savage" peoples. Yet the way this dissemination took place was itself anything but civilized, being intimately connected with the imposition of sovereign state authority and the forcible assimilation of non-European peoples into the society of states constituted by international law. Viewed from this perspective, new practices of globalized warfare can be seen as a return to earlier imperialistic forms, justified with reference to universal values and waged against the 'others' of international order by a host of different agents, public as well as private.[22]

IV

Most accounts of war and warfare seem to imply that the concept of war is timeless and immutable, and that it was invented in order to make the actual practices of warfare intelligible. Despite the fact that this concept is foundational in modern political thought, and has undergone a series of important changes between the sixteenth century and the present, it has attracted little attention from historians of political thought. Fortunately, historians of international law have made important contributions to our understanding of war's changing function in the context of the European states system, and how different justifications of warfare were operative in the relationship between the Europeans and non-European peoples. And yet, while historians of international law have attended to the difference between the ways in which war was understood and conducted within the European state system, and the ways in which war was understood and conducted in relation to non-European peoples, their focus has mainly been on *legal norms*, rather than on the underlying conceptions of war and the actual practices of warfare that these conceptions were used to justify. Missing from legal historiography are the links leading upward to conceptual meaning and downward to concrete practices.

By omitting these conceptual and practical dimensions, legal historiography has neglected the extent to which the identities of agents and the boundaries by which they are separated have been shaped by changing conceptions and practices of warfare, and how such processes of identity-construction and boundary-drawing have jointly constituted global order since the sixteenth century. Most importantly, we have yet to understand fully how changing conceptions of war affected the creation of political order in Europe and the simultaneous expansion of the European powers to other continents. In the current project, I will make an effort in this direction by comparing, on the one hand, the conceptions of war involved in the justifications of those wars believed to have been constitutive of the modern order of sovereign states, and, on the other, those operative in the justification of imperial expansion and colonial wars during the same periods.

Notes

1. Christopher Coker, *Barbarous Philosophers: Reflections on the Nature of War From Heraclitus to Heisenberg* (New York: Columbia University Press, 2010).

2. See *inter alia* Mary Kaldor, *New and Old Wars. Organized Violence in a Global Era* (Oxford: Polity, 2006); Christopher Coker, *The Future of War: The Re-Enchant-*

ment of War in the Twenty-First Century (Oxford: Blackwell, 2004); Mikkel Vedby Rasmussen, *Risk Society at War* (Cambridge: Cambridge University Press, 2003).

3. See Jens Bartelson, 'Philosophy and History in the Study of Political Thought,' *Journal of the Philosophy of History* 1 (2007): 101-124.

4. Peter Winch, *The Idea of a Social Science and its Relation to Philosophy* (London: Routledge, 1958), 114-115.

5. Nelson Goodman, *Ways of Worldmaking* (Indianapolis: Hackett, 1978), 3.

6. Ian Hacking, *Historical Ontology* (Cambridge, Mass.: Harvard University Press, 2002), 113.

7. See Judith Butler, *Frames of War. When Is Life Grievable?* (London: Verso, 2009), 1-32.

8. Augustine, *City of God* (Cambridge: Cambridge University Press, 1998), XIX. xiii, 939.

9. See Jens Bartelson, '"Double Binds": Sovereignty and the Just War Tradition", in *Sovereignty in Fragments*, ed. Hent Kalmo and Quentin Skinner (Cambridge: Cambridge University Press, 2010), 81-95.

10. See among others Jean Cohen, 'Whose Sovereignty? Empire versus International Law', *Ethics & International Affairs* 18 (2004): 1-24; Hauke Brunkhorst, 'The Right to War: Hegemonic Geopolitics or Civic Constitutionalism?' *Constellations* 11 (2004): 512-526; Jef Huysmans, 'International Politics of Exception: Competing Visions of International Order Between Law and Politics', *Alternatives* 31 (2006): 135-165; Wouter G. Werner, 'From *Justus Hostis* to Rogue State. The Concept of the Enemy in International Legal Thinking', *International Journal for the Semiotics of Law* 17 (2004): 155-168; Vivienne Jabri, 'War, Security and the Liberal State', *Security Dialogue* 37 (2006): 47-64.

11. See, for example, Uday Singh Mehta, *Liberalism and Empire. A Study in Nineteenth-Century British Liberal Thought* (Chicago: University of Chicago Press, 1999); David Armitage, *The Ideological Origins of the British Empire* (Cambridge: Cambridge University Press, 2002); Jennifer Pitts, *A Turn to Empire: The Rise of Imperial Liberalism in Britain and France* (Princeton: Princeton University Press, 2005); Jeanne Morefield, *Covenants Without Swords: Liberal Idealism and the Spirit of Empire* (Princeton: Princeton University Press, 2005); Duncan Bell ed., *Victorian Visions of Global Order. Empire and International Relations in Nineteenth-Century Political Thought* (Cambridge: Cambridge University Press, 2007). For an excellent overview, see Duncan S. A. Bell, 'Empire and International Relations in Victorian Political Thought', *The History Journal* 49 (2006): 281-298.

12. See, for example, Richard Tuck, *Rights of War and Peace. Political Thought and International Order from Grotius to Kant* (Oxford: Oxford University Press, 1999).

13. Carl Schmitt, *The Nomos of The Earth in the International Law of the Jus Publicum Europaeum* (New York: Telos Press, 2006), 93-4. For an interesting commentary, see Martti Koskenniemi, 'International Law as Political Theology: How to Read *Nomos der Erde?*', *Constellations* 11 (2004): 492-511.

14. Schmitt, *The Nomos of the Earth*, 100.

15. See Jordan Branch, 'Colonial Reflection and Territoriality: The Peripheral Origins of Sovereign Statehood', *European Journal of International Relations* 20 (2011): 1–21.

16. See Edward Keene, *Beyond the Anarchical Society* (Cambridge: Cambridge University Press, 2002); James Muldoon, *The Americas in the Spanish World Order. The Justification for Conquest in the Seventeenth Century* (Philadelphia: University of Pennsylvania Press, 1994).

17. See Martti Koskenniemi, *The Gentle Civilizer of Nations. The Rise and Fall of International Law 1870-1960* (Cambridge: Cambridge University Press), 98–178.

18. Antony Anghie, *Imperialism, Sovereignty, and the Making of International Law* (Cambridge: Cambridge University Press, 2005), 23.

19. Antony Anghie, 'Finding the Peripheries: Sovereignty and Colonialism in Nineteenth-Century International Law', *Harvard International Law Journal* 40 (1999): 1–71; Gerrit W. Gong, *The Standard of 'Civilization' in International Society* (Oxford: Oxford University Press, 1984); Edward Keene, 'A Case Study of the Construction of International Hierarchy: British Treaty-Making Against the Slave Trade in the Early Nineteenth Century', *International Organization* 61 (2007): 311–339.

20. Frédéric Mégret, 'From "Savages" to "Unlawful Combatants": A Postcolonial Look at International Law's Other', in *International Law and Its Others,* ed. Anne Orford, (Cambridge: Cambridge University Press, 2006), 265–317, at 294.

21. Mégret, "From "Savages" to "Unlawful Combatants"', 308.

22. For this suggestion, see Brett Bowden, 'Civilization and Savagery in the Crucible of War', *Global Change, Peace & Security* 19 (2007): 3–16.

On the Historicity of Concepts: The Examples of Patriotism and Cosmopolitanism in Ellen Key

REBECKA LETTEVALL

Studying the history of concepts is more than just the study of something past. It confronts us with the historicity of our own concepts, and makes us aware that our own premises are changeable, historical matter. Although analytical concepts are essential tools for any historian who wishes to give structure and coherence to the past, they can also obscure the particular historical context in question. In this essay, I will present a conceptual-historical background and analyse the concepts *patriotism* and *cosmopolitanism* in the Swedish author, educator, and social commentator Ellen Key (1849–1926). Key offers an illustrative example of the special historicity of these fundamental sociopolitical concepts.

A historical perspective on cosmopolitanism and patriotism as concepts

For both Hans-Georg Gadamer and Reinhart Koselleck, language and concepts are central to how we understand the past. Gadamer's notion of *Wirkungsgeschichte* and Kosellecks's project of conceptual history offer valuable insights into the historical study of ideas, insights which can move us beyond the simplified opposition between historical and ahistorical approaches to intellectual political history.

Any reflective conceptual-historical understanding which aspires to contemporary relevance will gain much from allowing itself to be guided by Gadamer's idea of *Wirkungsgeschichte*. This perspective focuses on historical phenomena and the effects of tradition as well as their historical repercussions, and ultimately also including the history of scholarship and academic research.¹ Koselleck's conceptual-historical approach opens up new possibilities for understanding both the past and the present. The changes in meaning and slippages exposed by conceptual-historical studies can illuminate not only the past but also the present.

A great many central concepts in modern politics, such as democracy, war, and peace, risk being misunderstood by an ahistorical approach.² Anyone discussing democracy today who turns for support to history can easily misunderstand Plato or Immanuel Kant, for example. Kant is often portrayed as an advocate of democracy, yet the form of government which he advocated was, more precisely, "republican"³. To be sure, Kant's republic has some of the features we today associate with democracy, such as power-sharing and citizenship. At the same time, the concept of democracy in Kant's writings has a clearly negative connotation; democracy, according to Kant, is characterized by incompetence and disorder, and, as for Plato, threatens to descend into anarchy.

Major political changes not infrequently lead to new interests and perspectives among scholars. An example of this is the idea of *cosmopolitanism*, which gained a new lease of life after the collapse of the Soviet empire in around 1990. *Cosmopolitanism* began attracting intellectuals from disciplines such as philosophy, sociology, political science, literary and intellectual history, and anthropology, in a varied and multifaceted discussion.

Its popularity stands in sharp contrast to the period before the fall of the Soviet Union, when the global political situation was defined by the Cold War, a situation that hardly encouraged visions of global unity and peace. With the end of the Cold War, globalization was able to make inroads freely into a number of areas. It is not unlikely that this has contributed to new perspectives on global development that have been shaped by cosmopolitanism.

Yet an important distinction must be made between globalization and cosmopolitanism. If the primary focus of globalization is economic relationships, then cosmopolitanism also includes theories about attitudes which can be applied to the consequences of economic globalization. Cosmopolitanism is often promoted as a means of achieving peace, or of living in peace.

The new theorists were quick to seek an affiliation with the conceptual-historical tradition of cosmopolitanism by invoking Stoicism and Enlightenment cosmopolitanism, with Kant as a particularly important influence. Such efforts, however, often lacked an understanding of conceptual history, and sometime used historical references more as ornamentation than as a conceptual resource for a more profound understanding the present.

The strong interest in pursuing various forms of cosmopolitanism among intellectuals today should be seen, in part, as historically determined. The historical situation since the fall of the iron curtain has re-actualized this idea and created a lively debate in the wake of globalization. At the same time, however, the twentieth century was to a large extent characterized by a profound myopia about cosmopolitanism as a concept, something that naturally raises the question of what other contemporary concepts have tended to arouse suspicion and can therefore be described as blindspots on the conceptual-historical map. Is it perhaps time to find out what else lies in the poisons cupboard of conceptual history?

It might seem as though changing historical-political situations force certain concepts to become invisible. While cosmopolitanism has been the object of interest during recent decades, *patriotism* as a concept has been made invisible, despite the fact that the two have historically often been lumped together. By contrast, it can be noted that during the eighteenth century these two concepts were often mentioned in the same breath and were taken to be mutually dependent.[4] As mentioned initially, Koselleck sees the task of conceptual history as tracing those central concepts which can enable a new understanding of the past so as ultimately to deepen our understanding of the present. From this perspective, the concept of patriotism may indeed be a significant tool for interpreting the past.

Twentieth-century usage of the concept of patriotism has contributed to its problematic status in European politics today. As is well known, patriotism in the twenty-first century has come to be associated with European populism, yet it is almost never mentioned in connection with cosmopolitanism. A quick search of the Internet in spring 2011 indicates that the term is used extensively by nationalist parties in Europe. There emerges an image of the patriot as an extreme nationalist, far removed from conventional nationalism: a Eurosceptic who is against immigration and international cooperation. At the same time, the portrayal of the patriot in American popular culture presents an important contrast. The image which emerges here is of an American soldier crawling on the ground in a foreign country, ready to fight to his last breath for his country, ready to sacrifice himself for something greater than himself.

Patriotism and cosmopolitanism in Ellen Key

In what follows, I will discuss the concepts of patriotism and cosmopolitanism in works published by Swedish author and commentator Ellen Key during the first decades of the twentieth century. Ellen Key (1849–1926) is important in this context for several reasons. It is often assumed that interest in cosmopolitanism evaporated from the public sphere in Europe at around the time of Kant's death. Scholars largely agree that nineteenth-century nationalism assumed such dominance of public discourse that it came to seem more or less impossible to advocate the ideals of cosmopolitanism.[5] Yet this assumption is only valid to a limited extent. Even if nationalist discourse was dominant throughout the nineteenth century, there existed at the same time a counter-discourse within the socialist and peace movements. Even after the First World War, the influence of nationalist voices remained strong, not least in the League of Nations, which was of course also a significant organ of international cooperation.

On the whole, however, cosmopolitanism as an ideal was rarely appreciated during the interwar years. Some even regarded it as a dangerous tendency. In *The Encyclopaedia of Sociology* (1931), for example, German sociologist Max Hildebert Boehm categorized cosmopolitanism as "abstract universalism".[6]

Patriotism, on the other hand, could be described in a considerably more nuanced fashion in this period than it can today. Key regarded patriotism as a significant and important part of life that was necessary for peace.[7] Several of her opponents criticized her definition of patriotism, however, and claimed that Key was unpatriotic. Key can thus be seen to interpret patriotism in a new way, and it could be argued that she develops a nuanced theory of patriotism. This theory can, I believe, also contribute to contemporary discussion of cosmopolitanism.

Key's view of patriotism is complex. In her central work *War, Peace, and the Future: A Consideration of Nationalism and Internationalism, and of the Relation of Women to War* (1916; published in Swedish as *Kriget, freden och framtiden* [1914]), she argues that the related concepts of *nationalitetskänsla* and *fosterlandskänsla* are too often conflated conceptually. Both are expressions of patriotism, yet *fosterlandskänsla* (a feeling of having been born in a particular country) represents belonging or affiliation, whereas *nationalitetskänsla* (a feeling of national political identity) represents a form of self-assertion. For Key, nationalism is a degenerate form of patriotism, while true patriotism is *fosterlandskänsla*, a "wonderful feeling" born from a person's earliest unconscious impressions in childhood. This kind of patriotism is ancient, argues Key, and already existed at the dawn of culture. As such, it has been of decisive importance for humanity and true cultural development.[8] Patriotism strives to create co-operation between different peoples.[9] Patriotism helps its own people to act justly, that is, in accordance with agreed principles of law. Nationalism is indifferent to the justice or injustice of an act, and its indifference can turn into contempt for the law. Thus the motto of the strong: My country first![10] The tree is an important symbol of patriotism: that which has no roots can neither grow nor develop, argues Key.

The most important aspect of love for country of one's birth, according to Key, is that instinct which cannot be governed by thought. It can have taken shape in various ways: in one person, from their place of birth; in another, in their relation to the people, language, history, or social order. These components may be conscious as well as unconscious. This feeling can be developed into a "sense of purposeful responsibility" and can be a good thing.

But Key also remarks on something that gives rise to a problematizing of these concepts:

> He who has not bonds of love in a particular childhood place, a particular mother-tongue, a particular people, he will truly become a cosmopolitan who lacks emotional depth. And the spiritual values elicited by him will be of the same impersonal kind as certain philan-

thropists, who have never loved another human being with all their heart.[11]

Thus, according to Key, a cosmopolitan is a superficial and callous person. And yet even while deprecating cosmopolitans, she remained strongly supportive of international cooperation and much of what is today called cosmopolitanism. So is Ellen Key a cosmopolitan, or not?

The concept of cosmopolitanism, like patriotism, is complicated and replete with contradiction, partly because of a long history in which it has been used in different senses. One sense of cosmopolitanism is almost synonymous with multicultural society. In another, cosmopolitanism represents a perspective, an ideology, or an outlook based on a conception of universal human rights and of their ethical and political consequences. A third meaning is the political effort to create a world republic or a political order in which the laws of the nation-state are supplemented by a cosmopolitan legal system.[12] But Key uses *cosmopolitan* in a completely different, albeit historically established, sense: someone ethically indifferent, rootless, and unfeeling.

Key is thus no friend of cosmopolitanism. "For most Europeans, *kosmo*politanism is merely a word without a corresponding emotional content," she claims. However, many of the contemporary senses of *cosmopolitanism* are close to what Key understands as *internationalism*:

> *Internationalism* is a reality which no scorn can dispel. Yet it has hitherto been only a material force, and it will take a long time for it to become an emotional force for the majority. What we in our corner of the world must achieve is good *Europeanism*: that feeling of solidarity and voluntary collaboration without which we will quickly find ourselves helpless against the East on one hand, and against the West on the other. And this is of vital necessity for the future of Europe, which war will destroy by whipping up national hatred into a frenzy.[13]

Key gives short shrift to arguments that might be used against the development of greater internationalism. The first is that national feeling is so fundamental a force that anything which might lead to its attenuation or eradication must be resisted. The second argument against nationalism is that the various nations of the world constitute a cultural resource, and that particularist views for this reason should be strengthened. For the foreseeable future, the best argument is that statesmen are directing politics so as to favour what she calls *sound nationalism*.[14]

It may be asked what makes Key prefer internationalism and repudiate cosmopolitanism. It cannot be just the emotional frigidity of cosmopolitanism: as the previous quotation indicates, internationalism also has no place in most people's emotional life. But before true internationalism can be attained, some kind of "Europeanism" must clearly be realized. This idea becomes comprehensible if we read it in the framework of Key's philosophy of history: the theory of history's organic development from smaller to larger communities, from family to nation to world. On this view, the nation-state stage cannot proceed directly to some world-encompassing stage. It has to go via Europe first. But in Key's day the road seemed long, since "the three most important civilized peoples" – for Key, Germany, France, and Britain – cannot unite against Russia, even in a time of revolution. But Key remained indefatigable in her ambition, according to contemporaries: "A defining feature of her love of her country is an unremitting effort to bring us into Europe, or bring Europe to us, at all events to relieve our spiritual isolation," wrote her friend Emilia Fogelklou in 1919.[15] A European community would help culture to develop.

But what would such a European community look like? Key does not believe in the idea of a European state, which she regards as far too imperialist. It is based on conquest, and would run the risk of eradicating smaller nations, since empires seek to gain economic and political power for its own sake. By contrast, *Europeanism*, which could strengthen Europe against the threat from revolutionary Russia on the one hand, and an expanding United States of America on the other, has a near-utopian quality. It is based on a pacifist idea of the state, and is meant to bring happiness to the younger generation:

> The pacifist idea of the state emphasizes *the unity of the people* instead of *the entity of the state*, *the popular will* instead of *state violence*. It holds up the *happiness and flourishing* of the younger generation as the ultimate ideal of state activity, and thus does not regard as worthwhile the acquisition of economic or political power by any means which impedes this happiness and flourishing.[16]

This distinction between social and political standpoints on the one hand, and moral standpoints on the other, had been noted by several of pacifism's pioneers. One of them was the Norwegian activist in the Interparlamentarian union Christian Lange, who discussed the matter in a 1905 speech to the Nobel Committee. He made other distinctions than Key had, claiming that internationalism was a social and political movement, while pacifism represented a moral position. Key tried to make internationalism into an ethical movement.

Key argues that those who think they are seeing the victory of nationalism over internationalism are wrong, since signs of the realization of internationalism can be seen "every day and in every corner of the world" in the form of: "business stoppages, shortages of goods, food price rises, unemployment, and every kind of restriction. Our entire economic life *is* already international, as is our scientific and artistic life."[17] For Key, the mutual dependence of nations was self-evident, a perspective which would subsequently be developed by many others.[18]

But it would seem that not every nation formed part of this reciprocity. Once again, it is a question of conflating the culture of a people with that of a nation. Their collaboration has developed into nothing less than a condition of life:

> Not even the most but narrow-minded nationalism can change the experience reconfirmed for us every day in a thousand ways: that there is no human being alive today who is not suffering in some way because reciprocity among different peoples has become a condition of life for all cultivated peoples. Their culture has grown within and by means of this reciprocity and, no more than it could have developed, can it continue without this international collaboration.[19]

Everyday reality, according to Key, offers proof of how the world is becoming intertwined. No man is an island, nor is any society or any state. But what does internationalism look like in Key's model? She rejects federation since it can be stifling for small states. For the same reason, she rejects empire, but also because it is based on strength rather than law. Internationalism instead seems to be built upon culture and moral tenets. This perspective, and the powerful demands which it makes, are articulated more fully in her concept of neutrality. It is a moral utopia.[20]

The claim that cosmopolitanism was weakened after Kant, and experienced its death-throes before the nationalist arms race of the nineteenth century began can be questioned. A reading of Key's texts from this era shows that the content of the concept did not disappear, even if it assumed a different name. Nationalist voices may have been raucous but they did not succeed entirely in drowning those voices that advocated collaboration, as, for example, in the pacifist and labour movements, for whom the emphasis in the word *internationalism* lay very much upon the prefix *inter-*. Besides, some of the presupposed nationalist voices might have been patriotist in the sense of Ellen Key and would thus strenghten the idea.

As was noted at the start of this essay, a critical conceptual history must always be prepared to reflect upon its own self-understanding. Problematizing concepts which now tend to be considered with scepticism can turn out to enable a new understanding of the past as much as of the present, thereby clearing the ground for new perspectives and courses of action. When situated in a different context, the family of concepts *internationalism*, *cosmopolitanism*, *patriotism*, and *nationalism* offer new perspectives on questions which still command our engagement. In sum, the historicization of concepts is not merely of historical value, it must form the basis for any attempt to problematize the contemporary world in which we live.

Notes

1. Hans-Georg Gadamer, *Sanning och metod (i urval)*, trans. Arne Melberg (Göteborg: Daidalos 1997).

2. See, for example, Jens Bartelson, "Ways of Warmaking" in the preceding volume. Also Rebecka Lettevall, "Turning golden coins into loose change. Philosophical, political and popular readings of Kant's *Zum ewigen Frieden*", 133–150 in J. Hrushka, S. Byrd (ed.) *Jahrbuch für Recht und Ethik*, vol. 17, 2008. (2009).

3. Volker Gerhardt, *Immanuel Kant's Entwurf 'Zum ewigen Frieden': Ein Theorie der Politik* (Darmstadt: Wissenschaftlicher Buchgesellschaft, 1995).

4. Pauline Kleingeld, "Kant's cosmopolitan patriotism", Kant-Studien (94), 2003, 299–316; Charlotta Wolf, *Noble conceptions of politics in eighteenth-century Sweden (ca 1740–1790)*, (Helsinki: Svenska litteratursällskapet i Finland, 2008).

5. Georg Cavallar, *Kant and the theory and practice of international right*, (University of Wales Press, 1999); Pauline Kleingeld, "Six Varieties of Cosmopolitanism in Late Eighteenth-Century Germany", *Journal of the History of Ideas*, (1999), 505–524.

6. Max Hildebert Boehm, "Cosmopolitanism", in Edwin R. A. Seligman (ed.), *Encyclopedia of the Social Sciences*, Vol. 4 (London: Macmillan, 1931), 457–461.

7. For a new reading of Ellen Key as a thinker, see Claudia Lindén, *Om kärlek: Litteratur, sexualitet och politik hos Ellen Key*, (Stockholm/Stehag: Symposium 2002), chap. 3.

8. Ellen Key, *Kriget, freden och framtiden*, (Lund: Ph. Lindstedts universitetsbokhandel, 1914) 5 f.

9. Key, *Kriget, freden och framtiden*, 29.

10. Key, *Kriget, freden och framtiden*, 15.

11. Ellen Key, "Fredens förverkligande", in Ellen Key, *Fredstanken*, (Stockholm: Bonniers 1899), 38.

12. In recent years, the literature on cosmopolitanism has assumed huge proportions. On cosmopolitanism in late-Enlightenment Germany, see Pauline Kleingeld, "Six varieties of cosmopolitanism in late eighteenth-century Germany," *Journal of the History of ideas* (1999): 505–524. For a discussion of different kinds of cosmopolitanism, see R. Lettevall (ed.) *The Idea of Kosmopolis*. During the Soviet-era pogroms in Russia, *cosmopolitan* was a term of abuse. The origins of ethical-political cosmopolitanism are usually traced to Immanuel Kant. It has been represented in recent years by Ulrich Beck, Thomas Pogge, and Martha Nussbaum. On cosmopolitan politics, see David Held.

13. Key, *Kriget, freden och framtiden*, 22f.

14. Key, *Kriget, freden och framtiden*, 4.

15. Emilia Fogelklou, "Ellen Key", 561–575 in *Ord och Bild*, årg. 28, 561.

16. Key, *Kriget, freden och framtiden*, 17.

17. Key, *Kriget, freden och framtiden*, 26f.

18. For example, this is the starting point for Ulrich Beck's theory of *Risksamhället* (1986), which was subsequently developed into a theory of cosmopolitanism (*Den kosmopolitiska blicken*, 2006). In 1795, Kant had expressed a similar position with regard to human rights, arguing that violating the rights of an individual is the same as the violation of the rights of all humanity.

19. Key, *Kriget, freden och framtiden*, 27.

20. Inga Sanner, *Att älska sin nästa såsom sig själv: Moraliska utopier under 1800-talet*, (Stockholm: Carlssons 1995).

Network and Subaltern: The Antinomies of Global History

STEFAN JONSSON

Modern historians, philosophers, and social scientists have often attributed historical agency to various collectivities. Consequently, terms such as "class," "nation," and "people" have shaped the historical consciousness of the global West. For reasons to be explored, these terms are today being theoretically and politically contested, with new ones emerging as scholars respond to an old question: who or what is the subject of history? Its mover, ultimate determinant, or driving force?

This essay will stage a confrontation between two possible answers to this question and discuss the preconditions and implications of each, not to determine their truth but to examine them as symptoms of a particular historical imagination. Put differently, I want to trace a vacillation between what we for convenience may designate as two ideal types of collectivity. On the one hand, I posit the category of the *network* as a predominant way of representing agency in the current world order. On the other hand, I propose the notion of the *subaltern* as a category frequently deployed to mark the subject of history.

Both categories are today widely used by those who seek to show how the world order is designed and transformed. Consider, for instance, the uprisings and revolutions in the Arab world in 2011. The events were explained as effects of popular organization by means of the Internet and other forms of wireless communication: network revolutions. But they were also explained as expressions of a national consciousness that had long been controlled by autocratic rulers, or they were interpreted as the actions of the hungry and the unemployed: subaltern revolutions.

Network and subaltern: that these are ideal types of collectivity implies that they are *representations*, providing an idea of what drives social change. Each period explains such transformations in terms consistent with its own discursive frames and constellations of power. Until recently, change was seen as being driven by other collective agents – states, classes, nations, peoples, or even races, if not simply by great individuals. What characterizes states, classes, nations, peoples, and races is that they are intrinsically temporal and historical phenomena. Emerging, flourishing, and vanishing, they unfold in historical time and enable narrations. States are histories of dynasties and coronations, inter-state relations and conflicts. Classes are narratives of labor and ownership, class struggles and revolutions. Races once invited evolutionary narratives about the vanishing of inferior peoples. As for the nation or people, Benedict Anderson states that it "is conceived as a solid community moving steadily up (or down) history".[1]

But what narratives can be told about a network or a subaltern? Are they historiographical categories? They appear rather like superimposed images, which take turns as the principal object of attention for the contemporary historian or theorist. This vacillation subtends a great deal of commentary on world culture and global society today, as I shall illustrate with examples from the visual arts, sociology, and postcolonial theory. My examples will demonstrate the difficulty, or impossibility, of conjoining network and subaltern into one "world picture." The thrust of my argument is that this difficulty indicates a failure to reflect on the current global situation in historical terms. In theories of globalization, the world is primarily grasped as a spatial or geographical constellation. It is symptomatic that Michael Hardt and Antonio Negri call their global analysis a "geography of power" while also asserting that the "cartography" of resistance remains to be written.[2] Examples could be multiplied, and all indicate some profound transformation of historical consciousness, such that historiography now finds itself in the awkward situation of having its object withdrawn.[3]

In 1982, Fredric Jameson, observing a crisis of historicity, argued that "our daily life, our psychic experience, our cultural languages, are today dominated by categories of space."[4] Göran Therborn, too, sees the 1980s as "the period when time imploded into space."[5] Both thinkers gesture toward a spatial turn. According to them, the discourse of globalization operates by means of two-dimensional frames in which the "mapping" of positions inside or outside an expanding network substitutes for a more properly historical representation.[6] Historical reflection being absent, our thinking ferries from one bank of the river of change to the other, without being able to describe the temporal medium itself – history – that both separates and connects them. Planted as signposts at the opposite sides of this river, network and subaltern then increasingly function as polar categories in relation to which our cultural imaginations as well as our discourses are organized.

Visual Arts: Cruel Disjunctures

Ferrying is quite literally the narrative mode in Renzo Martens' acclaimed and contested film *Episode III: Enjoy Poverty* (2008). For this Dutch artist, the dark waters of the Congo River serve as a metaphor for the impenetrable secrets of global trade and neo-colonialism, even as the work itself is an ironic take on the centuries-long tradition of European travel writing about Africa's heart of darkness.

On one side of the river, Martens maps the vast network of international actors shaping the Democratic Republic of Congo. The film presents the World Bank, Doctors Without Borders, the United Nations High Commissioner for Refugees (UNHCR), the United Nations Children's Fund (UNICEF), the mining company AngloGold Ashanti, the agribusiness company Groupe Elwyn Blattner, and additional actors as an entangled mesh, pinned with so many needles to the political map of Congo and even penetrating to its buried wealth. Every node of the network supports the others, in a single, predatory assault on this African country. How is it, for instance, that Pakistani UN peacekeepers are protecting the operations of a transnational mining company? How did Western news correspondents come to portray a mining company's press releases as "impartial" reports? And how is it that Doctors Without Borders has inserted itself into the fabric of Congolese life as yet another instance of Franco-Belgian supremacy? Martens shows how a global network creates facts on the ground. Yet the logic of the system exceeds the film's means of representation.

On the other side of the river are villages, plantations, and refugee camps populated by the wretched of the earth. As the film shows in harrowing close-ups, child malnourishment is caused by a wage-labor regime imposed by multinational agricultural and mining concerns, whereas traditional farming had at least enabled the rural population to subsist.

Martens' film has aroused controversy because of its stark disclosure of the cruel mechanism of human exploitation in campaigns masquerading as aid and development. Were we to mark out the precise location of this mechanism of cruelty, it would have to be at the juncture, or, rather, the disjuncture of the global network and the African subaltern. In Martens' film, the narrator, impersonated by the filmmaker himself, embodies this disjuncture. A Dutch artist-cum-journalist going upriver on a raft crewed by Congolese men, his aim is to help the poor help themselves by becoming entrepreneurs and connecting themselves to the international market. His mission is to integrate subalterns into the network.

What resources do they have that will attract the market? In one of the first scenes, the narrator visits a World Bank donor conference in Kinshasa, where he learns that the 1.8 billion dollars contributed by the donors to fight poverty far exceeds the state's combined earnings from cocoa, palm oil, gold, copper, coltan, and other exports. Following the functioning of the aid-and-business network to its logical conclusion, Martens' narrator then goes out into villages and camps preaching to the poor that they must turn their major asset to profit. Stop complaining about your poverty, he advices. Enjoy poverty, cultivate poverty, learn how to peddle the image of your poverty to Western media audiences – and billions will flow your way! Martens' counsel, though obviously absurd, is consistent with the laws of the market, which is precisely the film's point. Just as there is a demand for cocoa and coltan in the industrialized North, so, too, is African poverty a prized commodity that makes Westerners open their purses, especially since it is Africa's poverty that ensures their cheap access to Africa's resources.

This is hardly a new story, of course. Still, in mimicking the violence of a global coloniality that rolls out development and modernity in the name of humanitarianism, the film approaches a definition of the relation between network and subaltern. For the subaltern, inclusion in the networks of power and resources here comes at the price of existential humiliation and material destitution, if not death. The Congolese subject can connect to the European media only by becoming an "image" of poverty and violence. Furthermore, the subaltern can enter the capitalist economy only by becoming labor power, working at wages so low that he will be unable to feed his children. And this is exactly what the agents of development ask of the Congolese, according to Martens. Paradoxically and perversely, these agents also present this humiliating requirement as an opportunity. The concept is summed up neatly in the title: Enjoy Poverty!

That this command is impossible for consciousness to absorb – how does one celebrate the complete absence of everything as a condition of fulfillment and *jouissance*? – demonstrates that it is impossible for the subaltern to link up with the network. If Martens' film is controversial, it is surely because it reconfirms the idea of Africa as being, in Achille Mbembe's words, "the supreme receptacle of the West's obsession with 'absence,' 'lack,' and 'non-being,' [...] in short, of nothingness."[7] But what is even harder to digest is that Martens confronts us with the ultimate consequence of capitalist modernization – the annihilation of human life – even as the latter's victims are being asked to keep smiling.

Global Sociology: Black Holes and Countervailing Forces

In *The Information Society*, Manuel Castells describes how peoples and regions are "switched off" from the networks of power and wealth.[8] He argues that there is a "systematic relationship between the dynamics of the network society [...] and social exclusion."[9] A disjuncture between network and subaltern is how I have been describing it. Castells compiles empirical evidence of how "informational capitalism" impoverishes populations, territories, regions, cities, and neighborhoods. Network society thus becomes perforated by "black holes" into which a substantial fraction of the world's population disappears.

Castells, too, finds his account best illustrated by the Congo: "the exhaustion of mines or the devaluation of agricultural products on which a region was making a living."[10] Yet the Congo is just one extreme illustration of a global development. Now that the neoliberal promise of universal prosperity has turned to dust all over the world, it is a commonplace that capitalist globalization amasses unprecedented wealth in some corners even as it piles up disposable material and human waste in others. Although Castells' empirical analysis of the dual face of globalization remains unsurpassed, many other social scientists have noted the same contradiction. Accumulation of wealth and power at one end of the system relies on pauperization and death at the other end, with the result that whole regions of the world "fall away" and are left in camps, ghettoes, and decaying cities, with little chance of making a decent living or accessing the opportunities created by an economic system whose premise is that human communities can be written off as bad investments.

There is thus enough empirical evidence to support descriptions of the contemporary world as suspended between network and subaltern, the former comprising a global "inside" accommodating everyone with access to employment and communication power, while the subalterns may be "encountered everywhere, even though they belong nowhere," as Siegfried Kracauer once said of the masses in Weimar Germany.[11]

Network and subaltern, then, would be two categories representing an essential inequality of the world. Were this the only or major meaning of these categories, however, they would just be other names for rich and poor, inclusion and exclusion, North and South, or the like. Interestingly, this pair echoes all these divisions and yet something more. Castells identifies this additional feature when describing how the "downward spiral of poverty, then dereliction, finally irrelevance, operates until or unless a countervailing force, including people's revolt against their condition, reverses the trend."[12] Between the overlay of the network and the underlying geography of poverty, we thus glimpse a third category, a "countervailing force." Where does this force originate? It is hard not to see it as a "subject of history," given that Castells speaks of "people's revolt against their condition". Yet he does not clarify its emergence or offer a definition. He simply recognizes that contradictions may become so agonizing as to ignite a counterforce, springing directly out of that disjuncture I mentioned earlier. However, as long as network and subaltern are perceived as opposite poles in a global cartography of power, it will remain difficult to account for this collectivity except as some timeless resistance offered by social matter itself.

Postcolonial Theory: Where the Conflict Means Nothing

So far I have discussed the ways in which the categories of network and subaltern organize the empirical field surveyed in Renzo Martens' *Enjoy Poverty* and Manuel Castells' sociology. My third example is drawn from political and cultural theory, where we encounter Gayatri Spivak's canonical definition of subalternity. Remarkably, she defines "subaltern consciousness" as the effect of a "network":

> I am progressively inclined, then, to read the retrieval of subaltern consciousness as the charting of what in post-structuralist language would be called the subaltern subject-effect. A subject-effect can be briefly plotted as follows: that which seems to operate as a subject may be part of an immense discontinuous network ('text' in the general sense) of strands that may be termed politics, ideology, economics, history, sexuality, language, and so on. (Each of these strands, if they are isolated, can also be seen as woven of many strands.) Different knottings and configurations of these strands, determined by heterogeneous determinations which are themselves dependent on myriad circumstances, produce the effect of an operating subject. Yet the continuist and homogenist deliberative consciousness symptomatically requires a continuous and homogeneous cause for this effect and thus posits a sovereign and determining subject. This latter is, then, the effect of an effect, and its positing a metalepsis, or the substitution of an effect for a cause.[13]

Spivak relates "network" to "subaltern" because they represent alternative ways of thinking agency and collectivity. One alternative derives from the anti-humanist critique of European philosophy as developed by Jacques Derrida and Michel Foucault, who replaced the notion of a founding consciousness by notions of text and discourse. They thus repositioned "agency," "intention," and "authorship" within the frame of an "immense discontinuous network."

The second alternative is that of Subaltern Studies, the group of prominent historians addressed by Spivak in the essay quoted above. Their ambition was to help the subaltern or insurgent to "recover his place in history," as Ranajit Guha put it.[14] This entailed reading the historical archives against the grain so as to reinstate "subaltern consciousness" as a driving force in Indian history. As indicated in my quotation, however, Spivak is doubtful of the way in which Guha posits "subaltern consciousness" as historically foundational. Equating consciousness with historical origin amounts to a view of politics, knowledge, and social organization as the results of a discernable intention or rationality. Yet, as soon as that intention is identified, it will be tied to real human agents with precise rank and gender (typically, peasant movements or insurgents) to the exclusion of other agents of history (women).

But it is no less inaccurate to overemphasize the idea of the network as a medium in which history supposedly "happens." In Spivak's view, Indian historiography and European critical theory commit the same error. Both proceed by way of metalepsis, that is, by substituting an effect for an apparently unrepresentable cause (a subject of history). The Subaltern Studies group thus substitutes "subaltern consciousness" for the "heterogeneous determinations" and "myriad circumstances" that operate in the "text of history." European poststructuralists, meanwhile, substitute "network," "discourse," or some other formal category for the very same "heterogeneous determinations," thereby precisely reducing "history" to the operations of a network.

What narratives are possible, then, about a network or a subaltern? The probable answer is none – or all. Neither the category of network nor that of subaltern contains a tangible historical agent in relation to which events can be causally and narratively structured. This is why I want to suggest, finally, that network and subaltern are *post-historical categories*. Each category is useful, but mainly by virtue of showing what its polar opposite cannot. What the category of the subaltern cannot show is the systematic and global character of the contemporary world system. What the category of the network fails to register are the processes of exclusion that reinvigorate its own power. And what neither can record is the time of history.

In a later text, Spivak explicitly rejects the idea of an emergent subaltern counter-collectivity. "If you nominate collectivities that are questioning the power of the United States or the power of the West or whatever as immediately a subaltern counter-collectivity, I don't think you really know what it is like where this conflict *can mean nothing*. There are many millions of people in the world to whom this conflict means nothing, except in the lives they are obliged to lead. The search for subalternity has become like the search for the primitive."[15]

Network and subaltern: that they are post-historical categories implies that they are symptoms of an ideology for which history has in some sense ended, the historical dialectic having ground to a halt because of the sheer incommensurability of its antithetical powers. In this ideology, network and subaltern will then alternate as placeholders for an absent history, something I have so far indicated only as a disjuncture, a mechanism of cruelty, or a countervailing force. However, this "mechanism" and "force" may also be taken as a beginning in its own right, in an attempt to construe a more properly historical understanding of global society.

How to localize and represent this beginning? Perhaps by following Spivak's hint and seeking out collectivities "to whom this conflict means nothing, except in the lives they are obliged to lead"? Other categories of collectivity will then need to be engaged, which may sharpen our view of how power and resistance coexist at the complex frontiers of imperial globality. And if this engagement is to avoid once again running up against the antinomy of network and subaltern, I think it may be most rewardingly pursued in four directions. The first would be related to what is nowadays termed political ecology, the second to dialectical theories of globalization, the third to the politics of place in activist movements, and the fourth to documentary aesthetics. But these topics I must save for another occasion.

Notes

1. Benedict Anderson, *Imagined Communities: Reflections of the Origin and Spread of Nationalism*, rev. ed. (London: Verso, 2006), 26.

2. Michael Hardt and Antonio Negri, *Empire* (Cambridge, Mass.: Harvard University Press, 2000), xvi.

3. Additional examples range from Gilles Deleuze and Félix Guattari (*Milles plateaux*, vol. 2 of *Capitalisme et schizophrénie* [Paris: Editions de Minuit, 1980]),

Bruno Latour (*Reassembling the Social: An Introduction to Actor-Network-Theory* [Oxford: Oxford University Press, 2007]), and Arturo Escobar (*Territories of Difference: Place, Movements, Life,* Redes [Durham: Duke University Press, 2008]) to an array of empirical studies in the social sciences and humanities.

4. Fredric Jameson, *Postmodernism, or, The Cultural Logic of Late Capitalism* (Durham: Duke University Press, 1991), 16.

5. Göran Therborn, *The World: A Beginner's Guide* (Cambridge: Polity Press, 2011), 51.

6. See Fredric Jameson's chapter on Ricœur, "Making History Appear," in *Valences of the Dialectic* (London and Brooklyn: Verso, 2009), 546–612.

7. Achille Mbembe, *On the Postcolony* (Berkeley and Los Angeles: University of California Press, 2001), 4.

8. Manuel Castells, *The Rise of the Network Society*, vol. 1 of *The Information Age: Economy, Society and Culture* (Oxford: Blackwell, 1998), 1.

9. For Castell's definition of social exclusion, see *End of Millenium*, vol. 3 of *The Information Age*, 73.

10. Castells, *End of Millenium*, 164.

11. Siegfried Kracauer, *From Caligari to Hitler: A Psychological History of the German Film* [1947], rev. ed. (Princeton: Princeton University Press), 132. For a discussion, see my *Crowds and Democracy: The Idea and Image of the Masses in Germany and Austria between the Wars* (forthcoming from Columbia University Press), to which the present essay forms a sequel.

12. Castells, *End of Millenium*, 164.

13. Gayatri Chakravorty Spivak, "Introduction. Subaltern Studies: Deconstructing Historiography," in *Selected Subaltern Studies*, ed. Ranajit Guha and Gayatri Chakravorty Spivak (Oxford: Oxford University Press, 1988), 12–13.

14. Ranajit Guha, "The Prose of Counter-Insurgency," in *Selected Subaltern Studies*, 84.

15. Gayatri Chakravorty Spivak, *Other Asias* (Oxford: Blackwell, 2008), 247.

Historians' Picnic in Kurdistan

DAVID GAUNT

Puddles of rain on the pavement. A gypsy band bounces rhythms off a façade. It's the middle of the Istanbul night and three men can't sleep. Fighting jetlag and nerves, escaping to an all-night bar, they plan a panel for tomorrow's conference.

"I hate these huge Turkologist meetings" says Omar, the well-established professor at a German university. "Where do all these bores from provincial universities come from? Have they never done research or opened a book? Why must we put up with all these retired ambassadors and generals posing as historians?"

"Come out of the woodwork," goes Faik, a younger scholar struggling for tenure in America. "The right family, religion, politics – that's enough. What do you expect from this government? They probably won't come to our panel. They think we're too radical. Unless of course the Islamists and nationalists come to harass us."

"Well, I still wish we didn't have to come. And I know some will come just to make a fuss."

"Ah, let's get working!" exclaims Kenan, an independent scholar from Kazakhstan.

Omar takes control: "OK, tomorrow we present our findings on population movements in the Late Ottoman Period. Useful euphemism, eh? Faik does the settlement of Balkan Muslim refugees, Kenan covers the Chechen refugees. And I treat the Christians who were forced to convert to Islam."

Kenan: "Most of this is straightforward. Just the normal when, where and how. Just dotting the i's."

Omar: "Well, you know my pet question has always been, what happens when the forced converts want to return to their original religion? Do they have to go through a new baptism ceremony?"

"Hold on! You can't use the word 'forced,' the Islamists will lynch you."

"Hmm… I can say it in the panel, I just can't write it the finished article. Times are changing."

"You hope!"

"But you know that no-one can answer that question," replies Faik, trying to stop him. "You've asked everybody, and nobody knows. Anyway, it isn't an issue for many people. Once you are a Muslim, you can't change, on pain of death."

"I'm not so sure. We know there were thousands of forced converts, and some could change back just after World War I ended. It was a window of opportunity for a few who survived the genocide."

"My god, are you going to use the G-word tomorrow.[1] They'll throw eggs at us. This isn't Germany, you know."

"No, of course not. I've got a survival instinct, too. I promise not to say 'genocide'. But I do need to have my question raised."

"So what? You even asked that American guy G about it. And he didn't know."

"I thought he was Swedish."

"No, he just lives there. Some small university, something with a lot of dots."[2]

"Why Sweden?"

"Don't know. Must be running away from something"

"Well, he's the 'Where are the skeletons?' fellow who challenged Halaçoğlu."

"Really stupid move. How could he be so dumb as to get involved with those evil nationalists?"

"Eh? He must have done something right since Halaçoğlu got into deep trouble," replies Omar.[3] What a brute he was! How many careers did he ruin? I don't miss his face on the TV all the time going on about how sinful Armenians are. How treacherous they were. How Turks treated them so generously, and how they were so ungrateful. Pack of lies."

"I remember G," says Kenan. "I helped him at the Ottoman archives. We collected documents on the genocide. No idea how he got permission. We gathered a lot. Worked hard. He had these lists of names, dates, and keywords, a little Turkish dictionary. Pored over the catalogues, day after day. I could see him running back and forth to check dates in the reference book at the reception desk. Most of the findings went into a book."⁴

"I helped him, too," adds Faik. "Some years later, when the Second Section finally opened. Don't think he found much. Most of the important papers were gone. Probably when Halaçoğlu headed the archive."

Conversation peters out. Three tired men lean back with their drinks. Look around. The bar is empty. It is a converted old-fashioned patrician apartment. Carved woodwork, strange mythical paintings. On the walls, photos of Armenian families in antiquated headgear. The previous owners, now silent onlookers. Across the street, a sign on a building bears the inscription 'Pera Hellenic Association'. Witness to the overpopulated ghost town that is now Istanbul. A funny kind of nostalgia grows like moss here, feeling like a mix of melancholy, remembrance, and humourless absence. Not really good, but not truly bad. Memories don't help. Live for the moment.

"It's a strange story. I mean for academic historians," begins Kenan. "I met G's interpreter, Sabri, a while ago at a hotel in Diyarbakir. We were both staying there. He spoke something that wasn't Kurdish, so I asked. He said it was Turoyo, a local dialect. I asked him if he knew G, and we fell to talking. Sabri told me the story of how G and Halaçoğlu made that expedition to investigate the mass grave. G claimed the skeletons could have been Armenians – like the villagers said – or even Assyrians. Halaçoğlu insisted they were from Roman antiquity."

This was Sabri's account:

"It all began in October 2006. Kurdish villagers in a hamlet called Xirabêbaba⁵ were digging a hole. All of a sudden, they hit an opening, and one of them jumped in. What he saw was a mass of skulls and bones – the remains of perhaps twenty people. The skulls showed signs of stabbing and blunt force injuries. Somebody contacted the radical newspaper Ülkede Özgür Gündem.⁶ They sent out a reporter to write a story. According to the article, the villagers thought they had found a mass grave of massacred Armenians. They published pictures of the skulls and bones. This article circulated on the internet and was published on the WATS discussion forum.⁷ G had just finished his book and he suggested that if the victims were from 1915 then they could have come from Dara or from Mardin because there were witnesses who told of death marches from those places. He wrote this on the discussion forum. In no time at all, Turkish newspapers were reporting that a foreign historian believed that we had finally found a mass grave of Armenians or Assyrians.

That would be a sensation. It would prove decisively that there was an Armenian genocide. The controversy over genocide could no longer be denied. Speculation would stop. But it was impossible for Halaçoğlu to admit that there could be a mass grave with murdered Armenians. Well, you know Halaçoğlu everybody knows he really hates Armenians and uses racial slurs. When thousands marched in protest over the murder of Hrant Dink[8] he accused all the demonstrators of being crypto-Armenians. So all of a sudden he turns this hasty suggestion by G, into world news. It's in the papers, on the evening news, in the talk programs. It cannot be Armenians.

In Sweden an Assyrian lobbyist informs G of the goings on, shows him newspaper clippings. Gives him more photos of the site. He tells him this is an opportunity to prove that Armenians and Assyrians had been massacred. Why not issue a counter challenge to Halaçoğlu? Let's see if we can rattle his cage. And they come up with the idea of sending a very polite fax to the Turkish Historical Society proposing to make a joint investigation. After a few days G received a polite fax accepting the idea. Sabri thinks G deep down hoped that Halaçoğlu would never agree. But of course neither of them could back down. But you could see they hesitated, it took forever to agree on a date. In the end G played what he thought would be a dirty trick and proposed April 24, the day of Armenian Genocide Remembrance, hoping that this would be totally unacceptable. Surprise! Halaçoğlu accepted."

"Yeah," says Omar. "I get it. But there's another side, one the interpreter probably didn't know. At Munich airport, I ran into Elazar Barkan who used to be at the Institute for Historical Justice and Reconciliation.[9] He had been in contact with G for some time and they had been discussing how to start a dialogue among historians. Barkan had some experience of mediating with Yugoslav historians. Maybe it would be possible for honest historians to sift through the facts of the Turkish-Armenian conflict and find some sort of shared history to replace the disputed history. But there was a problem. G had promised a joint expedition. The Turks would easily organize a huge multi-disciplinary team. G couldn't turn up just by himself. Barkan suggested that G should work in association with the IHJR.

Next G tried to draw on a few Swedish government contacts. The minister for foreign aid had once listened to the idea of creating an independent commission. She had been sympathetic to the idea of Swedish mediation since political recognition of the Armenian genocide was such a diplomatic hot potato. But she was no longer in office. The Foreign Office listened to the idea of using the mass-grave expedition as a stepping-stone to an opening with the Turkish government. No-one had tried this, and Sweden, as a friend of Turkey, was in a good position to mediate. But no-one there would give G more than an encouraging pat on the back."

Omar concluded: "What was left was 'Track-Two Diplomacy', that is, negotiations on a non-government level aimed at solving an inter-governmental conflict through dialogue between concerned citizens. But this was a question of disputed history, so it had to be resolved by historians, who are seldom diplomatic. But how in the world did they think that our super-Turk would be willing to co-operate with professional historians? He can be accused of many things, but professionalism has never been one of them."

"Well, maybe it was a long shot. I might have done the same, it's worth the risk," continues Kenan. "After all, if you actually get the ultra-nationalists to the negotiating table, more moderate historians would also be able to work on this. But if Halaçoğlu isn't part of it, then life will be hell for any other participating historians. A friend of mine, a dental expert had promised to be part of G's team. But as the date neared, he got increasingly worried. He couldn't risk his entire career. He pulled out. Fact of life."

"Barkan told me that he fixed a really good contact for G with the Physicians for Human Rights (PHR).[10] They had done forensic work on mass graves in Bosnia and Iraq. They were very keen and promised to send some of their best people. And G consulted with Dutch experts who had excavated in Kosovo, and one volunteered. The PHR experts studied the photos and could see that the persons had been killed somewhere else. Then their bodies had been placed in a heap inside the hole. It was very important to understand that the site should be treated like a crime scene and the bodies not be tampered with. An investigation should not be limited to examining the bones; it is important to go through the soil underneath to see whether there are bullets and items of clothing that can help to date the find. This kind of careful investigation takes months. Obviously, this would not be possible, so the aim of the expedition was only to see if the site was suitable for a later study under the protection of the Turkish authorities. But all this depended on the outcome of the preliminary inspection.

As April 24 grew closer, G's team dwindled. The Dutch government would not let its expert go. One EU commissioner warned – like he always did - that this was just not the right time for a move that might upset Turkey. The worst possible outcome would be if the issue of the Armenian genocide exploded. Due to prior commitments the experts from the PHR could not come, and when they asked for postponement, Halaçoğlu refused. G went alone, armed only with an internet course in forensic investigation. Not happy."

Sabri met him at the airport. They both felt uneasy as they planned for an early night to catch the redeye to Diyarbakir. The telephone rang. Courteous, Halaçoğlu wondered when they would arrive. His team would be waiting outside Nusaybin. Then the chief of police called and requested that they stop at headquarters to pick up an escort for their personal security. Security? Who had thought of that? Sabri said that when they got to Mardin's police station, they waited. Out came guys in black suits and got into a car with Ankara licence plates. Big shots from the internal secret police. Once they got to the site, these guys would parade around with machine-guns.

They were late, because they had stopped in Diyarbakir to talk with people from the human rights NGO. The NGO people spoke of many mass graves and even places where skeletons had become exposed after heavy rain. But Sabri and G should not stop to look, because they were undoubtedly being shadowed. There were concerns about what they would find; the NGO people were sure the bodies were Armenian but the Turks would use this against the Kurds. They would blame the killings on Kurdish bandits.

The tiny expedition was greeted on the steps of the motel by Halaçoğlu's team of historians, archaeologists, local authorities, and dozens of journalists. Maybe forty people. It was now a media event. All went off in convoy in the pouring rain. Off the main road, onto a smaller road, then onto a dirt track that went on and on for what seemed like forever. Up and down rolling treeless hills dotted with stones, passing sheep and goats huddled in the rain. They came to six or so dwellings surrounded by stone walls. Just grey stones and red mud. A clutter of cars and vans. Even more journalists were waiting. And there were curious villagers. Sabri overheard them talking. G must be French, since he was interested in genocide. The security police assembledtheir guns. Bad beginning.

Any possibility of making a quiet and professional preliminary study to see if the site would be suitable for a full-scale forensic investigation, soon disappeared. This was a three-ring circus orchestrated by the Turkish Historical Society. Could G have imagined it in advance? Probably not. The crowd pressed on, down a path, across stones and rubble. Rain poured down. Finally, the spot: a hole in the ground one metre deep. A man jumped down, took an iron rodand shifted a flat stone covering another hole. Very black. Sides very muddy. How strange, G observed, no one-is rushing forward to look at the hole. Why is that? Aha, of course, everyone but me has already seen this hole many times! They've probably already been down here. That's why the path is so slippery. Then, one after another, they jumped down: an archaeologist, a research assistant, Halaçoğlu himself, and the district governor in a dark suit. All climbed down easily. Would G go down? He's not slim, and the others are younger. He hesitates, looks at the mud, wonders how deep the passage is. Slowly he slides down the incline, following the diagonal for at least two metres.

It took time to adjust to the dark. When he could see, he found himself in a circular space with niches on the side. Looking around, he made out the staring faces of the president of the historical society, his assistants and museum servants. Showtime! G rubbed his eyes, scanned the floor. It was very, very black. That's strange since the soil here is reddish. Has someone poured out a chemical? But, even weirder: where are the skeletons? No skulls at all, no leg- or armbones, either, some very black broken scraps lie scattered. On top, very clean fragments of antique pottery. They must be kidding! Is this a practical joke? They gesture to G to take a shovel. 'Take a sample of the soil, professor.' Stand still. Express surprise. 'What, you don't want to take a sample? Not get dirty? Well, let our archaeologist help you.'

No. No. G scrambles out of the grave. Rushes to get the photos he has so thoroughly memorized. For weeks he has focused on the position of the skulls, the injuries, and the placing of the bones. His primary goal was to determine whether the site was intact. The black chemicals showed it had been contaminated. The removal of the bones had destroyed the site. Grabbing the photos, he plunged back down into the grave and spread the photos out. 'Where are these bones?' he asked, pointing. The Turks grasped for answers. 'Oh,' said Halaçoğlu, these villagers are to blame. They left the grave open, and the winter rain brought in mud and covered the bones.' 'Is that so? Why is the soil black, then? And why is the antique pottery so clean and lying on top? I think you have tampered with this site. I won't take a sample. I'll touch nothing. I'm leaving.' Leaving the Turkish side bewildered.

Ground ZERO! Three days of travel and five thousand kilometres to come back empty-handed! Back on the surface, G felt as if he had just run into a reincarnation of all the school bullies he had ever met, all concentrated in an ugly hole in the middle of nowhere. If you find yourself in a hole, don't dig any deeper. Good advice to keep in mind, but what to do now? The point of the expedition was to build up a modicum of confidence to go on with planning a historians' commission. But how to build up confidence when one party had already destroyed the evidence?

Catatonic, G stands in filthy clothes, shivering in the pouring rain. The machine-gun-toting secret agents police the perimeter. Over by the hole, Halaçoğlu is orating. Tells all who will listen that this is a Roman grave and chemical analysis will prove it. A few yards away a villager is trying to catch G's eye, giving him a nod and wink. He wants to say that the gendarmes had taken the bones away months ago, but he can't. He's a brave man, but all the other villagers are petrified by fear.

G and Sabri gloomily ride the van back to the motel where a press conference is scheduled. What to say? There are numerous journalists squeezed into the lunchroom. At least three TV cameras. Halacoğlu immediately takes command. Says that we have taken samples of the soil. They will be sent to an independent institute for chemical analysis. It will show that the grave is from antiquity. G counters by saying that we came to analyze skeletal remains, not date the dirt at the bottom of a hole. Since there are no corpses, there is nothing to study. The site has been destroyed. It is a scandal that the Turkish authorities have not preserved it intact. After this confrontation, one would expect all dialogue to break down. Suddenly Halacoğlu changes his tone, gives G a glass bowl as a present and begins to talk abstractly about further co-operation. G rises to the bait; he needs one more meeting, at least. OK, he says, let's meet tomorrow. How about the Mardin museum? OK. Ten o'clock.

Phones start ringing. The leftist, liberal, and moderate newspapers all plan to run articles. And these prove to be overwhelmingly negative towards Halaçoğlu. Where are the corpses? They imply that the site has been manipulated. Once again, the Turkish Historical Society has shown itself to be incapable of cooperating with international scholars. Many print G's comment that there were no skeletons and that the enterprise was a fiasco. Most note that he had said: "This is the most expensive picnic I've ever been on."

Later that evening there is a telephone call. It's Timothy Ryback of the IHJR. "Have you seen today's Herald Tribune?"

"No, I've been rather busy. Don't think they sell it here anyhow."

"Good news. Abdullah Gül[11] has a full-page ad stating that the Turkish government encourages the setting-up of a historical commission. The timing is perfect. Probably they are following your doings. This could be our big chance."

"I sure hope so, because today was a total disaster. We meet again tomorrow morning. Maybe it will happen."

"What are your feelings about Halaçoğlu? Can we work with him?"

"Doubtful. I can't read him. Today I felt like I was back in the playground of my primary school surrounded by the school bully and his gang, with no way out. But I guess we need to have him on board if the more moderate historians will stand a chance."

"That's right."

"I'll try, but don't get your hopes up."

Sabri and G are halfway up the steps of the Mardin Museum when

Halaçoğlu sweeps down on them. Standing within spitting distance, an angry Halaçoğlu demands that G retract his statements. Why did he have to say that the bones were all gone, of course they were there, they were just buried in mud. Holds up a newspaper. "Look here at this twisted article in Radikal, it's out to get me! And it's not the first time!" shouts Halaçoğlu. Then he turns on Sabri. "Maybe it's you who gave out all these lies?" G realizes that the Turkish media are out of control and that Halaçoğlu is losing his grip and that all this is happening out in the open. He is heaping verbal abuse on a foreign colleague. After an intolerable tirade, G insists, "Have we come to discuss the Turkish media? Or have we come to discuss something more serious?"

"What's that?"

"Let's go inside."

They pull up chairs in the director's cave-like office. There were about twenty of them, including the secret agents, who are now unarmed. Tea is served all around. "OK," begins Halaçoğlu. "What do you want us to talk about?"

"You know that this grave thing was to be the first step towards a collaboration?"

"Yes, but you said yesterday you don't want to press that further."

"No, that's a dead end. Can't study a tampered site. Nobody would give you any credence. Do your chemical analysis of that piece of dirt if you want, but no one will ever trust your results."

"Well, what?"

"My mission is to see if the THS is willing to negotiate about forming an international commission on the Armenian question. There are many others who are interested. You must have heard of WATS already. This will mean a large-scale investigation like the Lithuanians have done for the Nazi period. Senior and young scholars getting free access to all the archives. Freedom to investigate all sorts of grave sites. No interference by authorities. Teams can be formed from all political, national and religious groups. What do you say?"

"This was expected."

"Oh, really?"

"You know we also have things we would like to access."

"That would be the Dashnak archive?"[12]

"Yes, of course. Such a commission must allow us access to their papers."

"We have such contacts. It will be possible. Shall we make a date?"

So it came about that a date in mid-June was chosen. The meeting was to be held at the headquarters of the IHJR at Schloss Leopold in Salzburg.

It is a magnificent archbishop's palace against the backdrop of snowy Alps. A good place for scholars to ponder intricate problems of disputed history. But would it be a good place for Track Two diplomacy and hard-nosed discussions between implacable opponents? There came three on the Turkish side: Halaçoğlu, his assistant Çiçek, and another academic who was there because he knew German. The mediators were Elazar Barkan and Timothy Ryback from the IHJR and a scholar who could eavesdrop on the Turkish discussions. The only person who couldn't come was a former archivist of the Dashnak archive, who backed down at the last minute. On the other side sat the inexperienced G. "To keep us honest," as Ryback put it, because building up a mutual respect often meant accepting outrageous statements from the other side. You let the other side state its case without correcting them. At least for the time being. G, however, tended to react to the slightest sign of denying or denigrating genocide and that could have a negative impact on building trust. So they played good cop, bad cop.

A one-day agenda. All agreed to form a commission. But at once the problem turned political. Who were to be the members? Halaçoğlu began by vetoing key Turkish scholars. No mention was to be made of Taner Akçam in his American exile. No, it was impossible to have anyone from the Tarih Vakfi. "We invite them to all of our conferences, but they never invite us to any of theirs", he complained. No, No, No. OK, can we have some of the scholars from WATS? Yes, some. Finally, after two hours, there was a preliminary list.

How many junior researchers? How many teams? And so the talk went on solving the simpler of the many complex problems. The practical ones. Should there be an executive board with respected names? Yes, of course. Let's talk names. Who would you like? Thus the morning session passed. Then the IHJR team sat down to make a budget. It would total several million dollars, to be funded equally by the Turkish government and, hopefully, the European Union. The Turkish team put together a draft of a letter of intent. They all reassembled at about four o'clock. The letter of intent was quite solid. The budget was presented, five million dollars over a five-year period. Halaçoğlu didn't bat an eyelid. "That's OK," he said. "I'll take it home to my masters." End of the day? Not quite. Barkan asked G to be the manager of the commission and, after several anxious walks around the palace duck-pond, agreed. For Halaçoğlu, this was the final insult. And the French scholar overheard another heated discussion. Not him, not G, no, never!

Everyone went home. Waiting. Weeks passed. Waiting for official signatures and confirmation of the agreement to set up the commission and apply for funds. Word never came. In August, the Turkish media began to write that Halaçoğlu should be fired. He refused to resign and it took until July 2008 before he was pushed out. Could it have anything to do with the commission? G, relieved not to have to manage a huge commission of warring Turkish and Armenian historians, withdrew into his own research like a Hobbit. Would he do it all again? Who knows?

Omar says, "Quite a mismatch. Halaçoğlu is the archetypical nationalist historian – half soldier, half preacher. Up against G, who is, who is …?"

"I know!" exclaims Faik "Haha, part Boy Scout, but the rest of him I just don't know."

Over in a corner, unnoticed, two journalists have been having a drink after sending their newspaper to press. They have eavesdropped on the conversation. Suddenly one, a tall, thin woman named Perihan, speaks up.

"Have you heard the latest about Halaçoğlu?"

"No, what's that?"

"He's going to run for the national assembly for the National Action Party. Finally showing his true nature."[13]

"Wow! Does that mean he was a Grey Wolf?"[14]

"Wouldn't surprise me. He was young back then, so he was the right age for it."

The historians ponder this in silence. It confirms their suspicions about the erratic behaviour of the Turkish Historical Society. But it also gives some idea over his unceasing aggression against anyone who showed interest in non-Turkish peoples

"Do you know anything about what happened when Halaçoğlu came to the government with the proposal for a commission on the Armenian genocide?" asks Kenan.

"Sure. I tried to do an article for Nokta, but by the time I had enough research, the government had closed us down for good.[15] Halaçoğlu was just the wrong messenger boy. Of course, Gül was waiting for him when he returned.

She continues. "But as far as I can see Halaçoğlu had no desire to push for it. So the future of the plan was droped into Gül's lap, and he got no further help. In fact, Halaçoğlu contacted his party friends to sabotage the whole thing. Turns out he had many like-minded friends among ambassadors, generals and judges."

"The cabinet discussions were violent. Prime Minster Erdogan[16] had never liked the idea in the first place, but that's because he has so little international experience. But Gül does and that's why the powers could pressure him to take an initiative,[17] and the Prime Minister let him. They probably both thought that nothing would come of it, that the Armenian government would instantly reject anything that started as a Turkish initiative. A state-level commission between two historic enemies was a ridiculous idea. The whole cabinet realized that. What they didn't count on was this track-two diplomacy thing. It came out of nowhere. No one quite knew how to handle it. No one knew if it was serious. If it really came from a serious and respected group, it would be a great danger for the Turkish government. Really there was a great risk itmight turn out to have really been genocide. The popularity of the ruling party would likely fall drastically. People like the tough stance on the PKK and the Kurds, and they wouldn't appreciate any sign of being soft towards the Armenians and Assyrians, to say nothing of the Greeks."

"In the end, it was money and power politics that put a stop to it all. Who would pay? The foreign ministry refused. So did the education ministry. There was an election coming up at the end of July, and Erdogan's party could not risk being perceived as soft, and it had to retain its Islamist voters. Members of the National Assembly began to talk of impeaching Gül.[18] For a time, it looked like Gül was in real trouble since the Kemalists were really active on preventing an Islamist from becoming president. So, all of a sudden, no-one was pushing for a historical commission. The idea died, and no-one seems to have regretted it."

"So, it is dead?"

"As a doornail."

"Why do the leaders keep on saying 'leave it to the historians'"?

"They never mean it. If the historians took over, the genocide issue would simply sink slowly into the everyday, boring history that doesn't matter. The politicians would lose a good flag-waving cause. So long as history is in dispute, you can win votes."

Epilogue

This text illustrates a growing problem in the field of history. Until fairly recently, nationalist historians have lived their scholarly lives in a favourable environment. They have had political backing, influence over school curriculum, access to the media on their own terms, and the privilege of setting the academic agenda, in addition to government funding. As a rule, when they write, they exclude or marginalize from the national-historical narrative ethnic and religious minorities as well as women and disadvantaged groups. When confronted with counter narratives, as in the case of the Armenian genocide, they enter a state of denial.[19] Left without scholarly-researched history, minorities have only recourse to their collective memories. By default, it becomes the task of internationally-oriented professional historians to pioneer their cause.

Notes

1. In Turkish *Soykerim*. Use of the term "Armenian genocide" was forbidden under a law that has since been amended to a prohibition of "insulting Turkishness".

2. Södertörn University, Stockholm, founded in 1997.

3. Then president of *Türk Tarih Kurumu* (The Turkish Historical Society THS), established in 1931 for the propagation of the Turkish Historical Thesis, has been the leading organ for denial of the Armenian genocide. Yusuf Halacoğlu (born 1949) was its president from 1993 to 2008. Previously head of the Ottoman

Archive, he is associated with *Aydılar Ocağı*, a group of right-wing intellectuals which champions a "Turkish-Islamic Synthesis".

4. *Massacres, Resistance, Protectors. Muslim-Christian Relations in Southeastern Anatolia during World War I* (Piscataway, N. J. Gorgias 2006). Turkish translation : *Katliamlar, Direniş, Koruyucular. I. Dünya Savaşında Doğu Anadolu'da Müslüman-Hıristiyan İlişkileri* (Istanbul: Belge 2007).

5. "Granddad's ruins", the official name is Kuru. An isolated hamlet near the Syrian border..

6. "The Country's Free Bulletin". The paper has been forbidden many times.

7. Workshop for Armenian Turkish Scholarship organized by University of Michigan since 2002. A book giving WATS position is: Ronald Grigor Suny, Fatma Müge Göçek, Norman Naimark, eds. *A Question of Genocide. Armenians and Turks at the End of the Ottoman Empire* (Oxford University Press 2011).

8. Turkish-Armenian journalist. Assassinated in January 2007.

9. IHJR, founded in 2004. See www.historyandreconsiliation.org.

10. Founded by healthcare professionals in 1986 to investigate the consequences of human rights violations on health, it has participated in the excavation of mass graves throughout the world. In 1997, it shared the Nobel Peace Prize.

11. Usually described as moderate Islamist. Then Turkish foreign minister in the AKP government, since 2007 president of Turkey.

12. Dashnakzoutiun, the Armenian Revolutionary Federation, formed 1890. Turkey claims that the Dashnaks had planned a revolt against the state and were legitimately punished.

13. Often described as a fascist party, the *Milliyetçi Haraket Partisi* was founded in 1969 with the goal of reuniting all Turkish peoples. He was elected in the election of June 12, 2011.

14. In the late 1960's, *Bozkurtlar*, the National Action Party's paramilitary youth section, launched a violent campaign of intimidation of leftist intellectuals, students and politicians. The campaign included bombings, robberies, kidnappings, and murders.

15. Nokta means "Dot" a weekly magazine started 1982 but closed in April 2007 under pressure from the military.

16. Born 1954, prime minister since 2003.

17. He studied in England and worked in Saudi Arabia.

18. He was elected president August 28, 2007 against the protests of the military high command.

19. Stanley Cohen, *States of Denial: Knowing about Atrocities and Suffering*. (Cambridge: Polity Press 2001).

4. Literatures of Time

Ambivalent Evolution: Euclides da Cunha, Olive Schreiner and the (De)Colonising of History

STEFAN HELGESSON

Evolutionism in southern hemispheric narratives

How are notions of historical time transferred between places?

In *Os sertões* (translated as *Backlands*), published in 1902, Euclides da Cunha represents Brazil as a nation of multiple temporalities. Whereas the inhabitants of Rio de Janeiro and other major cities along the south coast are contemporary, the *sertanejos*, or inhabitants of the northern backlands, are remnants of the past, three centuries behind the modern world. What Cunha sees as the historical necessity of social progress requires that the *sertanejos* either adapt or perish. Using an inclusive national "we", he states frankly: "Estamos condenados à civilização. Ou progredimos, ou desaparecemos." ("We are condemned to civilization. Either we progress or we become extinct.")[1]

This, at least, is Cunha's explicit claim, and it has continued to reverberate through history. *Os sertões* has long been, and remains, a foundational text in the Brazilian national canon.[2] Written as an essayistic account of the newly-formed republic's war against the insular, millenarian community of Canudos in the 1890s, it provides the reader with blatant examples of evolutionist and racist statements. And yet, these are contradicted and transformed as Cunha's peculiar narrative progresses. What we find in *Os sertões*, I will argue, is a misfit between ideology and identification – or, put differently, between the warring demands of scientific ambitions and what Salman Rushdie once called the "national longing for form".[3] The *sertanejos*, as many commentators have pointed out, are in fact the true heroes of Cunha's story, not primarily because of their bravery, but because they most authentically represent the Brazilian nation.

Across the Atlantic, in the Cape Colony, a contemporary of Cunha also grappled with concepts of historical progression. As she wrote her first novel in the 1880s, *The Story of an African Farm* – which also counts as the first South African novel – Olive Schreiner engaged with evolutionary ideas. By her own account, a chance encounter during adolescence with Herbert Spencer's *First Principles* reshaped her outlook on life: "I always think that when Christianity burst on the dark Roman world it was what that book was to me."[4] The comparison is even more striking when we recall that Schreiner grew up in a devoutly Christian environment. While *First Principles* can be read on an explicit level as a reconciliation of science and religion, it achieves this by insisting, agnostically, on the impossibility of acquiring absolute knowledge.[5] The appeal of Spencer's world-view, which is reworked in *African Farm*, can be attributed to a general nineteenth-century European assumption (articulated most clearly by Auguste Comte) that "humanity" progresses from religion to enlightened scientific knowledge.[6] Christianity, by implication, is Schreiner's own "dark Roman world".

The most transparently Spencerian section of *African Farm* is the "Times and Seasons" chapter at the start of Part Two, with its depersonalised allegory of growth and change. Yet the narrative as a whole often takes the evolutionary schema of human development for granted, notably in the racialised and racist depiction of "Kaffirs" and "Hottentots". The *degree* to which Schreiner can be charged with racism is open to debate – and there are significant changes in her later writing – but her language in *African Farm* is imbued with the racialised separation of times and peoples that is characteristic of late-nineteenth-century colonial discourse.[7] In the second chapter of Part One, for example, the children Em, Waldo and Lyndall play beneath some Bushman paintings, "their red and black pigments having been preserved through the long years from wind and rain by the overhanging ledge; grotesque oxen, elephants, rhinoceroses, and a one-horned beast, such as no man ever has seen or ever shall."[8] These reminders of a bygone era, colours on stone, prompt Waldo to insert the Bushmen into a timeline of evolutionary progress:

> [I]t seems that the stones are really speaking – speaking of the old things, of the time when the strange fishes and animals lived that are turned into stone now, and the lakes were here; and of the time when the little Bushmen lived here, so small and so ugly, and used to sleep in the wild dog holes, and in the sloots, and eat snakes, and shot the bucks with their poisoned arrows.⁹

There is, as we soon shall see, a supplementary observation to be made about Waldo's objectification of the "little" Bushmen as merely an episode in biological and social development. But it is crucial to first ask *why* evolutionism and Social Darwinism appealed so strongly to these very differently placed (post)colonial writers. The differences between them should in fact be underlined: whereas Brazil was an independent nation, the Cape Colony was an outpost of the British Empire; Cunha was highly educated, whereas Schreiner, her fierce intelligence and ultimate success notwithstanding, was largely self-taught; Cunha, of course, was a man, and unreflectingly male-centred and partriarchal in everything he wrote, which presents a sharp contrast to Schreiner, who is today known primarily a "New Woman" pioneer. Last but not least, Cunha and Schreiner wrote in two different "European" languages with discrete traditions and networks. And yet, in this short essay, I can only begin to enumerate the multiple concerns which their writings share, and which refract the global impact of nineteenth-century positivism and evolutionism.

My key hypothesis is that Social Evolutionism, as a reworking of and an *alternative* to European historicism, offered the white writer a cold, post-Christian narrative of belonging and purpose in territories where he or she, in genealogical terms, had a short history. Evolutionary time was free from the burden of European history yet justified the presence of the "European" on alien soil.¹⁰

However, and this is the second strand of my argument, Schreiner's and Cunha's literary endeavours also share incoherencies and tensions that push against not just evolutionism but, more significantly, some of the fundamental, racialised contradictions of inscribing the Cape Colony and the postcolony of Brazil as spaces of historical belonging. Just as the *sertanejos* are Cunha's heroes, so do we read in the continuation of Waldo's musings that

> [i]t was one of those, one of those old wild Bushmen, that painted those, said the boy, nodding towards the pictures – one who was different from the rest. He did not know why, but he wanted to make something beautiful – he wanted to make something, so he made these.[11]

This recognition of the paintings' aesthetic value, and the imagining of their maker as an individual, undercuts the objectification of the Bushmen. They are imagined not in terms of biology but as humans, belonging to the land, whose creative capacity has left behind something enduring. When Waldo subsequently concludes his reverie by brusquely pointing out that "Now the Boers have shot them all, so that we never see a yellow face peeping out among the stones", his grand and distant evolutionary vistas are short-circuited by current genocidal terror. There is a sudden shift from deep time to shallow time, and the Bushmen are inserted into colonial history albeit via radical negation. In this context, it should also be noted that the Boers are by no means positive harbingers of historical progress in *African Farm*.

Incoherencies such as these complicate, then, straightforward accounts of the colonial impact of evolutionism.[12] In fact, the textual labours of Schreiner and Cunha unravel many of their evolutionary presuppositions. Importantly, it is precisely in the *literary* aspects of their writing that this destabilisation is registered. The mixing of genres, the shifts in focalisation, and the ambivalent status of the imagination in *Os sertões* and *African Farm* speak volumes about the epistemological uncertainties that pervade their appropriation of evolutionism, and the need for a more nuanced understanding of what has been called the entanglement of temporalities in the postcolony.[13]

The problem of historicism

Before pursuing this any further, however, I must expand on the crucial distinction I am making between evolutionism and historicism. In colonial and postcolonial contexts, as is today well established, history easily becomes a problem at a conceptual level. The debates that were sparked by the Subaltern Studies Group in India in the 1980s and 1990s, resulting most famously in Gayatri Spivak's "Can the Subaltern Speak?" and Dipesh Chakrabarty's *Provincializing Europe*, demonstrate this. Their arguments revolve around the aporia of India's having emerged into a nationhood and a modernity that were intensely local in their effects, but alien and imperialist in their concepts. Spivak's subaltern cannot speak because the Enlightenment episteme of imperialism has denied her a position from which her speech would be audible.[14] Chakrabarty, who focuses more on the academic practice of historiography, claims that the very notions of nationhood and modernity were, at a *theoretical* level, the globally circulated products of local European histories, making it difficulty for historians to conceptualize India, say, without resorting to categories such as "lack" or "incompleteness".[15]

It is worth emphasising that Chakrabarty's target is not evolutionism but *historicism* in its liberal and Marxist guises.[16] Specifically, he is interrogating the "transition narrative" proposed by colonial and nationalist historians alike. According to this narrative, postcolonies need to undergo a transition from feudalism/barbarism/despotism to fully-fledged modernity, even as they invariably fail to complete such a transition. There is almost always something "lacking" in the transition, and this lack is measured against "a certain 'Europe' as the primary habitus of the modern".[17]

We should note that "history" here denotes more than simply "the past". Rather, this type of historicism is teleologically directed towards a known future. It evokes a time-frame in which societies move towards a goal *that has already been reached* by "Europe". It is historicism in this sense that becomes so ambiguous for white creoles such as Schreiner and Cunha – it is both a conceptual/philosophical resource and a threat, insofar as it complicates the desire for separation from Europe. The statement that Brazil is *"condemned* to civilization" gauges precisely the ambiguity of modernity in the postcolonial nation, even for someone as privileged as Cunha. But by inserting historicism into a far vaster temporal horizon, and by placing such a premium on geography and ecology, evolutionism offers a qualified means of reframing historicism on behalf of the (post)colonial territory.

Os sertões

The peculiar structure of *Os sertões* demonstrates with precision how evolutionism subsumes historicism: of its three parts, the first two – called "A terra" ("The land") and "O homem" ("Man") – are attempts at a scientific description and analysis of Brazilian geology, flora and fauna, and of the "races" that constitute the Brazilian population. It is only in Part Three, "A luta" ("The struggle"), that the story of the Canudos campaign gets underway. Although lacking any absolute generic or stylistic consistency, each section corresponds to a different time-frame: geological time in Part One, anthropological time in Part Two, and recent history in Part Three.

Part One effectively appropriates natural history on behalf of the Brazilian nation. The time-frame invoked through Cunha's reflections on the formation of mountain ranges covers hundreds of millions of years, but it is the newly-formed state of Brazil that marks the geographical boundaries of his account.

In "O homem", time contracts. Drawing on racist theories current at the time, Cunha paints a picture of Brazilian "man" as a convergence of Native American, African and European "races". More specifically, he offers a viciously objectifying explanation of the *sertanejo* as the backward product of miscegenation and isolation. In addition, this "mixed race" interferes with the process of evolution:

> É que nessa concorrência admirável dos povos, evolvendo todos em luta sem tréguas, na qual a seleção capitaliza atributos que a hereditariedade conserva, o mestiço é um intruso. Não lutou; não é uma integração de esforços; é alguma cousa de dispersivo e dissolvente; surge, de repente, sem caracteres próprios, oscilando entre influxos opostos de legados discordes. A tendência à regressão às raças matrizes caracteriza a sua instabilidade. [18]

> The mestizo is an intruder in the marvelous process of evolution, that endless competition between peoples, a struggle without truce in which selection refines attributes that are preserved by heredity. The mestizo has not struggled; he does not represent the integration of efforts; he is a disruptive and destructive element who appears without any characteristics of his own, caught between the opposing influences of his conflictive ancestry. The mestizo's instability is marked by his tendency to regress to his primitive origins.[19]

This view of the mestizo as a trickster figure in the grand scheme of evolution is analogous to the *sertanejo*'s intrusion into Cunha's own attempts at "scientifically" grounding his narrative of Canudos. The closer we get to actual historical events in *Os sertões*, and the more ethically compromised its the story of this bizarre Brazilian civil war becomes, the more the racial stereotyping of the *sertanejo* falls away as so much scaffolding. It is as though the very act of narration leads Cunha along unanticipated *veredas* (pathways) and prompts him to condemn what he at a theoretical level believes to be a historical necessity. Sometimes he tries to salvage the moral legitimacy of the campaign by warning that it "would turn out to be a barbaric, senseless act if the country did not follow the path of the artillery with a campaign of education" ("seria um crime inútil e bárbaro, se não se aproveitassem os caminhos abertos à artilharia para uma propaganda tenaz, contínua e persistente").[20] Elsewhere, the atrocities simply cause his world-view to implode: "In spite of three centuries of underdevelopment, the *sertanejos* did not rival our troops in acts of barbarism." ("Apesar de três séculos de atraso os sertanejos não lhes levavam a palma no estadear idênticas babaridades.")[21]

The Story of an African Farm

Olive Schreiner's *The Story of an African Farm* registers the ambiguities of evolutionist and historicist thinking somewhat differently. In her famous preface to the second edition, writing under the pen-name Ralph Irons, Schreiner spells out her suspicion of British representations of Africa, with their stories of "wild adventure". Such works "are best written in Piccadilly or in the Strand: there the gifts of the creative imagination untrammelled by contact with any fact, may spread their wings."[22] For the writer based in Africa, "facts creep in upon him. Those brilliant phases and shapes which the imagination sees in far-off lands are not for him to portray. Sadly he must squeeze the colour from his brush, and dip it into the grey pigments around him."[23] Imagination is invoked here as sheer fancy, opposed to the demands of truth.

Through this understanding of fiction as fictive, but not fanciful, that is, as being "true" in the sense of non-delusional, Schreiner inscribes her novel into nineteenth-century novelistic discourse.[24] This is contrasted in the narrative proper with a display of delusional discourse about *Europe*. When the devious Irishman, Bonaparte Blenkins, turns up at the farm, he tries to convince its inhabitants that he is related both to Napoleon and the Duke of Wellington, that he has travelled all over the world, and that he speaks "every civilized language, excepting only Dutch and German".[25] (Dutch and German, of course, are spoken at the farm.) In his conversation with the gullible German overseer – whom Bonaparte flatters by calling him "a student of history" – riffs fancifully on fragments of European history. His function as a character, which some critics see as symbolic of imperial intrusion into the lives of settlers, is clearly linked to this parody of history and, by implication, to historicist claims of European superiority.[26]

It is against such parodically devious history that we can appreciate the significance of Schreiner's emphasis *both* on the "fact" of the Karoo landscape *and* her Spencerian, quasi-phenomenological reduction of individual growth and existence to its barest features, most strikingly in "Times and Seasons", where she speaks of how in infancy, "from the shadowy background of forgetfulness start out pictures of startling clearness, disconnected, but brightly coloured",[27] or how at a later stage "[m]aterial things still rule, but the spritual and intellectual take their places".[28] In early adolescence

> the spirit-world begins to peep in, and wholly clouds it over. What are the flowers to us? They are fuel waiting for the great burning. We look at the walls of the farm-house and the matter-of-fact sheep kraals, with the merry sunshine playing over all; and do not see it. But we see a great white throne, and Him that sits on it.[29]

With maturity, finally, there is "a new time, a life as cold as that of man who sits on a pinnacle of an iceberg and sees glittering crystals all about him. The old looks indeed like a long hot delirium, peopled with phantasies. [...] Now we have no God." [30]

As a result of Schreiner's repeated attempts at matching form and truth, we find in her novel a generically unstable combination of realism, satire, and metaphysical speculation. This needs to be taken into consideration together with her use of the evolutionary time-scale as a means to disarm the authoritative claims of European historicism. If her invocation of the landscape and its harshness in the novel is one aspect of how she tries to "squeeze the colour from [her] brush", the technique of abstraction and suspension is another. In both instances, as in Cunha's *Os sertões*, we witness inconsistent attempts at articulating temporalities on terms derived in part from lived experience of entangled times in the colony and postcolony. Their writerly appropriation of evolutionism, read as an attempted departure from European historicism, is in this respect more ambiguous than colonial discourse analysis would have us expect.

Notes

1. Euclides da Cunha, *Os sertões: campanha de Canudos* (Rio de Janeiro: Francisco Alves, 1987), 52; Euclides da Cunha, *Backlands: The Canudos Campaign*, trans. Elizabeth Lowe (New York: Penguin, 2010), 62.

2. In a special issue devoted to Euclides da Cunha, Marcia Schuback speaks of *Os sertões* as the book that "laid bare the Brazilian literary consciousness" ("desnudou a consciência literária brasileira"). Marcia Sá Cavalcante Schuback, "Ao *rez das existências*, desapontamentos", *Tempo Brasileiro* 177 (2009): 53.

3. Salman Rushdie, *Midnight's Children* (New York: Everyman's Library, 1995 [1980]), 381.

4. Olive Schreiner, Letter to Havelock Ellis, 28 March 1884, in *Olive Schreiner: Letters*, vol. 1, ed. Richard Rive (Oxford: Oxford UP, 1988), 36.

5. Herbert Spencer, *First Principles*, vol. 1 (London: Williams and Norgate, 1911 [1867]).

6. John C. Greene, "Biology and Social Theory in the Nineteenth Century: Auguste Comte and Herbert Spencer", in *Herbert Spencer: Critical Assessments of Leading Sociologists*, vol. 2, ed. John Offer, (London: Routledge, 2000), 206.

7. Patrick Brantlinger, "Victorians and Africans", in *"Race", Writing and Difference*, ed. Henry Louis Gates (Chicago: U of Chicago Press, 1986), 185–222.

8. Olive Schreiner, *The Story of an African Farm* (Johannesburg: Ad Donker, 1975 [1883]), 37.

9. Schreiner, *Farm*, 42.

10. In respect of Cunha, it can be pointed out that Walnice Nogueira Galvão sees him as a writer concerned primarily with the conquest of space through language, comparing him in this regard with Joseph Conrad: Walnice Noqueira Galvão, "O fascínio dos confins", in *Moderno de nascença*, ed. Benjamin Abdala jr. and Salete de Almeida Cara (São Paulo: Boitempo Editorial, 2006), 88–99. In the case of Schreiner, Hannah Freeman has argued for the significance of land and landscape as a means of unmaking European and patriarchal histories in *The Story of an African Farm*. Hannah Freeman, "Dissolution and Landscape in Olive

Schreiner's *The Story of an African Farm*", *English Studies in Africa* 52.2 (2009): 18–34.

11. Schreiner, *Farm*, 42.

12. Brantlinger, "Victorians", 203-205.

13. The term "entangled" is used here advisedly, although I will not be able to expand on it in this essay. It is mainly Achille Mbembe's and Sarah Nuttall's theorization of the entanglement of temporalities in the postcolony that informs my own perspective. Achille Mbembe, *On the Postcolony* (Berkeley: U of California Press, 2001); Sarah Nuttall, *Entanglement* (Johannesburg: Witwatersrand UP, 2009).

14. Gayatri Spivak, *A Critique of Postcolonial Reason* (Cambridge, MA: Harvard UP, 1999), 266-293.

15. Dipesh Chakrabarty, *Provincializing Europe: Postcolonial Thought and Historical Difference* (Chicago: Chicago UP, 2000), 27–46.

16. It is, rather, in his current work on global warming that Chakrabarty has broached the issue of natural history vs. human history. Dipesh Chakrabarty, "The Climate of History: Four Theses", *Critical Inquiry* 35 (2009): 197–222.

17. Chakrabarty, *Provincializing*, 43.

18. Cunha, *Sertões*, 77.

19. Cunha, *Backlands*, 93.

20. Cunha, *Backlands*, 402; Cunha, *Sertões*, 350.

21. Cunha, *Backlands*, 431; Cunha, *Sertões*, 378.

22. Schreiner, *Farm*, 23-24.

23. Schreiner, *Farm*, 24.

24. Catherine Gallagher, "The Rise of Fictionality" in Franco Moretti (ed.), *The Novel*, vol. 1 (Princeton: Princeton UP, 2006), 336-363.

25. Schreiner, *Farm*, 52.

26. Freeman, "Dissolution", 23.

27. Schreiner, *Farm*, 127.

28. Schreiner, *Farm*, 128.

29. Schreiner, *Farm*, 130.

30. Schreiner, *Farm*, 138.

Histories Matter: Materializing Politics in the Moment of the Sublime

KRISTINA FJELKESTAM

The 1843 novel *Jenny* by German author Fanny Lewald contains a remarkable scene in which the main character, a Jew, is asked to sing at a social gathering. Just before stepping up, she overhears a derogatory comment on her Jewishness:

> For a moment Jenny seemed to be thinking, as if indecisive about which song to pick. Suddenly a thought appeared to come to her, she struck a few chords with steady hands and began to sing Byron's 'The Jewish Girl', which Kücken had so consummately set to music. Her strong, sonorous voice was made all the more enchanting by her inner pain. The deepest sorrow could be heard in her voice, and when she ended the second verse with the words, 'Oh! My beloved native home oh, Fatherland! when will Jehovah become your hand of vengeance?', no-one dared breathe; everybody was struck to their core by the deep pain in these notes that called out to God for revenge. Then the song turned into a melancholy lament; Jenny's voice became softer until it regained strength with the words, 'in slavery the Jews' enemies deride them', but eventually died out, exhausted, in a wish: 'Oh! My beloved native home, oh, Fatherland! Cannot death become our bond of union?'

Lewald continues as follows:

> The flush of inspiration that had painted Jenny's cheeks while singing, had vanished by the end of the piece. Calm but shaken, she stood up. No shouts of approval were heard, but many in the audience had tears in their eyes, and others looked at each other with surprise. They seemed to sense that, while expecting simple entertainment, they had seen Truth. A Truth which they feared the same way as they would fear a ghost in daytime, appearing suddenly among the living.[1]

Through her singing, Jenny communicates a deeply-felt sense of injustice. Flushed with emotion, she evokes pain and sorrow. Her overwhelming image of the horrors of death, and the ensuing call for revenge, is transformed into a heightened feeling of determination, with Jenny being described as "calm, but shaken." She pales when recalling the words of the girl in the song who nobly prepares to die for her people. The audience is struck by a sudden revelation: Jenny succeeds in conjuring up both a spectre of past injustice and a vision of future redress. The scene depicts an instance of what I will here be describing as the political sublime. As an aesthetic category, the sublime (*sub limis*) is what elevates us above everyday bodily mundanity, to disclose another dimension of humanity. But the sublime does not just reveal a different form of aesthetic experience, it can also be seen to function as a revolutionary political moment that enables new kinds of ethical and political sensibility.[2] It is precisely this *political* potential of the sublime experience that will serve as the starting point for my examination of this literary depiction of a moment in which a sudden materialization of historical issues leads to political consequences. Is it possible to bring history to life in order to change the future that lies dormant in the present? The answer is a rather complex "yes", following the literary representation of such a crucial moment that I will analyse here.

At the time of the novel's publication, Jewish emancipation was still a mirage – a hallucination or haunting ghost. Here, however, the ghost is materialized by Jenny's embodied sublimity. Thus the song scene is turned into a concrete, political act.

The song "The Jewish Girl" consists of F. W Kücken's musical setting of the poem "Das Mädchen von Judah". However, it was written, not by Byron, as Lewald suggests, but by Henriette Jeanette Paalzow, a German author famous at the time whom Lewald had met in Berlin. The poem is about a Jewish girl and her deep longing for redress for the historical persecution which began with the expulsion of Jews from Palestine: "Where are they now, the sons of the old tribe? / They have fallen in dark and bloody battle!"[3] It goes on to describe how the chains of the Jews rattle symbolically with a "hateful sound", and how the "[d]ays are long, the nights filled with fear, in slavery the Jews' enemies deride them."[4] When the girl calls out for revenge against her oppressors – the very lines which appear in *Jenny* – she is prepared to sacrifice her own life in the struggle for freedom: "Cannot death become our bond of union?".

This powerful scene in *Jenny* is echoed by a number of subsequent literary works in which sublime singing turns into politics in practice. The most famous of these is, of course, *Daniel Deronda* (1876) by George Eliot, a friend of Lewald's, in which a Jewish character named Mirah sings a Verdi aria and thus appropriates Italian nationalism for (proto)Zionism.[5] In *Jenny*, the aesthetics of the song scene are political on several levels. First, the song's depiction of the self-sacrificing girl recalls the taste for sublimely beautiful dead women in contemporary art.[6] Artistically, Jenny represents this familiar kind of aesthetic subject, which is recognized by the audience as marker of sublimity. The song's second political level is historical: the story of the Jewish diaspora and of the young men who have died in "bloody, dark battle", filling nights with fear and the "hateful" sound of rattling chains. The audience is touched by the deep pain Jenny now embodies in her now double sense of being both sign and reference. Then follows the level of the present, with statements on the continuing oppression. But the main ingredient here is the declaration at the end of the song, which comprises suggestions for future actions to end the oppression. All these aspects, together with the superior morals of Jenny as she resists prejudice, combine to conjure up a moment of supreme sublimity.

The ghost

The "truth" of the song scene, here defined as a sudden political insight, appears to the audience in the shape of a fearsome ghost. Ghosts or spectres are often used to evoke that which cannot be represented. In *Jenny*, the spectre is given a more specific, political meaning insofar as the "unpresentable" refers to an oppressed group in society. The most well-known spectre of this kind is, of course, that with which Marx and Engels open the Communist Manifesto (1848): "A spectre is haunting Europe the spectre of Communism."[7] Here, the repressed and the unnameable assuming the shape of a spectre stands for the proletariat, whereas the intimidating ghost in the song scene of *Jenny* has a specifically Jewish identity and the form of a beautiful woman.

During the revolutionary era, politically uncomfortable manifestations were sexualized and coded as female in terms of a "bad" sublimity. Edmund Burke, for instance, writes in *Letters on a Regicide Peace* (1796) that the French Revolution was comparable to "a hideous phantom", which he feminizes:

> Out of the tomb of the murdered monarchy in France has arisen a vast, tremendous, unformed spectre, in a far more terrific guise than any which ever yet have overpowered the imagination, and subdued the fortitude of man. Going straight forward to its end, unappalled by peril, unchecked by remorse, despising all common maxims and all common means, that hideous phantom overpowered those who could not believe it was possible *she* could at all exist...[8]

For Burke, revolutionary sublimity is thus something frightening and disgusting, and when he refers to it as a *"she"*, he gender codes what in it is politically provocative, much as was to happen in later representations of revolutionary *tricoteuses* and *petroleuses*. In Lewald's *oeuvre*, however, sublime femininity carries positive overtones since, as in *Jenny*, it is regarded as mediating an indisputable "truth". For instance, even in Lewald's reports from Paris during the revolution of 1848, *Erinnerungen aus dem Jahre 1848* (1850), political truth is represented as female. Here, in an episode that recalls the song scene in *Jenny*, Lewald chooses to let the revolution take the shape of the most famous *tragédienne* of the time.

The episode takes place on an evening when fighting on the barricades has ceased and the theatres have just re-opened. Lewald goes to see the celebrated Rachel Félix perform in a Greek tragedy in her characteristically elevated style of sublimity. But after the curtain has fallen, the sublimity of Félix is sharpened by political actuality. The audience begs her to return to the stage to sing the *Marseillaise*, which she does despite realizing with horror that the noble goal of freedom has put lives at stake:

> The curtain rose. In the same white garment, a tricolored sash wrapped around her waist beneath her bosom, her hair in the disorder of the last act, she stepped quickly out of the wings onto the stage. (...) Words cannot describe her. Her face showed what the rage of deepest oppression, what the anger of the dehumanized slave aware of his own human-

ity can imprint in an ominous expression upon the features of a human face. A Fury in battle, an unchained goddess of vengeance as the Greeks' concept of beauty had portrayed such creatures, beautiful as the paralyzing, petrifying face of a Medusa. Every nerve in me quivered as a light muffled drum-roll was heard behind the scene. Looking firmly at the audience and holding it under the spell of her magnetic gaze, pointing with her right hand into the distance, she sang or spoke the words – it was something in between: 'Entendez-vous dans les campagnes mugir ces féroces soldats – Ils viennent, jusque dans vos bras, égorger vos fils, vos campagnes!' A stream of gentle sadness flooded over her anger with these last words, and the avenging goddess had a mild soft lament for the fate of the sacrificed.[9]

Deeply moved by the sublimity of the performance, Lewald is at loss for words to describe Félix's immersion in the role, her fierce anger against the oppressors mixed with sadness at the memory of the dead. The ambience in the theatre is bursting from Félix's intense gaze and fearful facial expression, accompanied by the monotonous drum-roll in the background. After this elegiac mood passes, however, Félix goes on to rouse the audience's fighting spirit again. As the song ends, she begins waving the flag and conclude by expressing with sublime enthusiasm her desire to accomplish great deeds:

> The tone of this 'Liberté, liberté chérie!' cannot possibly be described. There was the most passionate enthusiasm, the deepest, most fervent love of her heart. Rachel is the personified human Marseillaise, the incarnate concept of the fight for freedom. In my mind I kept hearing: 'And the Word was made flesh!' Yes, that is what the word is supposed to do. It is supposed to, it *must* become flesh in order to be. And there is a God in the fact that this Marseillaise-incarnate is a Jewess, a daughter of the oppressed.[10]

Here, at the very end of the episode, Lewald introduces her main point. Not only is Félix a supremely gifted actress with sublime abilities, but she is also a member of one of the most exposed groups in society. She is a Jew, like the fictitious Jenny, and can therefore give voice to the oppressed, thereby mediating experiences that have hitherto been made invisible. And when the word of a Jew "was made flesh", that is, likened to the description of Jesus in the New Testament (John 1:14), more than just religious differences are being transcended.

When these experiences are materialized, Félix, like Jenny, also transcends the symbolic-allegorical function to which women had been confined, by assuming the form of a Marianne or "Liberty leading the people". Lewald stages the "Word" in its literal meaning, stressing the importance of the embodiment of political insights. Only when the ghost has materialized, suggests Lewald, does it become possible to put thought into action.

Materializing the past

In the song scene of *Jenny,* too, I would say that the road of political understanding from thought to action goes through embodiment. When Jenny represents a historical course of events in and through her singing, the ghosts of the past materialize. The hitherto unrepresented Jewish minority of the present is thus represented, and the Truth of their oppression – Truth with a capital T – now appears to the audience. But not until the most frightening and sublime moment of the song scene, the second verse, which concludes with the forward-looking "Oh! My beloved native home, oh, Fatherland! when will Jehovah become your hand of vengeance?", does Jenny suddenly become one with the "I" of the song – the word is made flesh.

For instance, the spectators are unable to breathe when confronted by this almost shocking metamorphosis. To be sure, the audience already feels the inexpressible sorrow of the Jewish people, but, unlike Jenny. they cannot become one with it because they are at the same time well aware of the fact that it is *they* that can be subjected to the vengeance of Jehovah. Thus, the ineffable grief that fills their eyes with tears is mixed with a profound dread which makes the experience ambivalent: "They seemed to have a feeling that, when expecting simple entertainment, they had seen Truth. A truth which they feared (...)".

Jenny's incarnation thus operates on two different levels, ontological and temporal. Ontologically, Jenny's embodiment of Jewish suffering signifies an ability to take political action, an agency which is produced by empathy, insight – and fear. The temporal aspect is founded on historical referentiality, which serves as the catalyst of future political action. Jenny's metamorphosis invokes ghosts from the past as well as the future, but the main point is that this spectrality is both a product and a producer of the present, an ongoing now. After all, the spectre's presence of absence consists of what no longer, and not yet, *is*.[11] But in telling histories we invoke the ghosts of the past, and this ghostliness can be put to use in order to challenge established history and its effect on what is coming. Consequently, spectrality can execute societal change. I maintain that this is the case in Fanny Lewald's *Jenny*. A more modern example would be Toni Morrison's *Beloved* (1987) which tells the story of a child ghost, inspired by the real Margaret Garner, who, as a runaway slave in the nineteenth century, killed her baby when she was about to be recaptured.

The phantoms of slavery still live among us here in the western world, writes Avery F. Gordon *à propos* Morrison's novel, but only in the present can we give any meaning to them and other spectres of the past: "The modus operandi of a ghost is haunting, and haunting makes its only social meaning in contact with the living's time of the now. (...) In other words, the ghost is nothing without you."[12] Consequently, both the present and the future are structured by ghosts of the past, Gordon claims. But she stresses that it is we who must act in the present, conscious of how we both create and are created by the representation of spectrality. Something similar is suggested by Karl Marx in the famous passage in *The Eighteenth Brumaire of Louis Bonaparte* in which he observes that humans actively form their future history but of necessity from that which cannot be controlled in the "directly encountered" present and the "transmitted" circumstances of the past.[13]

The memory of past sufferings inspires the emancipatory struggles of the present, but whereas Marx also considers *memory* as a *promise* of progress and victory, his later critic, the historian-philosopher Walter Benjamin, refuses to see the future as the goal of history in so teleological a fashion.[14] Indeed, Marx had secularized the messianic idea in his vision of the classless society, something which Benjamin supports, but his idea is still based on the progressive linear time-axis of historical writing in which past suffering constitute only one step towards an emancipated future. To a certain extent, the same critique can be applied to *Jenny*, at least as regards some of the emancipatory proclamations in other parts of the novel.

However, in the song scene this teleological, messianistic idea is problematized in its very representation of the sublime moment.

Benjamin claims that political imperatives emanate from historical memories in the shape of constantly varying images flashing up in the present, something I suggest are akin to moments of sublimity. These images depend on the time at which they are perceived, and do not describe "the way it really was"; first and foremost, they are brought to the fore at "a moment of danger," as Benjamin puts it in the sixth of his theses on the philosophy of history.[15] In this sense, the song scene in *Jenny* recalls the idea of historical memories appearing at "a moment of danger", i.e., the spectators' shocking realization that something is really at stake here. Thus every moment carries political possibilities, as Benjamin writes, and his messianic idea opens up the future as a promising potentiality without any deterministic adherence to law. History, then, is never completed, since it is continually being rewritten and reinterpreted in a present in which the future is still undecided.[16]

One thing is certain, however – a dominant power is always being haunted.[17] The distressing moment of the ghost's materialization contains both a threat and a dream of change, while at the same time being a call for action in the now. This turns the sublime moment into a political act, as happens in the song scene of *Jenny* when the representation of past oppression is compressed into the vision of future emancipation in a metamorphosis of the present where "the word was made flesh". The result is a shocking sudden realization, a "truth". This insight, like the spectre, is indeed transient yet leaves nothing unchanged. The embodiment of the ghost has thus transformed sublime aesthetics into politics, which leaves me with no other conclusion: Histories matter.

Notes

1. My translation from Fanny Lewald, *Jenny*, (Berlin: Zenodot, 2007), 195–196.
2. The political history of the sublime is unfortunately a rather neglected field of research, which has, however, lately benefitted from for instance Christine Battersby's excellent study as *The Sublime, Terror and Human Difference* (London: Routledge, 2007). I have also contributed to it with my recent book *Det sublimas politik: emancipatorisk estetik i 1800-talets konstnärsromaner* (Stockholm: Makadam, 2010; *The Politics of the Sublime: Emancipatory Aesthetics in Artist Novels from the Nineteenth-Century*). This essay consists of a translated and revised extract of this

book. The book was partially funded by The Foundation for Baltic and East European Studies (Östersjöstiftelsen).

3. Quoted from *Kücken-Album: Fünfzehn ausgewählte Lieder*, (Braunschweig: Litolff's Verlag), 12, my translation of: "Wo sind sie, die Söhne vom alten Geschlecht? / Gefallen in blutigen, finstern Gefecht!"

4. *Kücken-Album*, 13, my translation of: "ein widrig Getön"; "Die Tage sind lang, voll Grauen die Nacht, in Knechtschaft des Feindes der Jude verlacht."

5. Delia da Sousa Correa, *George Eliot, Music and Victorian Culture*, (New York: Palgrave, 2003), 170.

6. See for instance Elizabeth Bronfen, *Over Her Dead Body: Death, Femininity and Aesthetics*, (Manchester: Manchester University Press, 1993).

7. Karl Marx and Frederick Engels, *Selected Works in One Volume*, (London: Lawrence & Wishart, 1968), 35.

8. Burke is quoted in Barbara Claire Freeman, *The Feminine Sublime: Gender and Excess in Women's Fiction* (Berkeley: University of California Press, 1995), 47, my italics.

9. Fanny Lewald, *A Year of Revolutions: Fanny Lewald's Recollections of 1848* (Providence: Berghahn Books, 1997), 79–80. Fanny Lewald, *Erinnerungen aus dem Jahre 1848* (Frankfurt am Main: Insel Verlag 1969), 65, Lewald's italics.

10. Lewald, *A Year of Revolutions*, 79–80. Lewald, *Erinnerungen aus dem Jahre 1848*, 66.

11. See Jacques Derrida's concept of "hauntology"(*hantologie*) in *Specters of Marx: The State of Debt, the Work of Mourning, and the New International* (New York: Routledge, 1994).

12. Avery F. Gordon, *Ghostly Matters: Haunting and the Sociological Imagination* (Minneapolis: University of Minnesota Press, 1997), 179.

13. Marx and Engels, 97. Of course, Marx is but one of many thinkers, from Augustinus to Ricoeur and Koselleck, who have pondered the political significance of the various dimensions of time.

14. See Matthias Fritsch, *The Promise of Memory: History and Politics in Marx, Benjamin, and Derrida* (Albany: State University of New York Press, 2005).

15. Walter Benjamin, "Theses on the Philosophy of History", *Illuminations* (London: Fontana/Collins, 1973), 257.

16. In his *Spectres de Marx* (1993), Derrida has developed Benjamins's notion of the open potential of the future. He uses the category of the continually postponed or coming future – *l'à-venir* – that constantly apprehends the possibility of another (more radical) utopia beyond the utopias that we can imagine in the present. I also want to stress that here I am relying on Derrida's terminology when distinguishing between "messianistic", i.e. teleological, and "messianic", i. e. nonteleological.

17. Jacques Derrida, *Specters of Marx. The State of the Debt, the Work of Mourning, and the New International* (London: Routledge, 1994), 37: "Haunting belongs to the structure of every hegemony."

History and Mourning

VICTORIA FARELD

As historical beings, we exist in a field of tension between the desire to remember and the desire to forget, between a fear of forgetting and a fear of possibly remembering too much or of being unable to let go of the past. Nietzsche stressed the importance of forgetting in order to remember.[1] In the process of working through repressed memories, Freud saw the importance of remembering in order to release oneself from the power of the past.[2]

In what follows, I will reflect upon the relationship between historical thinking and the act of mourning. Through a reading of the Austrian-born writer and Auschwitz survivor Jean Améry (1912-1978), I discuss what *historicization* might mean for someone who refuses to forgive and to forget, who refuses the work of mourning. I will argue that a refusal to mourn is not always tantamount to a melancholic, repressed, or purely reactive position, but should be contextually interpreted in its specific manifestations. I claim that Améry's refusal to mourn, his clinging to the past, is to be understood, in his particular situation, as a revolt rather than a resignation in that it reveals a temporality possessed of critical potential. Thus conceived, Améry's position can be used to complicate a general view of historicization as analogous to the work of mourning, that is, a process of achieving critical detachment from the past.

History as an Act of Mourning. A Past Past

The current cultural and academic concern with the relation between notions of memory, history, and forgetting could to a large extent be seen as repercussions of the traumatic experiences of the twentieth century. In light of the *Shoah*, there has been an increasing interest in exploring the existential foundations of historical consciousness. Psychoanalytic vocabularies have turned out to be an important resource for historians seeking to represent experiences which transcend the boundaries of traditional historical narrative. In recent decades history has been understood not only in its monumental, antiquarian, and critical modes, as Nietzsche had it, but also in terms of trauma, melancholia, and mourning.[3] When experiences of the past are traumatic, German historian Jörn Rüsen observes, "historical thinking should become a procedure of mourning".[4] Mourning has become "a new mode of making sense of history".[5]

Even without referring to traumatic experiences or using a psychoanalytical language, it is common to see the writing of history as analogous to the process of mourning on a more general level, since historicization and mourning are both attempts to deal with loss; in the work of mourning, we remember the deceased person by translating the loss into words, by filling the absence with presence, silence with speech. Similarly, we try to remember and make sense of times past by transforming their many events into coherent stories, restoring the lost past by translating it into a language that we can understand and by giving it a form we recognize.

If one accepts the general analogy between historical thinking and mourning, one can easily see the writing of history as a way of positioning oneself in relation to the deceased. Tellingly, Paul Ricoeur compares the writing of history to a funerary rite. In considering "the historiographical operation to be the scriptural equivalent of the social ritual of entombment", he sees history as an "enduring mark of mourning" organized around absence.[6] It is a permanent mourning insofar as "[t]he historical operation" is understood to be "an act of repeated entombment".[7] Importantly, however, this act of repetition does not chain us forever to the past since "[t]he work of mourning definitively separates the past from the present and makes way for the future".[8] Historical thinking, when conceived of in terms of mourning, is thus similar to an activity which enables the future by transforming the past into a past that *is* past, detached from the present.

In a similar vein, Rüsen points out that "[t]he relationship to the past can be compared to the relationship to deceased persons or objects in the mourning process", associating history with death but also resurrection since the act of mourning makes the lost subject or object return "in the form of the presence of absence".[9] This prompts him to declare that "in historical consciousness the dead are still alive".[10]

Viewed against this background, history can be seen as not only conserving the past but making it alive and vital by treating it as, in a sense, dead (as something that no longer is or occurs) in order to make it resurrect (as something that has been and therefore always will be); a presence of absence. It is a past that we, by the very act of losing it, can reclaim as a past past, as our appropriated history. A movement of loss and regain thus seems to be at the core of the historiographical operation itself. Indeed, the word *historicization* is often related to words referring to life and to the act of animating, implying a past that is lifeless, lost, or absent, and that is restored to life by history. This refers not only to a past which is gone or lost to us in a purely temporal sense, but a past that is detached from the present and treated as lost yet revived in the writing of history.[11]

In *Mourning and Melancholia*, Freud develops the concept of mourning as a process of "working-through" in which the lost object is detached from the mourning self and transformed into something lost with which one can form an independent relation. Through the mourning process, distance to the past is acquired, enabling us to see the latter as something lost to us. Freud contrasts mourning with melancholia, a state in which past experiences are "acted out" rather than worked through. Unable to mourn, the melancholic clings to the past and refuses to let go of the lost object or person.[12]

For the melancholic, the past is, in the words of Julia Kristeva, "*un passé qui ne passe pas*", a past that does not pass.[13] Interestingly, "The Past That Will Not Past" is the title of the article by German historian Ernst Nolte which launched the so-called Historians' Debate in Germany in 1986. In it, Nolte critically describes Germany's National-Socialist past as a "*Vergangenheit, die nicht vergehen will*" – without, however, referring to melancholia or mourning – precisely because it has not been transformed into history by the passage of time. Only when the past has lost its "vividness", Nolte states, can it be "left to the historians".[14] The problem is that the National-Socialist past is still too vivid, too alive, to become history. Allowing the past to pass away, he argues, is necessary for us to be able to appropriate it as critically examined history.

In Nolte's article, vividness refers not to a lost past revived as history but a past so present that it resists historicization. His notion of a past too vivid to become history rests upon an underlying assumption that temporal distance grants us the objectivity and detachment needed for historical thinking. The National-Socialist past is exceptional, however, since it does not become historical merely by virtue of its temporal distance from the present. This past, Nolte argues, has established itself in the present and does not pass away with the course of time. We have to actively make it pass by detaching ourselves from it, emotionally and morally, in order to be able to appropriate it as objective history.[15] Nolte's article reveals a past from which we have to liberate ourselves in order to be historical. The implicit suggestion is that we should bury the morally burdensome past so that historians can turn it into history.

Different as they are, these examples share the idea that the historicity of the past, the very concept of historicization, implies that the past is conceived of as no longer happening in the present. This shared model of temporality does not merely refer to a past which is gone in the temporal sense of being beyond the recollection of those now living; it refers to a past which must be "infused with a definite quality of pastness" in order to become historical.[16]

By seeing the past as no longer happening in the present, the reciprocal relation of influence between past and present is severed: we who live in the present can do something with the past, (study it, develop it, use it, abuse it, etc.), thereby making it alive and present again (in its absence). The past, however, cannot do anything with us (have an uncontrolled impact on our lives, etc.) since it is no longer happening. Through the process of historicization, which is similar to the process of mourning, we achieve a critical distance that enables us to see the past as something lost to us. In the process, we come to possess the past even as the past no longer possesses us.

HISTORY AND MOURNING

Disordered Time. Past as Present

In 1966, Jean Améry published *Jenseits von Schuld und Sühne* ("Beyond Guilt and Atonement"), a work that became his literary breakthrough.[17] In this "phenomenological description of the existence of the victim", Améry insists upon remembering as an ethical and critical force directed towards the moral amnesia that characterized postwar German society, which, in his view, had dismissed the memory of its own past by seeking to forget the crimes of the Nazis.[18]

Jenseits von Schuld und Sühne has the telling subtitle *Bewältigungsversuche eines Überwältigten*, which might be translated as "attempts to master [by implication, the past] by one who has been overpowered [by it]". The metaphor is violent: both words derive from *walten*, meaning to "rule" or "govern"; a person who has been overpowered or overwhelmed – implicitly, by the past – tries to regain control over it or take possession of it. Today, the word *Bewältigung* is familiar to us primarily as part of the German notion of *Vergangenheitsbewältigung*, mastery of the past and, specifically, Holocaust historiography and a broad debate that began in the 1980s about how to come to terms with Germany's National Socialist past. The word conveys an image of the past as an uncontrolled force which one has to master in order not to be mastered by it. In contrast to *überwältigen* (overpower, overwhelm), which signals a play of forces that can take new forms and whose outcome ultimately remains open, the word *bewältigen* (master, overcome) expresses a movement towards closure or completion in which the act of successful overcoming also implies that something has been settled, got rid of, or left behind.

By adding the word *Versuche* (attempts) to the title, Améry raises a crucial objection against the double meaning of *Bewältigung* – to settle and to get rid of. Améry's *Bewältigungsversuche* are unending attempts. In that sense, they are failed attempts to master the past. In the preface to the second edition in 1977, he writes:

> I do not have [clarity] today, and I hope that I never will. Clarification would also amount to disposal, settlement of the case, which can then be placed in the files of history. My book is meant to aid in preventing precisely this. For nothing is resolved, no conflict is settled, no remembering has become a mere memory.[19]

For Améry, what has been, still is. In demanding that we cling to the past, he appears to be the melancholic *par exellence*, unable to let go of the past and writing about an experience of loss that cannot be lost. In insisting upon remaining a victim by refusing to forget and to forgive, Améry not only adopts an attitude of irreconcilability towards the past, he questions the very notion of linear time by demanding the impossible, "that the irreversible be turned around, that the event be undone".[20] His claim that "[t]he moral person demands annulment of time" entails an ethical imperative: to disrupt society's chronological time in favour of a disordered moral time in which the past is inseparable from the present.[21] Viewed against this background, Améry's call for the disruption of linear time can be seen as a protest against not only the desire to forget but the attempt to bring closure to an historical event: the past does not provide closure. It remains unfinished and should therefore not be separated from either the present or the future.

The temporal disruption has several meanings in Améry's text. His clinging to a disordered sense of time could be seen as a response to a state of trauma or deep alienation. Améry is chained to a past which is experienced as an eternal now: "Whoever was tortured, stays tortured".[22] Time cannot bridge the moral abyss between himself and the world: "Twenty-two years later I am still dangling over the ground by dislocated arms".[23] Améry's distorted body – he was beaten while hanging in a hook in the ceiling so that his shoulders were dislocated – leads to a distorted time and a distorted narrative.

Disrupted time is not only a shattered temporality or a frozen now beyond time. Time has lost its unity for Améry also through its ambiguous presence: "For two decades I had been in search of the time that was impossible to lose", he writes in the preface.[24] It is a time which is both present and absent, which cannot be forgotten neither entirely remembered.

Living in exile in Brussels since 1938, he was in 1943 imprisoned and tortured by the Nazis for his activities in the Belgian resistance, and subsequently, when his Jewish origin was revealed, deported to Dachau, Auschwitz and in the end of the war to Bergen-Belsen. Améry's disordered time reflects the existential rupture caused by torture and his indescribable experience of the concentration camps. As such, it might be seen as a phenomenological description of trauma, although Améry himself insists: "I [...] am not 'traumatized', but rather my spiritual and psychic condition corresponds completely to reality."[25]

As a reader, I choose to take him at his word, not because I reject the medical classification of his situation but because I see his position as involving a claim which transcends personally lived experience. Therefore I understand it not only, nor even primarily, as an inner state of mind but, rather, as a revolt against historic-political circumstances – an existential revolt, indeed, but also a social revolt, a reaction against how a society treats its relationship to the past.[26]

The historical function which Améry ascribes to the faculty of remembering – the power to disrupt chronological time in favor of a shattered moral time in which the past is present – hinges on a refusal to allow past events to become history. "I rebel", he writes, "against my past, against history, and against a present that places the incomprehensible in the cold storage of history and thus falsifies it in a revolting way".[27]

Améry's choice of words ("the cold storage of history") indicates that the past – which, for him, is still occurring in the present – has been relegated to an inert history, a lifeless object to be stored in a cold space suggestive of the morgue rather than the archive.[28] The past as history is a closed case: dead and buried, with no possibility of revival. Améry wrote in an era characterized by near-complete silence about the crimes committed by National Socialism. In 1950, Adorno claimed that "the mention of Auschwitz already provokes bored resentment. Nobody is concerned with the past anymore".[29] In a situation in which the past is already treated as lost, yet without the loss having been acknowledged as such, the process of historicization as an initial act of losing the past (in order for it to return as history) has no sense. Améry must stick to his loss. It is the only thing he has left in a society which neither mourns nor clings to its past but treats it as if it has never been present. Society's forgetting is Améry's moral incitement to remember by reliving the past rather than by mourning it as lost.

Améry was writing during a period of transition, however. His series of five talks about his experiences in Auschwitz (published in 1966 as *Jenseits von Schuld und Sühne*) were broadcast on West German radio in 1964 and 1965 while the Frankfurt Auschwitz Trials were in progress, making public hundreds of detailed testimonies about life in the camps. The trials, which received massive media coverage, forced Germans to confront the reality and the extent of the crimes committed. When, a year after the appearance of Améry's book, Margarete and Alexander Mitscherlich initiated a public discussion about Germans' inability to mourn, German society was undergoing a profound transformation.[30] The fact that *The Inability to Mourn* remained on bestseller lists in West Germany for over a year was clear evidence of a cultural climate that had not existed when Améry wrote his radio manuscript.

Viewed against this background, Améry's insistence upon remembering the past as present can be seen as a return of the repressed in post-holocaust culture of the 1950s and 60s. Indeed, only in the light of the specificity of this culture does Améry's refusal to mourn appear as a political and emancipatory act, rather than a melancholic, reactive, and passive position. His situation reveals that German society and the victims of the *Shoah* had to acknowledge two different kinds of loss, each with its own work of mourning. Ultimately, Améry's refusal to mourn, to regain himself, and recover through to history, is an attempt to enable post-war German society to do just that, by forcing it to remember what it had already forgotten.

Améry writes about a past that has to resist historicization, historicization understood as analogous to the work of mourning in the Freudian sense, that is, as an achievement which establishes an independent and critical relation to the past as something that is lost. For Améry, the past is not lost to history but retrievable as present. However, using his critique as the basis for questioning general assumptions about historicization is not the same as granting it general validity. On the contrary, it is an attempt to stress the particularity of his situation, for which a general assumption about historicization cannot account.

Améry's critique can nevertheless be taken as an invitation to reflect upon how we conceive of ourselves as historical beings: What does it mean to exist in a historical space of experience? What does it mean to historicize the past? What do we "do" with this thing called the past for it to become historical? His insistence upon a past that has to resist historicization, as a call for acting out, reveals history's ambiguous relation to the past as its object of representation, and the tension at the core of the writing of history in that history provides that which the past does not: closure.

Notes

1. Friedrich Nietzsche, "On the Uses and Disadvantages of History for Life"[1874], *Untimely Meditations*, ed. Daniel Breazeale, trans. R.J. Hollingdale (Cambridge: Cambridge University Press, 1997 [1876]), 57–124.

2. Sigmund Freud, "Mourning and Melancholia", *The Standard Edition of the Complete Psychological Works of Sigmund Freud*, vol. 14, trans. and ed. James Strachey (London: Hogarth, 2000), 237–260.

3. Cf. Saul Friedländer, *Memory, History and the Extermination of the European Jews* (Bloomington: Indiana University Press, 1993); Cathy Caruth, *Unclaimed Experience: Trauma, Narrative, and History* (Baltimore: John Hopkins University Press, 1996); Dominick LaCapra, *History and Memory after Auschwitz* (Ithaca, NY.: Cornell University Press, 1998).

4. Jörn Rüsen, "Mourning by History: Ideas of a New Element in Historical Thinking", *Historiography East & West* 1 (2003): 15.

5. Rüsen, "Trauma and Mourning in Historical Thinking", *Journal of Interdisciplinary Studies in History and Archaeology* 1 (2004): 17.

6. Paul Ricoeur, *Memory, History, Forgetting*, trans. Kathleen Blamey and David Pellauer, (Chicago: University of Chicago Press, 2004), 365–366.

7. Ricoeur, *Memory, History, Forgetting*, 499.

8. Ricoeur, *Memory, History, Forgetting*, 499.

9. Rüsen, "Mourning by History", 17.

10. Rüsen, "Mourning by History", 18.

11. For an example of historization as an act of bringing alive in the above sense, see the Swedish public authority The Living History Forum, "About Us: Forum för levande historia", last modified June 17, 2011, http://www.levandehistoria.se/english.

12. Freud, "Mourning and Melancholia", 237–260.

13. Julia Kristeva, *Soleil noir: dépression et mélancolie*, (Paris: Gallimard, 1987), 70.

14. Ernst Nolte, "The Past That Will Not Pass: A Speech That Could Be Written but Not Delivered", in *Forever in the Shadow of Hitler?: Original Documents of the Historikerstreit, the Controversy Concerning the Singularity of the Holocaust*, trans. James Knowlton and Truett Cates, (Atlantic Highlands: Humanities Press, 1993), 18.

15. Nolte, "The Past That Will Not Pass", 18-23.

16. Rüsen, "Historizing Nazi-Time: Metahistorical Reflections on the Debate Between Friedländer and Broszat", in Rüsen, *History: Narration, Interpretation, Orientation*, (New York: Berghahn Books, 2005), 168.

17. Jean Améry, *Jenseits von Schuld und Sühne: Bewältigungsversuche eines Überwältigten. Werke in neun Bände*, ed. Irene Heidelberger-Leonard, vol. 2. ed. Gerhard Scheit, (Stuttgart: Klett-Cotta, 2002). In 1980 it appeared in English translation *At the Mind's Limits: Contemplations by a Survivor on Auschwitz and Its Realities*, trans. Sidney Rosenfeld and Stella P. Rosenfeld, (Bloomington: Indiana University Press, 1980).

18. Améry, "Preface to the First Edition, 1966", in *At the Mind's Limits*, xiii.

19. Améry, "Preface to the 1977 Reissue", in *At the Mind's Limits*, xi.

20. Améry, "Resentments", in *At the Mind's Limits*, 68.

21. Améry, "Resentments", 72.

22. Améry, "Torture", in *At the Mind's Limits*, 34.

23. Améry, "Torture", 36.

24. Améry, "Preface to the First Edition, 1966", xiii.

25. Améry, "On the Necessity and Impossibility of Being a Jew", in *At the Mind's Limits*, 99.

26. I don't dismiss that Améry suffered from depression or posttraumatic stress, or that his position could be seen as pathological. However, to regard someone who rejects reconciliation and who refuses to forget as someone who primarily is in a need of care or treatment – rather than as a social agent whose position is a moral and political answer to a situation – means that one risks failing to see the social criticism expressed by this position.

27. Améry, "Preface to the 1977 Reissue", xi.

28. Cf. the German original: "gegen eine Gegenwart, die das Unbegreifliche geschichtlich einfrieren lässt", Améry, "Vorwort zur Neuausgabe 1977", in *Jenseits von Schuld und Sühne*, 18.

29. Thedodor W. Adorno, "Spengler after the Decline" [1950], in *Prisms* (Cambridge, Mass.: MIT Press 1981 [1967]), 58.

30. Alexander Mitscherlich, Margarete Mitscherlich, *The Inability to Mourn: Principles of Collective Behavior* (New York: Grove Press 1975 [1967]).

Derrida on the Poetics and Politics of Witnessing

IRINA SANDOMIRSKAJA

The Problem of the Witness

This essay is a reading of Jacques Derrida's *"A Self-Unsealing Poetic Text": Poetics and Politics of Witnessing*.[1] Derrida's text sums up a long period of work on Paul Celan that resulted in numerous essays, lectures, and seminars on witnessing (one of which I myself witnessed during his visit to Moscow in 1991 at the dawn of post-Soviet Russia). An aspect of the essay that was important at the time of its writing is its response to claims by Holocaust revisionism to the status of historical research.[2] Today, Holocaust revisionism is regarded as a discourse of politically motivated denial, not as history. Is Derrida's critique still valid, and how is the issue in question – that of "politics and poetics of witnessing" – still problematic?

The central assertion of Holocaust revisionism specifically concerned the status of witnessing and testimony as a historical source. It denied the truth of testimonies by Holocaust survivors and, on the basis of this, the truth of the Holocaust as a historical fact.

It is precisely because witnessing has both a poetics and a politics – a provocative statement Derrida makes in the title of his essay – that the witness has been doubted as a source, and not only by deniers. In *Eichmann in Jerusalem*, Hannah Arendt disqualifies witnesses as inadequate precisely because they have a political and aesthetic agenda.[3] Her criteria for a qualified witness are difficult to meet: a true witness should be a "righteous" man with an ability of dealing with the story, its "poetics and politics",

> ...the rare capacity for distinguishing between things that had happened to the storyteller more than sixteen, and sometimes twenty years ago, and what he had read and heard and imagined in the meantime. ... [The court found out] how difficult it was to tell the story, that – at least outside the transforming realm of poetry – it needed a purity of soul, an unmirrored, unreflected innocence of heart and mind that only the righteous possess.[4]

It is not because of the absence of righteousness among the witnesses, but because of the nature of testimony itself in its relation to the world, that Primo Levi speaks of a "lacuna" and that Giorgio Agamben uses this notion to construct the paradox of the impossibility of witnessing. According to Levi,

> ...witnesses are by definition survivors and so all, to some degree, enjoyed a privilege...I must repeat: we, the survivors, are not the true witnesses – we are those ... who did not touch the bottom. Those who did so, those who saw the Gorgon, have not returned to tell about it or have returned mute – the submerged, the complete witnesses...[5]

The survivor's ability to witness, and, moreover, to make a judgment, is also questioned by Tzvetan Todorov in his discussion of Primo Levi's project "to understand the German mind", that manifested itself in Levi's aborted attempts to exchange views with Albert Speer (described in *The Drowned and the Saved*.)[6] According to Todorov, this project collapsed under the weight of its unstated goal: "not to understand the others [the Germans] but to convert them." (Ibid., 270)

The witness appeals to the immediate presence of truth in his statement ("I have been there!"), and feels bitterly betrayed when confronted with a dismissive attitude in the listener. An old Russian saying seems to be confirmed in all its cynical realism. A man who lies through his teeth, it says, "lies like an eyewitness". A similar line of reasoning disqualifies the witness as witness, not only in the falsifications of the denier but in the constructions of bona fide theorists as well as, it would seem, in the testimony of the witness himself: the impossibility of surviving *and* witnessing, of surviving *and* judging. The witness is essentially unreliable precisely because there are always a poetics and a politics in the act of bearing witness.

Derrida seems to confirm this view when he chooses as his point of departure a phrase from a poem by Paul Celan, "No-one bears witness for the witness".[7] Indeed, one testimony cannot be affirmed by another in which a second witness attests to the former's capacity or incapacity of bearing witness. Testimony has no meta-level. It is, by definition, no proof, and this is why revisionism, as if in agreement with Primo Levi, rejects survivors' testimony by alleging that

> ... the survivor cannot be a certain and reliable witness to what happened, in particular of the existence for this purpose, the purpose of putting to death, of gas chambers or ovens for cremation – and that therefore he cannot bear witness *for* the only and true witnesses, those who have died, and who by definition can no longer bear witness, confirm or disprove the testimony of another. (200–1)

What, then, is the meaning of Celan's "no one bears witness for the witness", if we refuse to hold this "revisionist thesis to be fundamentally indestructible or incontestable" (ibid., 202)? Derrida proposes an affirmation of the problematic, paradoxical nature of witnessing and testimony – and a warning about the perversity that allows us to disregard its complexity. Testimony is not information, and witnessing is not a speech act that produces knowledge. By asserting this thesis repeatedly, Derrida seems to defeat the witness himself and the latter's claim to the immediate truth of the testimony ("I have been there"). Where does his affirmative gesture actually lead us?

Derrida proceeds from the hypothesis that "all responsible witnessing involves a poetic experience of language" (ibid., 181). Two components of this hypothesis require discussion. Firstly, what is "a poetic experience of language"? And, secondly, what is "responsible witnessing"? To answer the first question, Derrida defines "poetic experience" as a constellation of three singularities: "a *singular* act, concerning a *singular* event and engaging in a *unique*, and thus inventive, relationship to language" (199, emphasis added). Thus, testimony as a speech act is determined by a triple irreproducibility: the singularity of the event means that there is no collective experience or memory of it, hence no sharing, and hence no "witnessing for the witness". Whether it produces a poem or a piece of undecipherable traumatized speech, the relation between language and singular experience is also unique. "Responsible witnessing", on the other hand, presupposes the presence of politics – but how, in this case, does it relate to truth? Should truth be entrusted to a traumatized, possibly fabricating narrator?

As if to confirm "the indestructibility of the revisionist thesis", Derrida questions the direct relationship between witnessing and truth, "...whether the concept of witnessing is compatible with a value of certainty, of assurance, and even of knowing as such..." (182) Testimony, he agrees, is not proof. Moreover, the act of bearing witness only makes sense when the witness is testifying to something unprovable because witnessing to what can be proved is not testamony but simple tautology, just as forgiving the forgivable is not forgiveness, as Derrida argues elsewhere. A real act of real forgiveness would be forgiving the unforgivable. Likewise, "...as soon as it is assured as a theoretical proof, a testimony cannot be assured as testimony." (ibid.)

That "bearing witness" is not "proving" is a fact universally acknowledged in legal practice, where testimony can be checked against other testimonies, confirmed or invalidated, accepted or rejected as evidence – evidence that, in turn, may or may not qualify as proof. However, as Carlo Ginzburg insists, the work of the historian is different from that of the judge: even though history was strongly influenced by the imagery of the courtroom, history does not judge, but understands, i.e. collects a different kind of evidence and interprets it in a different way.[8] Revisionism occurs in the general context of "the debate about the status of bearing witness and of survival". For Derrida, these are different modalities of the same phenomenon. One is testifying in the sense of 'being present as a third person in the deal of the two' (Lat. *terstis*, 'third', in the root of *testes*, 'witness'). The other is *superstes*, 'survivor', a figure that connects the reality of now (the moment of bearing witness) with the reality of then (the event testified to); a figure endowed with a double presence, present there and present here at the same time. As *terstis*, he is present to "the dealing of the two", as *superstes,* to the horror of the past, and hence cannot be "objective" and "impartial".

Incidentally, the etymologies of these terms in other languages do not confirm Derrida's Latin etymology, and "language cannot of itself alone ... be guardian or guarantee of a usage." (p. 188) "Bearing witness is not proof" is "an axiom we ought to respect" (ibid.) and not seek to prove. "Witnessing appeals to the act of faith with regard to a speech given under oath, and is therefore itself produced in the space of sworn faith" (ibid.), not in the space of objective knowledge and proof. "I bear witness" means, first of all, "I swear": "I swear that I have seen/heard/touched/felt", "that I have been present". Since testimony is given under oath, perjury is possible, yet perjury only confirms the structure of the situation in which it is committed. Since testimony is the statement of a perception, mistakes made in good faith are also possible. Such are the risks involved in the very situation of bearing witness. The perlocutionary force involved in the production of testimony hinges on the fact that in bearing witness one appeals to the good faith of the addressee. Every statement of witnessing is preceded by a vocative: "*You* have to believe me." The listener can refuse to believe, but, once again, without eliminating the general framework of sworn faith.

But what is believing? The truth of a proof, as well as that of a syllogism, does not require "belief" as a necessity ("you *have to*"). "To believe" can refer to two different acts: namely, an act of faith in which a testimony (or a poem) is effective by virtue of being a signature or a unique attestation of a singular event; or, alternatively, as an intellectual act pertaining to the order of knowledge. "Truth" is similarly ambiguous referring as it does to a non-lie on the one hand, and to justice, i.e., the order of law, on the other. Believing is necessity constructed within the relationship between witness and addressee, the two actors, who in the act of bearing witness, are joined by a sworn contract involving law, faith, and conscience (190–1). Testimony "... must not essentially consist in proving, confirming a knowledge, in assuring a theoretical certainty, a determining judgment. It can only appeal to an act of faith." (191)

For what is conscience? It is "a presence to oneself." (192) No testimony affirming one's presence would qualify as testimony in the space of sworn faith if it did not presuppose the presence of the witness to himself.

> A witness can only invoke having being present at this or that, having tried out or experienced this or that, on condition of being and having being sufficiently present to himself, as such, on condition of claiming, at any rate, to have been sufficiently conscious of himself, sufficiently present to himself, to know what he is talking about. (192)

Thus, "responsible witnessing" is present to its conscience and aware of its own politics and poetics. It is only guaranteed by the witnesses' critical awareness in three modes of attentiveness – of attending, in good faith – to the internal truth of the act of bearing witness: presence to the self, presence to the event, and presence to the listener. Such is the triple condition of answerability:

> In witnessing, presence to oneself, classic condition of responsibility, must be coextensive with presence to something else, with having-being-present to something else, and with presence to the other, for instance to the addressee of the testimony. It is on this condition that the witness can be answerable, responsible, for his testimony, as for the oath by which he commits himself to it and guarantees it. (Ibid.)

"A Past Citable in All of Its Moments"

Thus, indeed, "no one bears witness for the witness" in any sense of "for". Not in the sense of "in favor of", nor in the sense of "in place, or instead of", nor even in the sense of "in front of, before" (199–200). The witness stands alone and is irreplaceable. The necessity of faith – "you *have* to believe me" – is addressed to the listener and obligates him. It is this "you" upon whom the project of bearing witness entirely depends. The truth of the witness, even supported by his triple answerability of conscience (presence to himself), memory (presence to the event), and communication (presence to the addressee), still does not become the truth until the "you" of the listener commits to his part of the contract and responds to the imperative of faith. In this sense, Carlo Ginzburg's opposition between the judge and the historian (and, alongside this, the opposition between the judgment of law and the so-called "judgment of history") ceases to apply. The judge and the historian coincide in the figure of the "you" who, in the act of bearing witness, is of necessity required to believe. In the face of this necessity of faith, such a listener becomes a second-degree witness, attesting as he does to the very act of bearing witness. His position in listening amounts to the same triple answerability as that of the original witness i.e., presence to oneself, to the potential listener, and to the event of witnessing. It is only by their answerability that the judge or the historian can justify their verdicts or claims to understanding. As formulated by Derrida,

> ...the judge, the arbiter, or the addressee have to be *also* witnesses; they do have to be able to testify, in their turn before their consciences or before others, to what they have attended, to what they have been present at, to what they have happened to be in the presence of; the testimony of the witness in the witness box. (200)

The answerability of the addressee, – the "you" involved in the act of sworn faith, an actor in the *sacramentum* of bearing witness – is such that the addressee, even when rejecting the testimony or denying the survivor's right to testify, does not disentangle himself from the framework of relations imposed by the ethical foundations of the act of bearing witness:

> ...he (the addressee, the you. – I.S.) remains a witness even if he contests the first testimony by alleging that, since he has survived, the survivor cannot be a certain and reliable witness to what happened, in particular of the existence for this purpose, a purpose of putting to death, of gas chambers or ovens for cremation – and that therefore he cannot bear witness *for* the only and true witnesses, those who have died, and who by definition can no longer bear witness, confirm or disprove the testimony of another. (200-1)

Thus, even a Holocaust denier is a witness: he can deny the fact of the Holocaust yet cannot extricate himself from the position of being a "you": a second-degree witness in the performance of bearing witness. His is a "you" in bad faith, someone who desecrates the *sacramentum* and whose revisionist claims violate the courtroom oath and cannot be justified to others (just as David Irving failed to justify himself in court in 2000).

By thus eliminating the difference between the judge and the historian, Derrida returns us, on a new level, to Schiller's idea of universal history, *Die Weltgeschichte ist das Weltgericht*, in which *Weltgericht* means 'judgment of the world' both in the sense of the ultimate historical interpretation and in the sense of the Last Judgment. In assigning so prominent a role to the "you" of the addressee – the listener, the arbiter, the judge, the historian – Derrida resolves the paradox of witnessing by relocating history into the sphere of messianic time. In messianic time, all history seeks to achieve what Walter Benjamin referred to as completeness of citability, i.e., a fullness of the past that is granted only to a redeemed humanity.

> The chronicler who narrates events without distinguishing between major and minor ones acts in accord with the following truth: nothing that has ever happened should be regarded as lost to history. Of course, only a redeemed mankind is granted the fullness of its past – which is to say, only for a redeemed mankind has its past become citable in all its moments. Each moment it has lived becomes a *citation à l'ordre du jour*. And that day is Judgment Day.[9]

Citability not only refers to literary quotation but has a legal sense. To cite means 'to summon to appear before a court of law' or 'to refer to or mention as by way of example, proof, or precedent'. To quote Hannah Arendt, "Everyone, everyone should have his day in court"[10], and especially "the anonymous", because, as Benjamin remarks,

> It is more difficult to honor the memory of the anonymous than it is to honor the memory of the famous, the celebrated ... The historical construction is dedicated to the memory of the anonymous ...The eternal lamp is an image of genuine historical existence. It cites what has been – the flame that once was kindled – in perpetuum, giving it ever new sustenance.[11]

Notes

1. In *Revenge of the Aesthetic: The Place of Literature in Theory Today*, ed. Michael P. Clark (Berkeley Los Angeles London: University of California Press, 2000), 179-207.

2. See, for instance http://www.hdot.org/trial for a detailed documentation of the legal process Irving *v.* Lipstadt in 2000. The historian Barbara Lipstadt was accused of libel by David Irving when she described him as a "a dangerous spokesperson" for Holocaust denial. In the verdict, the judge declared that Irving "misrepresented, misconstrued, omitted, mistranslated, misread and applied double standards to the historical evidence in order to achieve his ideological presentation of history." (ibid., accessed May 7th, 2011). Irving was thus defined as an ideologist, in contrast to his own self-identification as a historian.

3. Hannah Arendt, *Eichmann in Jerusalem: A Report on the Banality of Evil* (New York:Penguin Books, 1994 [1963]), 223-4.

4. Though imperfect, witness accounts nevertheless afford redemption, as in the moment of silence that occurs when one witness tells a story about a German sergeant who helped to save his life. These moments of silence "were like a burst of light in the midst of impenetrable, unfathomable darkness" (ibid., p. 231).

5. Primo Levi, in *The Drowned and the Saved*, quoted in Giorgio Agamben, *Remnants of Auschwitz: The Witness and the Archive* (New York:Zone Books, 2008), 33-4. Agamben's detailed discussion of Levi's notions of complete vs. incomplete witnessing (op. cit., 15-40) confirms Derrida's idea about its politics and poetics: the impossibility of ("complete") witnessing is what makes possible a poem (as with the poem by Celan which Derrida analyzes in this essay). Unfortunately, however, Agamben's reasoning does not seem to be fully convincing in the eyes of the survivor who wants her memory to be, not exclusively encrypted in "obscure writing" (Levi's description of Celan), but narrated and ethically reflected in plain words. In a seminar recently, I witnessed just such a discussion concerning Agamben's concept of the *Muselmann* in which one participant, a former inmate of Auschwitz, expressed dissatisfaction with Agamben's thesis about the impossibility of witnessing. The seminar failed to provide an answer to her question, "What am I, a former *Muselmann*, to do?"

6. Tzvetan Todorov, *Facing the Extreme: Moral Life in the Concentration Camps* (New York : An Owl Book, 1996), 268-271.

7. Paul Celan, *Aschenglorie,* quoted in the same essay by Derrida. Even though both the poem and Derrida's reading of it deserve a special discussion, I have set them aside in order to concentrate on Derrida's account of the structure of witnessing as a performative act.

8. Carlo Ginzburg, *The Judge and the Historian: Marginal Notes on the Late-Twentieth-Century Miscarriage of Justice* (London and New York : Verso., 2002), 12-18.

9. Walter Benjamin, "On the Concept of History" in *Selected Writings. Volume 4. 1938-1940* (Cambridge, Mass. and London, England : The Belknap Press of Harvard University Press, 2003 (1940), 390.

10. Hannah Arendt, *Eichmann in Jerusalem*, 228.

11. Walter Benjamin, "Paralipomena to "On the Concept of History"", ibid., p. 406-7. The "eternal lamp" is a citation from Exodus 27:20, on the need to maintain a lamp at all times in a sanctuary as a sign of God's presence.

Event, Crack-up and Line of Flight – Deleuze Reading Fitzgerald

FREDRIKA SPINDLER

Through a sequence of influential works on philosophy, cinema, art, and literature from the early 1960s to the 1990s, Gilles Deleuze contributed to the rethinking of, among other things, time and different temporalities. This is true in particular of how he develops the concept of the event, *l'événement*. In this article, I will explore two variations of the event – as "crack" (*fêlure*) and as "line of flight" (*ligne de fuite*) – through the particular lens of Deleuze's interpretations of F. Scott Fitzgerald, in order to establish their close but qualitatively different values and implications. In both processes, the event signals change and becoming, thus involving a loss of ground and of identity. But where the crack inevitably implies a disintegration of sense, the line of flight opens toward a possible, albeit not necessary, becoming-other. At stake, therefore, is our understanding of the differential element that allows the line of flight to become a value of life.

At the core of Deleuze's philosophy of the event, there is his beautiful reading of F. Scott Fitzgerald. It is not difficult to understand what appeals to Deleuze in Fitzgerald's work: the rapidity and the elegance, the nomadism and the perpetual high-speed immobility, but also, first and foremost, the way Fitzgerald always dwells in the heart of the paradox joining strength and fragility, vitality and decline, lightness and gravity, creation and destruction. In Fitzgerald, Deleuze finds both an affirmation of the tragic and the absolute absence of resentment, and loss as the non-negotiable condition of all that pretends to be life. All these particularities characterize an art of writing that is more preoccupied with painting than with telling a story. Reading Fitzgerald, Deleuze could not help but find the themes on which he himself feeds: the exploration of surfaces, deviating trajectories, disjunctive becomings and infinite conjunctions, leakages and transformations, alienation as principle of life and death, and, always, the battle of a body embracing the Great health at the cost of its own. In *The Logic of Sense*, Deleuze develops the question of the event, its temporality and, most of all, its quality: its value, but also its charge. In the junction with Fitzgerald, the event finds its fatal characteristic against the backdrop of the creative but destructive abuse constituted by alcoholism, or as Deleuze would express it: the event as drama, war, plague, death. When Deleuze, together with Guattari, again writes on Fitzgerald in *A Thousand Plateaus*, this very charge or value of the event makes possible a turning-point, a leaving of itself, something that is also explored as "deterritorialization" or "counter-effectuation". Thus it is rendered not only less fatal in the deadly sense, but also, and above all, as constitutive of all real creation, of an opening in becoming toward the infinite. In the tension between these two versions of the Deleuzean event, mediated through Fitzgerald, we thus find a profound ambiguity underlying each ingredient that goes into it: surface and its depth, loss of identity and the becoming-other/multiple, the twofold relation between crack and perfection, between break-up and continuation.

The event as a crack-up

In *The Logic of Sense*, in the 22nd series, "Porcelain and Volcano", Deleuze pursues his development of the notion of the event by referring to Fitzgerald's autobiographical essay *The Crack-Up,* in which the author tries to understand how he lost himself. What initially captures Deleuze's interest is precisely the very first sentence of the essay in question, where Fitzgerald states that all life is a process of breaking down, *of course*. This *of course* is not to be taken in a defeatist or resigned sense, but rather as a statement of fact. What is at stake here is not, as one might think, the inevitable relation between life and death in general, but rather, a process inscribed into the very activity of living. The great events of our life, the blows and the hazards that strike us – war, crisis, the loss of loved ones, etc – constitute but one side of a process, of which the other is far more insidious. Coming from the inside, things happen, so discreetly that they might not even be noticed, and thanks to their invisibility and impalpability, they are entirely free to pursue their destroying activity, the breaking down. When one finally perceives what is going on, it is only through the effects of the traces that these events have left behind, in other words, when it is always already too late. Echoing Fitzgerald, Deleuze states that what shatters us in the end are never the great accidents that strike us: "all these noisy accidents already have their outright effects; and they would not be sufficient in themselves had they not dug their way down to something of a wholly different nature which, on the contrary, they reveal only at a distance and when it's too late, – the silent crack."[1] Hence, the crack becomes that in us which constitutes the failure, loss and decay, the open yet hidden wound where the work of destruction is pursued without our knowing it. Yet the crack is not internal, as if in contrast to that which comes from the outside, being rather that which dwells and operates on the surface: it is "it is imperceptible, incorporeal, and ideational".[2] Situated at the frontier, constituting it even, the crack is the backdrop against which the great events play out, and through which they effectuate themselves. All the while it constitutes and hollows out the interstices through which the internal events effectuate and propagate themselves towards the exterior. The crack, thus understood, is at the same time that on which things occur, and that which allows them to make sense. Moreover, it is that which, under the three-fold pressure of interior, exterior and of the surface, will eventually crack up once and for all: "in the shattering and bursting of the end [...] the entire play of the crack has become incarnated in the depth of the body, at the same time that the labor of the inside and the outside has widened the edges."[3]

In Fitzgerald's viewpoint, it is not death that is at stake. Death, on the contrary, would only constitute the most banal and final aspect of the process of breaking down in which all life is *of course* engaged. More delicately, and more dramatically in a sense, what is at stake is a transformation – subtle but from which no return is possible – through which one becomes other, without landmarks or reference points, void of the past as well as of any future. The desolation has a Biblical resonance, hence Fitzgerald quotes Matthew: "Ye are the salt of the earth. But if the salt hath lost its savor, wherewith shall it be salted?" (ch 5 v 13).[4] The earth is without salt and all savor is gone; one is alive but without any of the qualifications that so far defined life. Fitzgerald, realizing that he is cracked, can only diagnose himself as no longer being a man, only a writer: neither a subject nor a person, but at best a dog, correct, but devoid of any vitality or enthusiasm. "Life will never be very pleasant again, and the sign Cave Canem is hung permanently just above my door. I will try to be a correct animal though, and if you throw me a bone with enough meat on it I may even try to lick your hand."[5]

This fate is not only Fitzgerald's own, retraced in this text as in many others – *Early success*, *Echoes of the Jazz Age* and *My Lost City* – but most of all that of all his characters. The same point of no return is reached, irretrievably, by the beautiful Southern Belle, who one day realizes that the promise of love held out by life will never have been kept (*The Last of the Belles*); by the rich and infinitely promising young man who realizes that nothing has been accomplished, nor ever will be (*The Rich Boy*); in the inevitable relapse of the converted drinker, cancelling suddenly the conversion for ever (*Babylon Revisited*); and of course the complete demolition of *The Great Gatsby*.[6] All are seized, caught up by their crack, and it dawns upon them as if they had just woken up after a bad drinking binge: the moment is gone and will never come back – and through the decline of the past one is also dispossessed of the future. Indeed, all Fitzgerald's work explores the nuances of this theme, depicting decline that is at the same time its realization, always three steps behind by the one who is subjected to it. In the novels this theme is first outlined as the subtle and hallucinatory advent of the little man in *This Side of Paradise*, with the nightmarish vision of his curling toes, anticipating the slow curve of going down. This is marvelously perfected later in the tragic destiny of Dick Diver, dissolving before disappearing in *Tender is the Night*. And, like all his characters, the genius of Fitzgerald drinks, literally, at the source of that which constitutes also his failure; drinks his brilliance until it has been consumed, dried out, run dry.

Deleuze's concern is not just to state that Fitzgerald appears to be struck by the same affliction as that of his characters, alter egos transformed into pure and luminous art, falling stars which cannot be rescued, caught or salvaged. As Deleuze carefully underlines the distinction in nature between internal or external accidents, on the one hand,

and, on the other hand, those that really make sense in the end, he also notes that this distinction is, in fact, impossible to maintain. No matter how justified, it is always made by the observer, the theoretician, the "abstract thinker" whose concern is precisely to keep the two phenomena at a distance.[7] It seeks not to have the crack coincide with the blows, not to be subjected to the irretrievable falling-apart, the irreparable loss of the self and the world, to be shattered and suddenly find oneself having become a dog. If it is true, as Deleuze argues, that the one condition for the creation of a work of art or of a thought is absolute risk, if a thought can be conceived only at the limit of what is thinkable, then how could it be possible for the crack at a certain moment *not* to incarnate itself in the depths of a body, thereby shattering it? Indeed, he says, "if there is a crack at the surface, how can we prevent deep life from becoming a demolition job and prevent it from becoming it as a matter 'of course'?"[8]. This 'of course', pronounced with all the elegance and the nonchalance of a Fitzgerald who in his own view has already gone down, is what attracts Deleuze, whose entire thought affirms its necessity all while insisting, relentlessly, also on the fact that the value of "of course" always has to be subjected to yet another throw of dice making it possible to go beyond the breaking up. It is necessary that the breaking up is transfigured into something else, since "the crack is nothing if it does not compromise the body, but it does not cease being and having a value when it intertwines its line with the other line, inside the body."[9]

How, then, are we to think the crack in order for it to become something else than destruction; how are we to think the event in order for it to not be necessarily fatal, and to transform instead into life? The term employed by Deleuze for this transformation is "counter-effectuation", allowing the event to break loose from itself as it is incarnated. Perhaps this is the movement suggested by Fitzgerald when he writes of himself in *The Crack-Up*, of his becoming-writer, becoming-dog, as in fact signifying a radical becoming-other?

From crack to line of flight

In the short text concerned with Fitzgerald in *A Thousand Plateaus*, Deleuze and Guattari return to the question by introducing some new distinctions. The event, here understood as the impalpable form of "what happened?", must be understood and valued, no longer in relation to the interacting trinity of interior/exterior/surface, but as what is at play in the intertwining of three kinds of lines, lines recalled by Fitzgerald himself in the same short story, according to Deleuze, "traversing us and composing 'a life'."[10] There is the line of hard or molar segments, composed of binary, institutional and identitarian distinctions, working as instruments of control, segmenting the world into men or women, rich or poor, working or idle, but also, from an identity-shaping point of view, as being part of a couple (or not), being successful (or not), being young (or no longer). Life as a process of breaking down *of course*, say Deleuze and Guattari, consists in the inevitable hardening of this segmentarity, as we grow older, rendering each segment more and more terse and clear-cut. Hence the blows and fates that we are stricken by.

The second line, molecular and supple, is now where micro-cracks take place, far from the noisy events. Rather than concerning intimate structures contrasted to those more public or even relating to states and institutions, this line is traced as slight changes of perspective, subtle variations of colors and light, as the gradual event of sunset, resulting in dark night even before one has wholly realized its process. Here, all of a sudden, nothing has necessarily changed, and yet the value of the whole has changed, and the game is no longer the same as before: "In truth, nothing assignable or perceptible: molecular changes, redistributions of desire such that when something occurs, the self that awaited it is already dead, or the one that would await it has not yet arrived."[11] Yet this crack, fatal as it might seem, no longer necessarily implies the final break-up as was the case previously. As Fitzgerald remarks, it can probably still be about another possible redistribution: although irreparable and absolute as a loss of self and of the world, the crack still makes possible an existing in the world. Alive, but as *another* life – this is the formula of the micro-crack.

It is however the third line that makes all the difference. It marks an absolute break-up, a mad tangent, and a cancellation of the hard as well as of the supple segments, but without substituting them with something else. It is a line of flight through which all structure and identity have been transformed into an unknown. For Deleuze this final line is definitely the most decisive. If the first operates by the brutality of an either-or, the second, through shifts and minor displacements, the third is the only one that allows for sense to be constituted at the cost of previous sense. It marks a line of creation and of sense, of radical loss in the sense that what is lost does no longer even exists as memory or past. At the same time Deleuze underlines repeatedly that nothing predestines it to produce sense *necessarily*, at least not in a "constructive" sense. To evaluate it, we need to know from what it is breaking loose, from what it deterritorializes itself and to what it gives birth, and thus reterritorializes itself. When understood in this way it is clear why it cannot be considered apart from the two others, and why all three lines co-determine each other's value. Or perhaps the question would rather be how is value, or that which has value, conceived? Once again, it appears that we are walking a very thin line. On the one hand, the line of flight *makes* sense, no matter whether this sense is constructive or not, precisely because it sweeps away any precedent sense. On the other hand, as Deleuze repeatedly remarks, its value is much more measured in relation to what it is yet capable of generating, continuing, transforming or transfiguring: a blown-up brain or body no longer makes sense; nor does a life destroyed by alcohol. The line of flight must, and this should come as no surprise, be weighed on a Nietzschean scale, capable of determining the nature of the forces at play.

What, then, are the elements pertaining to Fitzgerald's line of flight? In *The Crack-Up*, there are, indeed, three movements, distinct yet linked together. If the first one consisted in how he deals with vitality and hope in relation to the accidents that do occur, the second is expressed in depression and burn-out, as void, solitude, cracks and fragility. The third, departing as a tangent from the two others, accomplishes the break and the deterritorialization. Fitzgerald is no longer neither empty nor alone, since he has obliterated the very subject that could be subjected to void and solitude. Dressed in the costume of Everybody, wearing Everybody's smile and even his vocal tonality, shattered (but alive), he is but Nobody. Yet, emptied of affection, he is still full of affectivity whenever his state is that of "qualified unhappiness". One might think that the line of flight didn't lead anywhere and that it has been arrested, if it wasn't for the fact that he continues to write, at least for a while.

Line of flight, deterritorialisation, reterritorialisation

To conclude, let me indicate how the tension between the crack and the line of flight operates in one of Fitzgerald's major novels, *Tender is the Night*. The story, like most of those of Fitzgerald's, is easily summarized. Narrated in the present tense, but nourished by a past that is equally present, it concerns the ongoing history of gilded couple Nicole and Dick Diver. He is a non-practicing psychiatrist, she a very rich heiress, the couple drifting between the French Riviera, Paris, and the Swiss Alps. Together, they adopt people, subjecting them to the magical talents of Dick, who "works them over" in order to make them, at least for a moment, as golden, lustrous and sparkling as their creator. In these transformations, the subjects-objects find themselves transfigured, enveloped by a process whose *acmé* comes about as the blossoming of a flower in which all that can be perceived is a change of quality that has already occurred. At one of the famous dinners at the Divers, it is in this way that the world suddenly gains more relief: "[...] The two Divers began suddenly to warm and glow and expand, as if to make up to their guests, already so subtly assured of their importance, so flattered with politeness, for anything they might still miss from that country well left behind. Just for a moment they seemed to speak to every one at the table, singly and together, assuring them of their friendliness, their affection. And for a moment the faces turned up toward them were like the faces of poor children at a Christmas tree. Then abruptly the table broke up – the moment when the guests had been daringly lifted above conviviality into the rarer atmosphere of sentiment was over before it could be irreverently breathed, before they had half realized it was there."[12] Discreet but definitive, this movement is undoubtedly that of supple segmentarity. But when the decline becomes noticeable, it was in fact always already there. Behind Nicole's beauty, there is her psychiatric condition; behind Dick's human genius the lack of all anchorage and foundation. Co-dependent, the one determining the other, the couple starts to sink, and in their sinking, they bring down a whole world.

Two lines are traced here, different and clear-cut, co-determining each other, no doubt, but deviating from each other in the end. In this couple, it is the strong element that will effectuate the radical fall. Dick, whose qualities suddenly start to escape and leak away from him, thereby causing him not only to lose the power to define Nicole but also his own power of transfiguration, can do nothing but flee in the literal sense. Losing his vitality, even his process of breaking down ceases to be spectacular. As he disappears, he does so without leaving any trace. If ever there was a line of flight, it has ended up turning on itself. As Deleuze says, it's time to die. But Nicole, the weak element – wearing her condition as her secret, fighting against all the ways in which her condition, over and over again, manages to seep out, leaking through the cracks and fissures – takes off in another direction. Leaving Dick even before he has disappeared (yet, however, he already had), she literally loses her identity, loses her face, but also her secret. Alone, dead to her past, but radically new: a line of flight of which the reterritorialisation creates a sense hard as a diamond, but bereft of all devastation. By all its micro-political shifts – in the relationship of love, in the displacement of the elements of dependency and autonomy, in the definition of beauty and the understanding of health, this line responds to all the criteria of the real line of flight, reterritorializing itself on nothing but the deterritorialisation itself.

Notes

1. Gilles Deleuze, *The Logic of Sense* (hereafter, LS), (transl. M. Lester), London/New York: Continuum 2004, 176.
2. LS, 177.
3. LS, 177.
4. F. Scott Fitzgerald, *The Crack-Up, with other pieces and stories*, (hereafter, CU) London: Penguin Books 1988, 45.
5. CU, 56.
6. LS, 178.
7. LS, 178.
8. LS, 182.
9. Gilles Deleuze and Félix Guattari, *A Thousand Plateaus* (hereafter, TP), (transl. B. Massumi), Minneapolis/London: University of Minnesota Press 2005, 200.
10. TP, 198–199.
11. F. Scott Fitzgerald, *Tender is the Night*, London: Penguin Books 1986, 44.

5. Rewriting Time

Rethinking the Industrial Revolution and the Rise of the West: Historical Contingencies and the Global Prerequisites of Modern Technology

ALF HORNBORG

In this essay I want to explore the role of the concept of "technology" in the way we write world history. Over the past two decades, several persuasive critiques of Eurocentric narratives, which explain the "rise of the West" in terms of uniquely European conditions, have offered perspectives emphasizing the global conjunctures and contingencies which provided opportunities for European expansion.[1] The latter mode of writing world history is one that most anthropologists like myself would endorse, because it relativizes cultural historiographies and deconstructs the essentialist legacy of Eurocentrism which can be traced back to colonial ideologies and even racism. In fact, my agreement with this shift in perspective extends to the point that I suspect it of not having been radical enough. In scrutinizing the arguments challenging Eurocentrism, I have found that the aspect of Western cosmology most resistant to deconstruction is the concept of "technology". I thus want to focus this brief discussion on the way technology is treated in the seminal works of James M. Blaut, Andre Gunder Frank, and Kenneth Pomeranz.

Scornfully, James Blaut and Andre Gunder Frank review the modern history of Eurocentric historiography, from Adam Smith, Karl Marx, and Max Weber, to Lynn White, Robert Brenner, and Eric Jones. Their call for a shift of perspective, which builds on the work of earlier critics such as Eric Williams, Janet Abu-Lughod, and Edward Said, is incontrovertible. The economic and technological expansion of Europe in the nineteenth century cannot be explained in terms of conditions or characteristics specific to Europe, whether cultural or environmental. Such accounts, which refer to putatively "European" attributes such as "rationality" or "inventiveness", commit the error of essentializing what appear to be geographically circumscribed developments as local (i.e., national or continental) accomplishments, rather than recognizing their emergence as conditioned by global processes. The latter recognition is fundamental to world-system analyses and sufficiently uncontroversial not to require recapitulation here. Instead, we shall look more closely at the specific role of "technology" in these non-Eurocentric accounts. Because the so-called "Industrial Revolution" is a pivotal phenomenon in these deliberations, any scrutiny of mainstream understandings of technology has significance. Even if non-Eurocentric historiographers have managed to extricate themselves from discursive assumptions about European superiority, I shall argue, they have arguably not succeeded in dispensing with a definition of "technological progress" that is no less characteristic of the modernist worldview.[2] The very materiality of technological superiority evidently makes its deconstruction extremely difficult.

The understanding that artefacts such as commodities are in some sense "social" goes back at least as far as Karl Marx, who observed that relations between people in capitalist society assume the appearance of relations between things. It is thus paradoxical that the notion of "technological progress", which holds that technological objects can be arranged along a normative scale of generalized improvement, continues to constrain mainstream discourse on development and history. We know that the most "advanced" technologies may have disastrous social, political, or ecological implications at the global level – not least in terms of shifting burdens to other populations – yet only rarely do we allow such insights to contaminate our assumptions about "technological progress". Rather than view modern, capitalist technology as a specific social strategy for accumulating power through the appropriation of (human) time and (natural) space from other people – i.e., as a strategy of elite *capacitation* – technology itself tends to be viewed as exempt from political critique.[3] This is particularly evident in some Marxist discourse, which acknowledges that machinery represents the exploitative accumulation of appropriated labour time even while glorifying that same technology as a path to global proletarian emancipation. A similar contradiction pervades the discourse on ecological sustainability, which generally assumes that the environmental degradation caused by technology will be alleviated by further "technological progress". I hope to illustrate how even non-Eurocentric world-system analysts, while earnestly struggling to dethrone Europe and the "West" as intrinsically generative of "technological progress", tend to encounter difficulties when they reframe such progress in terms of global power-relations.

The general thesis on technology pursued by Blaut, Frank, and Pomeranz is that by the late eighteenth century Europeans were no more inventive than people in other core areas of the Old World, such as China or India, and that technologies previously attributed to Europeans were generally invented elsewhere. While this is, of course, a valid way of countering the opposing claims of Eurocentric historians of technology such as Lynn White, Eric Jones, and David Landes, arguments over the priority of inventions do not address the more fundamental question of what technology *is*. Although Blaut and Frank only touch upon this latter issue briefly, their intuitions about the world-systemic nature of modern technology deserve to be elaborated. Rather than viewing technological capacity as an essentialized attribute of a given population, such an elaboration entails understanding the specific social application of a technology, as a kind of "field phenomenon" emerging at certain points in the global system, i.e. as an expression of processes involving the system as a whole.

Blaut's main point seems to be that technological inventiveness is not a specifically European feature that can be traced back to the Middle Ages. In an argument directed mainly at the work of Lynn White, Blaut lists allegedly "European", pre-industrial inventions that in fact derived from – or were, at least, developed to an equal stage – elsewhere: iron-working (Middle East, West Africa); ploughs (Middle East, China); the horse-collar (Eurasia); textile production (China); mechanical clocks (China); ship-building (China); cannons (China); printing with movable metal type (Korea); and so on.[4] Blaut concludes: "It was only after 1492, with its utterly revolutionary consequences, that European technology acquired the beginning of an edge over Asian and African."[5] In other words, this technological "edge" only began to crystallize as a consequence of the consolidation of the modern world-system.

Andre Gunder Frank reaches exactly the same conclusion.[6] Frank observes that technological developments in Europe had very little to do with a European propensity for science: indeed, technology contributed more to the advancement of science than the reverse.[7] Like Blaut, he goes on to list a number of technologies in which early modern Europe, if anything, lagged behind other core areas of the Old World: ship-building, printing, textile production, metallurgy, overland transportation, etc. Frank takes an important step toward de-essentializing technological capacity when he notes that "armaments technology was rapidly diffused to *anyone in a position to pay for it*" (italics added).[8] For Frank, the expansion of Europe was founded on accidents of geography and history that gave it access to the New World, particularly its silver, which (temporarily) shifted the balance of global economic power from East to West. For our present purposes, his most important conclusion is that "there was no *European* technology!"[9] Technological inventions are not attributes of specific populations, but capabilities that are rapidly adopted by any population that can afford them. "That is", he continues, "technological development was a *world economic process*, which took place in and because of the structure of the world economy/system itself." This is the closest that any world-systems historian has come to radically reconceptualizing technology as a total socio-ecological phenomenon.

Like Blaut and Frank, Pomeranz[10] shows that Europe in 1750 was not "technologically superior" to China, India, or Japan, for instance, and was struggling to "catch up" with these regions in fields such as agriculture, textile production, porcelain, medicine, sanitation, and even iron-making.[11] The relevant question is why Europe by the nineteenth century had absorbed what Pomeranz refers to as the "best available technologies" developed elsewhere in the world. There was obviously something about this particular geographical region at this point in time that encouraged the adoption and refinement of mechanical devices capable of increasing production per invested unit of domestic labour and land. If this was the essence of the Industrial Revolution, a world-systemic perspective should prompt us to ask not only whence these inventions derived but, more importantly, what were the global consequences of the European strategies for saving labour and land to which they were applied. Given their implications for populations and ecosystems in Africa, Asia, and the Americas, we may need to nuance our definition of "technological progress". Were Europe's industrial technologies in the nineteenth century "best," not only for Europe but for the world as a whole? Inevitably, the answer will be different in a so-called "full world" in which technological rationality arguably can no longer be geared to the economic success of nations competing ruthlessly for market shares, and should reflect a concern with managing finite resources in order to allow humanity to live sustainably on a single planet.

Although it has often been argued that the rationale of the Industrial Revolution was the application of labour-saving innovations, which enabled Europe to oust competitors such as the Indian textile industry, Pomeranz[12] argues that the most important innovations were in fact *land*-saving ones. The so-called "progress" or "development" of the Industrial Revolution was prompted by the cul-de-sac of ecological constraints that England faced, together with other populous core areas of the Old World in the eighteenth century, but that it was able, uniquely, to transcend by means of access to the Americas and domestic coal deposits. In displacing their environmental demands onto other continents and into the future,[13] industrialized societies have from the start pursued a radically different strategy for dealing with the "land constraint" than, say, that of eighteenth-century China. Although Pomeranz[14] characterizes this strategy as "abolishing" the land constraint, the "ecological relief" that Europe gained through the Industrial Revolution occurred at the expense of other populations, ecosystems, and future generations.[15]

Pomeranz[16] concedes that "the application of coal and steam power to all sorts of processes eventually led to enormous labour savings", but proposes that "(i)f the makers of the Industrial Revolution were primarily economizing on expensive labour, they were unaware of it." Rather, they were struggling with the "bottleneck" represented by constraints on the expansion of textile production. Pomeranz[17] observes that "it is unlikely that the necessary land to relieve this bottleneck could have been found in Europe." The fibre for textiles demanded land, and "competition for land among Malthus's four necessities

– food, fuel, fibre, and building materials – was growing ever more intense in much of eighteenth-century Europe".[18] Soil degradation, deforestation, and overgrazing in western Europe at this time brought erosion, dust storms, declining yields, waterlogging, acidification, and adverse climate change. Even if such ecological constraints were common to other core areas in the Old World, which all imported land-intensive commodities in exchange for manufactures (particularly textiles), Europe was able to use the New World and the Atlantic slave trade to turn "manufactured goods created without much use of British land...into ever-increasing amounts of land-intensive food and fiber (and later timber) at reasonable (and even falling) prices".[19] The Americas offered Europe not only vast areas of conveniently depopulated land but also huge quantities of silver with which to purchase additional "ecological relief" from the rest of the Old World.[20]

Pomeranz[21] provides tangible measures of how, in various ways, the Industrial Revolution brought "ecological relief" to nineteenth-century Britain. Citing Mintz,[22] he observes that replacing the calories from sugar consumed in the United Kingdom in 1831 with food energy from domestic harvests would have required up to 2.6 million acres of average-yield English farmland. Farming the sheep to replace the cotton fibers imported in 1830 would have required over 23 million acres of pasture and hay, a figure which by itself "surpasses Britain's total crop and pasture land combined."[23] Pomeranz calculates that Baltic and American timber imports in the early nineteenth century substituted for the output of over 1.6 million acres of British woodland, and he cites E.A. Wrigley's calculation that, as early as 1815, England's annual consumption of energy from coal was equivalent to at least 15 million acres of woodland.[24] These land-saving strategies grew tremendously in significance through the nineteenth century. Between 1815 and 1900, Britain's sugar imports increased eleven-fold, its coal output fourteen-fold, and its cotton imports "a stunning twenty-fold".[25] What these three commodities alone meant in terms of millions of acres of "ecological relief" is easily estimated,[26] but over the same period Britain also imported huge quantities of American grain, beef, timber, and other land-intensive products.

Pomeranz[27] concludes: "it seems likely that the exploitation of the New World, and of the Africans taken there to work, mattered in many ways above and beyond those reflected in our ghost acreage figures. Taking all the indices together, it seems likely that this exploitation did more to differentiate western Europe from other Old World cores than any of the supposed advantages over these other regions generated by...institutions within Europe." In other words, "forces outside the market and conjunctures beyond Europe deserve a central place in explaining why western Europe's otherwise largely unexceptional core achieved unique breakthroughs and wound up as the privileged center of the nineteenth century's new world economy."[28]

The reconceptualization of world history since the sixteenth century proposed by Blaut, Frank, and Pomeranz has implications far beyond the abandonment of Euro-exceptionalism. Not only must Europe and the "West" be dethroned as intrinsically generative of economic growth, modern technology, and civilization, these phenomena must in themselves be recognized as contingent on specific global constellations of asymmetric resource flows and power relations. In other words, not only was the "rise of the West" a geographical coincidence of world history – Europe's location as middleman between the Old and New Worlds – but its economic, technological, and military *means* of expansion, generally viewed as European "inventions" and as contributions to the rest of humanity, were products of global conjunctures and processes of accumulation that coalesced after the articulation of the Old and New Worlds. Thus the very existence of industrial technology has been a global phenomenon from the very start, intertwining political, socio-economic, and environmental histories in complex and inequitable ways. If historical hindsight can help to clarify this often neglected fact, the next challenge must be to spell out its ramifications for our perceptions of economic growth and technological progress *today*. This chapter has argued that technology is not simply a relation between humans and their natural environment but, more fundamentally, a way of organizing global human society. To reconceptualize in this way the material artefacts that surround us – as crystallized relations of unequal exchange – would be to pursue a fundamentally Marxian understanding of capital accumulation beyond the Cartesian boundaries that have hitherto exempted technology from political critique.

Notes

1. James M. Blaut, *The Colonizer's Model of the World: Geographical Diffusionism and Eurocentric History* (New York: The Guilford Press, 1993); James M. Blaut, *Eight Eurocentric Historians* (New York: The Guilford Press, 2000); Andre Gunder Frank, *ReOrient: Global Economy in the Asian Age* (Berkeley: University of California Press, 1998); Kenneth Pomeranz, *The Great Divergence: China, Europe, and the Making of the Modern World Economy* (Princeton: Princeton University Press, 2000).

2. Michael Adas, *Machines as the Measure of Men: Science, Technology, and Ideologies of Western Dominance* (Ithaca: Cornell University Press, 1989); Michael Adas, *Dominance by Design: Technological Imperatives and America's Civilizing Mission* (Cambridge, Mass.: The Belknap Press of Harvard University Press, 2006); Ben Marsden and Crosbie Smith, *Engineering Empires: A Cultural History of Technology in Nineteenth-Century Britain* (Houndmills: Palgrave, 2005); Robert Friedel, *A Culture of Improvement: Technology and the Western Millennium* (Cambridge, Mass.: MIT Press, 2007); Daniel Headrick, *Power over Peoples: Technology, Environments, and Western Imperialism, 1400 to the Present* (Princeton: Princeton University Press, 2010).

3. Alf Hornborg, *The Power of the Machine: Global Inequalities of Economy, Technology, and Environment* (Walnut Creek: AltaMira Press, 2001); Alf Hornborg, *Global Ecology and Unequal Exchange: Fetishism in a Zero-Sum World* (London: Routledge, 2011).

4. Blaut, *Eight Eurocentric*, 31–38.
5. Blaut, *Colonizer's Model*, 115.
6. Frank, *ReOrient*.
7. Frank, *ReOrient*, 191.
8. Frank, *ReOrient*, 197.
9. Frank, *ReOrient*, 204.
10. Pomeranz, *Great Divergence*, 43–48.

11. In fact, even steam engines "of a sort" had been developed by non-European societies, including China, before the eighteenth century; Pomeranz, *Great Divergence*, 61–62.

12. Pomeranz, *Great Divergence*, 49–68.

13. Combustion of fossil fuels not only relies on "ghost acreages" of the distant past, it reduces future access to such fuels and generates future problems with carbon dioxide emissions, ocean acidification, and climate change.

14. Pomeranz, *Great Divergence*, 264.
15. Hornborg, *Global Ecology*.
16. Pomeranz, *Great Divergence*, 52.
17. Pomeranz, *Great Divergence*, 55.
18. Pomeranz, *Great Divergence*, 56.
19. Pomeranz, *Great Divergence*, 242–3, 269.

20. Pomeranz, *Great Divergence*, 274.

21. Pomeranz, *Great Divergence*, 274-8, 313-15.

22. Sidney Mintz, *Sweetness and Power: The Place of Sugar in Modern History* (New York: Penguin, 1985).

23. The total arable land of Britain at this time was roughly 17 million acres (Pomeranz, *Great Divergence*, 275).

24. Pomeranz, *Great Divergence*, 59. Pomeranz (ibid., 276, n.50) believes that 21 million "ghost acres" would be a more correct figure.

25. Pomeranz, *Great Divergence*, 283-4.

26. Building on figures provided by Pomeranz (*Great* Divergence, 274-8, 313-15), we can conclude that the "ghost acreages" available to Britain in the year 1900 through imports of sugar and cotton alone amounted to over 195 million acres. In the same year, the combustion of coal would have equaled 210 million acres of woodland. In 1900, these three commodities combined thus represented 405 million acres of ecologically productive land. The total land surface of Great Britain is about 59 million acres.

27. Pomeranz, *Great Divergence*, 282-3.

28. Pomeranz, *Great Divergence*, 297.

Enlightened Prejudices: Anti-Jewish Tropes in Modern Philosophy

JAYNE SVENUNGSSON

In November 1894, Alfred Dreyfus, a young artillery officer of Jewish descent, was convicted for military treason against the French state. When in 1896 evidence came to light that proved Dreyfus innocent, high-ranking officials in the military tried to suppress the new information. The event evolved into a major political scandal which divided French society into Dreyfusards and anti-Dreyfusards. Thanks to the involvement of a number of leading liberal intellectuals, all the accusations were finally shown to be false and Dreyfus was exonerated and reinstated in the French army.

In history books in Europe, the Dreyfus Affair is presented as one of the defining moments of the Enlightenment legacy: a prime example of how rationality, tolerance, and universal ideals of justice finally conquered prejudice, intolerance, and nationalist sectarianism. Indeed, this portrait of the Dreyfus Affair is a portrait of how, in one particular case, modern liberal ideals prevailed against ideological prejudice. It is also, however, part of a larger ideological narrative which recounts how modern Europe came into being through a process of successive universalization of ideals such as freedom, equality, and fraternity.

In the wake of the atrocities of the twentieth century, this standard account of the Enlightenment, as a warranty of universal ideals of rationality and morality, has been challenged from a number of different angles. As long ago as 1947, Theodor Adorno and Max Horkheimer advanced the bold thesis that fascist and Nazi barbarity was, in fact, the dialectical other of the Enlightenment project.[1] Even the "Dreyfusards" – the defenders of tolerance and justice – had subtly perpetuated prejudices that had paved the way for modern anti-Semitism and other forms of ideological prejudice. The malign logic of this dialectic ultimately concerns the way in which a seemingly universal Enlightenment idea tends to obfuscate its own particular conditions, thereby excluding ideals and identities which these conditions implicitly challenge or contradict.

In this article, I want to highlight this dialectic further by demonstrating how, to a significant extent, two of the greatest philosophers of reason, Kant and Hegel, underpin their universal principles with prejudiced stereotypes about Jews and Judaism. More particularly, I will illuminate the way that both Kant and Hegel secularize and politicize a number of age-old anti-Jewish tropes which are deeply rooted in the Christian tradition; tropes which serve to reinforce their notions of freedom and enlightenment. Clearly, these tropes take on a different meaning once they are removed from their original theological context. The target of the stereotyping is no longer the individual Jew but, rather, Jewishness as a particular identity which stands in the way of universal ideals of freedom and rationality and which must be overcome in order for Jews to become free individuals. Even so, the same dialectics, between the universal and the particular, is at work – and particular Jewish individuals are still affected by the prejudices of a seemingly formal universalism.

In the last section of the article, I will draw attention to the recurrence of this troubling dialectic in still more subtle fashion, namely, when the universalist heritage of Christianity is invoked as a resource in contemporary philosophical debate. I am thinking in particular here of the efforts by Alain Badiou and Slavoj Žižek to formulate a new political universalism. What is striking about their efforts is how "Jewishness" is once more invoked as a signifier of particularity. However, it should be clarified immediately that "Jewishness", less even than for Kant and Hegel, here refers to particular Jewish individuals. Rather, it is used as a rhetorical marker which is interchangeable with any particular predicate that obstructs a truly universalist political order. Nevertheless, it is a good question as to whether the use of these long-standing anti-Jewish tropes does not reveal the lasting tensions generated by a universalist legacy that is dialectically reliant upon eliminating conflicting claims on definitions of the universal.

The Idealistic Body Politic

In his celebrated work *The Stillborn God*, Mark Lilla lucidly illustrates the "great separation" between religion and politics that took place in early Western modernity. With the Enlightenment, religion was severed from both politics and philosophy in an unprecedented fashion, and new ideals – focusing exclusively on human nature and human needs – replaced theological speculations about society, morality, and knowledge.[2]

Lilla's narrative of the subordination of religion by political philosophy forms part of the standard account of the Enlightenment alluded to earlier. What makes his work original, however, is that he does not end the story there but goes on to illustrate how the process toward secularization was partly reversed when the Enlightenment reached German soil. In contrast to most English, Scottish, and French Enlightenment thinkers – who opposed religion in the name of reason – the major proponents of the German *Aufklärung* sought to reconcile religion with reason by incorporating religious truths into their rational discourses.

This process is perhaps nowhere more clearly manifested than in the philosophy of Immanuel Kant. Unlike Hobbes, Locke, or the French *encyclopédistes*, who saw in religion nothing but man's stubborn ignorance and emotional flight from pain, Kant recognized religion as a permanent human need and even a precondition for man's moral improvement. He did so, however, only by placing its doctrines well "within the boundaries of reason," as the title of his most famous work on religion indicates.[3] Kant's basic idea concerning religion is that it exclusively deals with the practical aspects of human life. Religion offers no valid contribution to rational knowledge; its only contribution is to the history of morality. As Yirmiyahu Yovel has observed, Kant borrowed this idea from his Jewish friend and colleague, Moses Mendelssohn.[4]

In locating the essence of religion solely in practical commands, Mendelssohn endeavored to demonstrate that the particular creeds of the religion of his fathers need not stand in conflict with the Enlightenment ideal of universal reason. Unlike Mendelssohn, however, Kant was not particularly interested in seeking harmony between a specific religious tradition and universal reason. Rather, he made use of Mendelssohn's argument only in order to reinforce his own conviction that religion *per se*, being a purely practical affair, offers no rational grounds for morality or knowledge. The only legitimate ground for morality, Kant famously proposed, lies in the purity of the human will (as opposed to blind obedience to an external law). Nonetheless, positive religion *can* be a source to morality, precisely to the extent that it mirrors the moral law which issues from free human reason. The task of the moral philosopher is thus to reveal the kernel of morality that lies beneath the creeds, ceremonies, and historical narratives of each religion.

Kant's argument also has a historical aspect. Like many subsequent philosophers and anthropologists in the nineteenth century, Kant placed the historical religions on an evolutionary scale. The more a religion expressed the universal kernel of morality, the higher its place on the historical scale. At the bottom, Kant placed Judaism, distinguished by its legalistic and "statutory" traits; then, in turn, came Orthodox and Catholic Christianity, Protestantism, and, finally, the universal religion of reason embodied in the philosopher's own system.[5] However, if we look closer at the fate of Judaism in Kant's philosophy of religion, we find that not only does it lie at the lower end of the scale, it is, strictly speaking, not a religion at all. Unlike the other religions, which in varying degrees give expression to what would ultimately develop into the pure religion of reason, "[the] Jewish religion stood out for Kant as having no moral content at all; it was merely legalistic, a *political* constitution only."[6]

This denial of Judaism's moral and spiritual value notwithstanding, Kant willingly admitted that particular Jewish individuals, like his friend Mendelssohn, were able to develop moral minds. But such magnanimity was extended to them precisely as *individuals*, i.e. as members of universal humanity, not as *Jews*. This apparent conflict between particular Jewish identity and the universal ideals of reason is perhaps most famously – or, rather, infamously – expressed in Kant's late work *The Conflict of the Faculties* (1798). Kant here argues that the Jews ought to adopt the "religion of Jesus" and interpret the Bible in the spirit of the Enlightenment. In this way, he concluded, the Jews would finally be assimilated into European culture and be relieved of their archaic religious tradition. Kant termed this process "the euthanasia of Judaism."[7]

As Michael Mack has suggested, Kant's argument about the euthanasia of Judaism can be seen in the light of an elaborate pseudo-theological body politic. "Pseudo-theological" here refers to the way in which Kant develops his social theory using Christian theological imagery that he secularizes and politicizes. For instance, Kant draws, implicitly and explicitly, on Paul's theological anthropology centered on notions of flesh and spirit – the old Adam, and the new. Paul's idea is that the "old Adam," i.e. the fallen human being, must become dead to the sinful temptations of this world in order to prepare for the new, resurrected life in Christ. Kant is not interested in the heavenly salvation for which Paul hopes; his interest lies in the construction of a perfected body politic in the here and now. Nonetheless, he repeats the structure of Paul's argument, as seen most clearly in his definition of autonomy as liberation from the desire to rely upon the empirical world (in which he employs the phrase "to die away from the world," alluding on Christ's rejection, symbolized by the cross, of the happiness of the sensuous).[8]

Kant's construction of rational autonomy, Mack continues, parallels his attempt not only to do away with the Jewish foundations of Christianity but also, more importantly, to exclude Jewishness from his body politics. If Christianity paved the way for universal rational and moral freedom, Kant "targeted the Jews as the empirical obstacle to the establishment of a rational order in which heteronomy would be overcome."[9] Historically as well as in the present, Jews remained oriented towards the material world, immutably bound to their God and their particular way of living. As such, they were unable to transcend their empirical conditions and, in consequence, inevitably excluded from any idealist model of the body politic.

The Spirit of Judaism

One thinker who was profoundly influenced by Kant's late writings on religion was the young Friedrich Hegel. From his earliest writings, Hegel shared the older philosopher's conviction that the goal of humanity was not to be found in an other-worldly divine kingdom, but consisted, rather, in rational and moral freedom in this world. Like Kant, Hegel believed that religion, in part, posed an obstacle to realizing this freedom. Religion, in its manifest form, thus needed to be re-interpreted and rendered compatible with philosophical reason. Only in this way could its rational and moral kernel be uncovered.[10]

Hegel's early affiliation with Kant's philosophy soon came to an end, however, and this is perhaps nowhere more detectable than in his views on religion in general, and on Christianity in particular. Whereas Hegel in his earliest writings had shared Kant's criticism of historical religion, he began in the late 1790s to reconcile himself with at least one religion in its positive form, namely Christianity. In opposition to Kant, who denied that any religion offered reconciliation between human needs and moral duty, Hegel now started to discern in Jesus's Sermon on the Mount a "religion of love" which made it possible to live a moral life while also experiencing existential plenitude. This shift in emphasis foreshadowed what would become a fundamental conviction in Hegel's mature philosophy – that both rational and moral freedom must be embodied in specific communities and institutions.[11]

Despite abandoning Kant's condescending view of historical religion, Hegel did not reject Kant's offensive portrayal of Jews and Judaism. On the contrary, his newfound esteem for Christianity only hardened his antipathy towards Judaism. In "The Spirit of Christianity and its Fate" (written in 1797), Hegel managed, in John Caputo's words, "to say the most hateful things about the Jews in the course of defining Christianity as the religion of love."[12] At the same time, we need to remind ourselves that Jews were routinely described in disparaging terms in everyday cultural discourse of the eighteenth century. This contextualization notwithstanding, "The Spirit of Christianity" stands out as one of the most disparaging texts in modern philosophy ever written on Judaism.

As a contrast to his elaboration of the spirit of Christianity, Hegel in the beginning of this work offers an account of the "spirit of Judaism," which he traces back to the patriarch Abraham. Although the word "alienation" had not yet fully entered Hegel's philosophical vocabulary, Abraham seems to perfectly embody what he would come to understand by this term. Abraham, the restless wanderer, is a "stranger on earth, a stranger to the soil and to man alike."[13] Abraham cuts himself off from the world in order to obtain freedom but instead ends up utterly dependent upon an immense God before whom he is nothing. The Jewish spirit, symbolized by the patriarch, is thus characterized by a *double* alienation – from nature and from God.

Despite distancing himself from Kant, Hegel thus shares the other's view of the Jewish people as the very acme of heteronomy. Even the Exodus, one of the most powerful epics of liberty in human history, is turned into its opposite in Hegel's account. Having depicted the flight from Egypt as the act of cowards profiting from other people's agony, Hegel concludes: "It is no wonder that this nation, which in its emancipation bore the most slavelike demeanor, regretted leaving Egypt, wished to return there again whenever difficulty or danger came upon it in the sequel, and thus showed how in its liberation it had been without the soul and the spontaneous need of freedom."[14]

Among the anti-Jewish stereotypes present in both Kant's and Hegel's philosophies, we also find a linking of the Jews with materialism. In discussing the receiving of the Torah – in Hegel's reading, yet another expression for the Jewish people's deeply servile character – Hegel alludes to a beautiful image in Deuteronomy (32:11), in which God is likened to an eagle who protects her young and trains them to fly. He then remarks: "Only the Israelites did not complete this fine image; these young never became eagles. In relation to their God they rather afford the image of an eagle which by mistake warmed stones, showed them how to fly and took them on its wings into the clouds, but never raised their weight into flight or fanned their borrowed warmth into the flame of life."[15]

All these instances of derogatory characterization of Jews and Judaism are taken from Hegel's early philosophy. To do justice both to the subject matter and to Hegel, one must, of course, take into account his later philosophy, too. As already indicated, the mature Hegel rejected Enlightenment ideals as too abstract, and, increasingly, recognized that rationality in its highest form is always embodied in particular practices and institutions. What is more, Hegel's view of Judaism became less dismissive in his mature works; as he developed his dialectical notion of history, he attributed the Jewish religion a major role in the evolution of the Spirit. Still, Judaism is not assigned a flattering role; its essential contribution is to prepare the stage for Christianity, while its own historical project is aborted. Like Kant, Hegel was thus unable to find a place for Jews as *Jews* in the ongoing march of history.

Neo-Paulinism and the Recurrence of Anti-Jewish Stereotypes in Philosophy

In the last two decades, European intellectuals have increasingly turned to traditional theological discourses for politico-philosophical insights. This somewhat unexpected development has found its most spectacular expression in the revived interest in the Pauline corpus of the New Testament. Beginning with the publication of Alain Badiou's original work *Saint Paul: The Foundation of Universalism* in 1997, fascination for Paul has grown into a major philosophical trend, uniting thinkers as different as the neo-Leninist philosopher Slavoj Žižek and the neo-orthodox theologian John Milbank.[16]

As the subtitle of Badiou's work indicates, Paul's attractiveness to these thinkers on the resurgent radical left-wing of political thought lies in the way in which he offers a foundation of a new political universalism. After decades of fruitless identity politics supported by deconstructivist philosophy, what is needed is an emancipatory politics that interpellates subjects *universally*, i.e. irrespective of ethnic, social, or gender factors. And this is where Paul turns out to be the man. In his famous declaration that there is "neither Jew nor Greek, slave nor free, male nor female, for you are all one in Christ Jesus" (Gal. 3:28), the apostle reveals the framework for a universalism that demands fidelity, not to any particular tradition or identity, but simply to the revolutionary event itself.[17]

In my view, Badiou and Žižek ought to be given credit for raising the question of a new political universalism. At the end of the day, localist pragmatism and identitarian strategies have not always proved to be effective solutions to global (or even just European) problems, and in our increasingly fragmented societies the need for a powerful vision of the common good has never been more urgent. Yet there is an uncomfortable flip side to Badiou's and Žižek's argument, not unlike the paradoxical aspects of the Enlightenment philosophical legacy mentioned earlier. Accordingly, if universal freedom and rationality in Kant and (early) Hegel presupposes exclusion of our inclinations toward the empirical world, so, too, does "fidelity" to the revolutionary "event" for Badiou and Žižek imply the elimination of any kind of particularity, ethnic or other. Still more remarkable, however, is that both thinkers repeatedly use "Jews" and "Judaism" for rhetorical effect when explaining why this particularity is so problematic for the universalist point of view.

On second glance, however, this situation may not be so remarkable. As some acute historians have observed, Badiou's – and, by extension, Žižek's – reading of the Pauline epistles depends heavily on an exegetical paradigm established in early modernity.[18] Deeply rooted in German idealist philosophy, this paradigm is characterized by a false and implicitly anti-Jewish dialectics that pits law against grace, letter against spirit, Old Testament against New, and so forth. The paradigm was predominant in the so-called Tübingen School and to a significant degree laid the foundation for the modern Protestant image of Paul. Following Hegel's interpretation of God's incarnation as a bridge from the alienated religion of the Jews to the Christian religion of love, these early New Testament scholars based their biblical hermeneutic on a dialectical opposition between a Petrine legalist position and a Pauline universalist position, the former being doomed to obsolescence with the passage of time.[19]

Though Badiou and Žižek both seem unaware that they are subscribing to a Protestant paradigm for interpreting Paul's notions of law and grace, they simultaneously inscribe themselves in a broader Christian narrative which throughout history has associated Judaism with particularity and exclusiveness – in sharp contrast to Christianity, which has been presented in terms of universality and openness. To be fair, however, it should be emphasized that both philosophers recognize that Judaism does also include an impulse towards universality. As Žižek reminds the reader in the opening section of his vast study *In Defense of Lost Causes*, Jews throughout history have represented strongly particularizing currents as well as far-reaching universalizing impulses: "sometimes they stand for the stubborn attachment to their particular life-form which prevents them from becoming full citizens of the state they live in, sometimes they stand for a 'homeless' and rootless universal cosmopolitanism indifferent to all particular ethnic forms."[20]

It is telling, however, that both Badiou and Žižek identify the more constructive impulse – i.e. the universalist one – with figures who in one way or another departed from Judaism: Spinoza, Marx, Freud, and Trotsky. To be a good Jew, it seems, is to be a Jew no longer. This is precisely the idea conveyed by Kant in his lamentable expression "the euthanasia of Judaism." Žižek, with his strong predilection for iconoclastic rhetorical twists, expresses the same idea in the following manner: "the only true solution to the 'Jewish question' is the 'final solution' (their annihilation), because Jews *qua objet a* are the ultimate obstacle to the 'final solution' of History itself, to the overcoming of divisions in all-encompassing unity and flexibility."[21]

Does universality really demand the overcoming of particularity? If we are to show the critical historian's "fidelity" to the "event" proclaimed by Paul, the answer will most likely be no. Paul's aim was never to abolish the particular Jewish covenant; it was to universalize its messianic promise to include all nations. In this sense, Paul merely unfolded the universalist impulse inherent in Jewish messianism since the days of Jeremiah. This impulse – to reach out for universal ideals of justice and wisdom while maintaining fidelity to a particular way of life – has also distinguished subsequent Jewish thought, from Maimonides to Mendelssohn and Emmanuel Levinas. One of the many merits of such "embodied universalism" is that it avoids, in Michael Mack's words, "the prejudicial aspect of a seemingly universal concept of enlightenment that obfuscates its own particularity and thus excludes that against which it defines its identity."[22]

Notes

1. Theodor W. Adorno and Max Horkheimer, *Dialectic of Enlightenment*, trans. Edmund Jephcott (Stanford: Stanford University Press, 2002).

2. Mark Lilla, *The Stillborn God: Religion, Politics, and the Modern West* (New York: Alfred A. Knopf, 2007).

3. Immanuel Kant, *Religion within the Boundaries of Mere Reason*, trans. Allen Wood and George di Giovanni (Cambridge: Cambridge University Press, 1998).

4. Yirmiyahu Yovel, *Dark Riddle: Hegel, Nietzsche, and the Jews* (Cambridge: Polity Press, 1998), 6–7.

5. Kant, *Religion*, 129–151.
6. Yovel, *Dark Riddle*, 7.
7. Immanuel Kant, *The Conflict of the Faculties*, trans. Mary J. Gregor (Lincoln and London: University of Nebraska Press, 1992), 95.
8. Michael Mack, *German Idealism and the Jew: The Inner Anti-Semitism of Philosophy and German Jewish Responses* (Chicago and London: University of Chicago Press, 2003), 27–35.
9. Mack, *German Idealism*, 39.
10. See, above all, G.F.W. Hegel, "The Positivity of the Christian Religion," in *Early Theological Writings*, trans. T.M. Knox (Philadelphia: University of Pennsylvania Press, 1971), 67–181.
11. Yovel, *Dark Riddle*, 32–33.
12. John D. Caputo, "Spectral Hermeneutics: On the Weakness of God and the Theology of the Event," in *After the Death of God*, ed. Jeffrey W. Robbins (New York: Columbia University Press), 80.
13. G.F.W. Hegel, "The Spirit of Christianity and its Fate," in *Early Theological Writings*, 186.
14. Hegel, "Spirit" 190.
15. Hegel, "Spirit" 199.
16. See *inter alia* Alain Badiou, *Saint Paul: The Foundation of Universalism*, trans. Ray Brassier (Palo Alto: Stanford University Press, 2003), and John Milbank, Slavoj Žižek and Creston Davis, *Paul's New Movement: Continental Philosophy and the Future of Christian Theology* (Grand Rapids: Brazos Press, 2010).
17. Badiou, *Saint Paul*, 4–15.
18. See, for example, the contributions of Paula Fredriksen, E.P. Sanders, Dale B. Martin and Daniel Boyarin in John D. Caputo and Linda Martin Alcoff (eds.), *St. Paul among the Philosophers* (Bloomington and Indianapolis: Indiana University Press, 2009).
19. See further Horton Harris, *The Tübingen School* (Oxford: Clarendon Press, 1975).
20. Slavoj Žižek, *In Defense of Lost Causes* (London & New York: Verso, 2008), 6–7. A similar position is articulated by Badiou in *Circonstances, 3. Portées du mot "juif"* (Paris: Éditions Léo Scheer, 2005), 14–15.
21. Slavoj Žižek, *In Defense*, 5.
22. Mack, *German Idealism*, 12.

Identity and Collective Memory in the Making of Nineteenth-Century Feminism

ULLA MANNS

According to the historian Maria Grever, analyzing feminist sites of memory is a way of shedding new light on the women's movement in the West. It calls attention, she writes, "to how these memories define a feminist identity", and to how certain women "did not earn a place in the pantheon of feminist culture".[1] Historical monographs offer an important means for the movement to produce a collective memory about itself. Read by people who wish to improve the conditions of women and to change the ongoing construction of gender, the accounts of feminism and reform told in these monographs also serve as something to relate to and identify with. For Grever, these narratives produce a certain memory that can be added to, maintained, and commemorated as well as contested or rejected.[2] In this article I will explore this function of the historical monograph, taking as my example the Finno-Swedish feminist Alexandra Gripenberg.

A central figure in the International Council of Women (ICW), Gripenberg participated in a huge European-American feminist network.[3] On the eve of the rise of the international struggle for women's suffrage in 1904, she published a three-volume monograph, *Reformarbetet till förbättrandet af kvinnans ställning* (1893–1903) (Reform Work for the Improvement of Women). It was originally meant to be published in English, but for some reason this did not happen. Nevertheless, as a lengthy study of reform work undertaken to change the conditions for women throughout the Western world, it serves as one of many continued feminist memories, to use Grever's typology. Gripenberg offers repeated advice on how to achieve strategic progress, not merely local goals. Doing this identity markers are implicitly put forward for the reader, showing what it takes to identify with the movement. The first volume, published in 1893, was devoted to a series of countries: the US, Britain, Germany, Austria, the Netherlands, Belgium, Switzerland, Russia, Poland, Bohemia, Hungary, and Greece. The second volume, published in 1898, was dedicated to France, Italy, Spain, and Portugal. The last volume, published in 1903, covered the Nordic countries (Norway, Sweden, Denmark, and Finland) and is far longer than the others. Even though the monograph does not conceal its Western focus, its stated ambition was to offer a general analysis of the state of the Woman Question and of the possibilities for progress. Changing gender conditions around the world were seen as crucial for progress since the development of women "from sexhood to humanhood" was regarded as a question that involved "half of humanity".[4]

Gripenberg's universalist approach to the Woman Question was quite typical for the time. By and large, women's rights and needs were generally discussed and written about with few concessions to social, economic or religious conditions. In Gripenberg's analysis, the situation of women was intimately connected to modernity and civilization. The women's movement in different countries was portrayed in a largely unreflective, Western/Eurocentric way. First and foremost, the ethical basis for feminism was made clear: Christianity in general and Lutheranism in particular. Implicit but notable was the absence of remarks about its middle-class, white, and liberal character, prerequisites that were taken for granted. Such identity markers were something to which readers could relate, creating feelings of affinity or exclusion. As Sara Ahmed notes, the women's movement described functioned as an institution orienting around particular bodies, that is around certain kinds of women.[5] These women were indisputably white, Christian, and liberal. But, as the following analysis will show, the text also contained less predictable markers. Relating the absence of the almost compulsory feminist stress on innate feminine qualities and motherliness to the many contemporary feminists living either as single or engaged in same-sex relations, Gripenberg also offered possibilities for identification for women who chose to live without men.

This article will not pursue an analysis of the geopolitical framing of the West in contrast to "the rest". The construction of imaginary

Western and non-Western women, as well as of a hyperreal West and a hyperreal Orient, will be addressed elsewhere.[6] Instead, this article argues that Gripenberg's monograph can be read as one of many that contributed to the collective memory of First Wave feminism in the West.[7] *Reformarbetet*, it will be argued, functioned as an effective means of social cohesion participating in the construction of a feminist space, a particular space to relate to or depart from. As Grever remarks, memory production was by and large an outcome of knowledge production, historical consciousness, and invented traditions within the movement. The events and people which eventually gained a place in the pantheon of feminism was an effect of an ongoing production of collective memory. Collective memory is in itself a result of prior selections, agreements, and decisions about what and whom to remember, what to document, and how to display events and people. Besides the production of historical knowledge about the women's movement and the struggle for reform, a major role in shaping and upholding feminist identities was also played by invented traditions within the movement. As inventions, such traditions functioned not only as a means of countering the construction of narratives from outside but also served as traditions shaping feminist ideals. As Grever notes, analysis of the women's movement and the functions of its memory production and invented traditions: "throw[s] considerable light on how people relate to the past. All 'invented traditions' use history to legitimate action and cement group cohesion. In addition, 'invented traditions' illuminate processes of inclusion and exclusion within power relations."[8]

Progress for Christ's sake

Time and space have an important place in the work of Gripenberg, who consistently relates societal progress to contemporary historical and political conditions. Based upon a trinity of foundational ideals consisting of Enlightenment philosophy, the Gospels, and the Reformation notions of individual freedom, care for others, and civic responsibility are made ethical precepts for political and feminist change. The text evinces a firm belief in reason that is, however, not entirely secular (that is, left-wing). The religious ethical dimension is constantly present and contrasted with secular, materialist ethics. Having no doubt that Christian, or rather Lutheran Protestant, ideals are necessary for progress, Gripenberg emphasises that these must be combined with the belief that all humans are individuals and capable of personal development as well as of moral and political agency. Evident in a number of paragraphs women are seen as fully capable of becoming educated human beings and future citizens, not the least when the United States is discussed and when conditions for women in countries dominated by the Catholic or Greek Orthodox church is analysed.[9]

Gripenberg had a firm belief in progress. Paraphrasing Hegel on the title page, the whole enterprise sets off: once an idea has appeared, it eventually conquers the world, not without resistance or struggle, because it is ethically right.[10] Women's entitlement to freedom and justice is justified by ideals of Enlightenment philosophy and Christianity that have already been accepted. It is unjust to treat women as other than human, and hence unjust to suppress and exploit a fellow human being because of her gender, race, or class. This line of argument is evident throughout Gripenberg's discussion of political and social rights for African-Americans, the European working class, and women in general.[11] Science and rational thought are, moreover, seen as crucial for progress and will accelerate progress. The barrier to progress is quite clear: ethical inconsistencies in society, women's lack of formal education, the protection of male privilege, and the lack of feminist consciousness.

For Gripenberg, the idea of progress – the gradual realization of ethical principles and political ideals inherent to the West – provides the matrix for general change. As already noted, she quickly narrows this matrix down to Christianity (in contrast to "the Oriental"), thereafter to Protestantism (in contrast to Catholicism), and, eventually, to Lutheranism (in contrast to Calvinism and the Greek Orthodoxy). This narrowing tendency is particularly discernible in the chapters on Russia, the Netherlands, Belgium, France, and Greece. Interestingly she makes no comment on Anglicanism or Judaism in Europe and the US. Nor is the role of contemporary Jewish feminists commented upon.[12] Religious and cultural heterogeneity is thus made invisible at a national level, with the exception of Greece, whose religious heterogeneity Gripenberg regards as too important to leave unremarked. Regardless of education or class, Muslim women are portrayed as less advanced, a result of ethical deficiencies and sexual morals in Muslim societies. Although Gripenberg was a fierce advocate of social and political reform, socialism was ranked alongside Oriental ethics as one of Western feminism's greatest enemies, mainly because of its long neglect of women's claims for equality, and its atheism.[13]

Gripenberg's story is not just an optimistic narrative about inevitable, albeit hitherto contested, progress towards full justice and gender equality in the West. The analysis centres on hindrances to a progress that ought to be, if given possibilities to prosper without gendered prejudices, male resistance, formal and informal hindrances of different kind. Lack of formal possibilities for women to earn a living of their own is alongside with the decisiveness of women to act and carry out changes, put forward as main tools for social change, eventually leading to a world of equality and independence for women.[14] Freedom is the overall goal: freedom for all women. Once again, as a liberal feminist Gripenberg is not exceptional in this respect, nor is her concept of freedom. Freedom is contrasted with the secular variety for which socialists were assumed to be striving. Freedom is, first and foremost, freedom from exploitation and different kinds of injustice, and the right for all people to find happiness in an ethically just world. As noted, for Gripenberg, Lutheranism provides the basic ethical foundation for the right kind of freedom because of its starting-point in ideas about equality and care for others. The idea of freedom becomes politically intertwined with equality: no one is to suffer because of the freedom of others. In Gripenberg's argument this perspective came to include women of different classes, even though she was fiercely opposed to wider social change. As an outspoken opponent of socialism, Gripenberg carefully avoided socialist ideas, rhetoric, and analysis.

Space and belonging

The space claimed was universal and free, where women of all classes were regarded as agents. This space also had a private and corporeal dimension. The stress was on women's agency as citizens, as rational, moral, and embodied beings as well as wage-earners. Liberate women, give them the opportunity to make choices, to act and live independently. Gripenberg offers few normative prescriptions about roads to be followed after liberation. Recommendations about suitable areas to act or perform within are few even though the cultural, religious and political framework is evident. It is noteworthy that Gripenberg does not choose to point out certain areas for women to exercise their future rights as citizens. When not stressing women's complementary duties or innate feminine capabilities, Gripenberg leaves open an imaginary space in which women will be counted as individuals, whatever they choose to do, even beyond the matrix of marriage and motherhood. If read as part of an identification forming contribution, Gripenberg's monograph thereby provides a possibility for women to relate to feminism without the almost compulsory prerequisites of nineteenth-century feminism where women are first and foremost seen as mothers, as the bearers and rearers of children.

The feminist identity processes in Gripenberg's work are complex: make women reflect, act and mobilise. Let them loose and trust them as agents, capable of acting on behalf of their own! Gripenberg presents this idea without specifying what kind of feminists are to be produced or which particular women are to be included. At the same time, the text specifies a number of aspects of feminist identity. Cultural and religious norms are explicitly held within the realms of Western, protestant ethics. Bringing in Gripenberg's own feminist context, the international women's movement in general and the leadership of the ICW in particular, other identification markers become manifest. The group of transnational feminists in the ICW leadership consisted largely of Protestant, bourgeois, middle- and upper-class white Western women. Despite their national differences, they came together in a politically somewhat vague but liberal enterprise to improve women's conditions worldwide.[15] This enterprise fitted well with ideas about progress and femininity elsewhere. According to T.J. Boisseau, at the World's Fair of 1893 in Chicago, where the ICW held its constitutional meeting, a strong, relatively new, feminine ideal along ethnocentric lines was presented:

> The exposition presented an opportunity to invent a model of modern American womanhood in keeping with its modern ethos. *Modern* did not denote only contemporaneity in the context of the exposition. The adjective implied the attainment of civilised moral standards and social relations as well as the development of industry and technology.[16]

The ICW very much continued to work along this path. But at the same time, as Leila Rupp has shown, the feminist "we" produced within the ICW leadership also provided a space for women to live and work without men. For the leadership itself, the ICW functioned as a transnational all-female and feminist space where women, often slightly controversial on a national level, could carry out political work and form personally important networks and relations. This transnational, almost cosmopolitan space enabled friendships across national borders outside of marriage and even same-sex relations. Rupp shows how many of the prominent feminists within the ICW leadership, and, later, in the international suffrage organisation as well as in the international peace movement, formed intimate relations with women in the organisation as well as lifelong friendships across national borders. This seems not to have posed a problem for either the movement or Gripenberg.[17]

The feminist identity processes at work in Gripenberg's monograph are both clear and vague as regards normative and implicit prescriptions about how to be a feminist. This was most often effected through displays of ethical and religious ideals contrasted to non-desirable qualities, creating a picture of a feminist *persona non grata*. A genuine belief in women's agency makes the recommendations and thereby the construction of the other stops at a general, overall ethical level. The goal was to let women become citizens in all respects. As such they were supposed to be good, independent Christians, just and responsible persons who did not misuse or exploit others. Christianity, social awareness, reflection, agency and selflessness were displayed as necessary components. Beyond these prerequisites, women were free to choose and the feminist space was open to anyone. At the same time, the general ethical framework dismissed women on racial grounds as well as on class/caste, religious, and cultural grounds. The overall narrative argues for a successful transnational feminism based on Protestantism, liberal political values, and women's agency. In many respects, Gripenberg's historical representation of Western civilisation as progress is unsurprising. In many respects, it follows other nineteenth-century Western narratives. What stands out is the particular feminist space Gripenberg carves out, where consequences of regarding women as individuals and agents supported the idea of women living as single, outside of marriage and children, even to choose a life in partnership with other women.

To elaborate further: Gripenberg did not draw on national solidarity among women. Common ethical, political, and religious ideals are instead presented as the glue that could unite women across the world. Mobilisation of women, co-operation, networking, feminist solidarity, and ethical unity are important, regardless of nationality. The political importance of a particular transnational space for women, a place within which to act as well as a space in which to exist, was considered crucial for long-term feminist change. Although Gripenberg strongly believed in working with feminist men, she did not overlook the importance an all-female space. She herself felt at home in the ICW, which represented a massive female network at the turn of the twentieth century, providing a transnational space in which women of different nationalities, cultures, and sexual orientations could meet. While Alexandra Gripenberg was a strong believer in the possibility of solidarity among women, the feminist "we" that she put forward had its limits. She thereby participated not only in cementing group cohesion but also in producing a cultural memory of the nineteenth-century women's movement.

Notes

1. Maria Grever, "The Pantheon of Feminist Culture: Women's Movements and the Organization of Memory", *Gender & History* vol. 9, no. 2 Aug (1997), 372. My italics.

2. Ibid.

3. Gripenberg was a board member of the ICW at the turn of the nineteenth century and was considered for the chair when Lady Aberdeen resigned. However, she turned down the offer. Ulla Wikander, *Feminism, familj och medborgarskap: Debatter på internationella kongresser om nattarbetsförbud för kvinnor 1889–1919* (Göteborg/Stockholm: Makadam förlag, 2006), 232.

4. Alexandra Gripenberg, *Reformarbetet till förbättrandet af kvinnans ställning* (Helsinki, 1903) vol. 3, foreword.

5. Sara Ahmed, "A Phenomenology of Whiteness", *Feminist Theory* (2007).

6. "Hyperreal" is here used to denote an imaginative trope whose geographical referents remain somewhat indeterminate. See Dipesh Chakrabarty, *Provincializing Europe: Postcolonial Thought and Historical Difference* (Princeton, NJ: 2008) 27. See Manns, "Time, Space and Place in the writings of Alexandra Gripenberg", *Scandinavian Journal of History* (f.c).

7. The term "collective memory" refers to group identity within a social movement. See, for example, Verta Taylor & Leila J. Rupp, "Loving Internationalism: The Emotion Culture of Transnational Women's Organizations, 1888-1945", *Mobilization: An International Journal* vol. 7, no. 2 (2002).

8. Grever, 367.

9. See particularly "Introduction", 8f. and the chapters on the US, Belgium in vol. 1, France in vol. 2.

10. Detailed reference to Hegel is not given. See title page, vol. 1. Quote in original: "En idé framträder, förvandlar verlden, medför kamp och strid, framkallar sin motsats, luttras och renas, blir ändtligen segrande, och verlden har dermed blifvit en annan."

11. See the chapters on the US, Britain, Belgium, France, and the Nordic countries.

12. Ernestine Rose (1810-1892), for example, daughter of a Polish rabbi and an international feminist, is the only one mentioned, and very briefly, in the chapter on the US. Rose was a free-thinker and outspoken atheist who had married a British Owenist. See Bonnie S. Anderson, *Joyous Greetings: The First International Women's Movement, 1830-1860* (Oxford: Oxford University Press, 2000).

13. On misogynic writers, vol. 1, 110ff., 136, vol. 3, 72. On socialism, see vol. 1, 117f. in the chapter on Germany, and vol. 2, 67ff. on France.

14. This is discussed in several chapters of the monograph.

15. Leila J. Rupp, *Worlds of Women: the Making of an International Women's Movement* (Princeton, New Jersey: Princeton University Press, 1997).

16. T.J. Boisseau, "White Queens at the Chicago World's Fair, 1893: New Womanhood in the Service of Class, Race, and Nation", *Gender & History* vol. 12, no. 1 (2000), 36. Cultural and ethnical homogeneity in the international suffrage organisation is discussed by Charlotte Weber (2001) in "Unveiling Scheherazade: Feminist Orientalism in the International Alliance of Women, 1911-1950", *Feminist Studies* vol. 27, n. 1. See also Rupp, *Worlds of Women*.

17. Leila J. Rupp, "Sexuality and Politics in the Early Twentieth-Century: the Case of the International Women's Movement", *Feminist Studies* vol. 23, n. 3 (1997). I make this observation without any suggestion about Gripenberg's personal life. On the stress on motherhood in the emotional life of the ICW, see Taylor & Rupp.

Temporality and Metaphoricity in Contemporary Swedish Feminist Historiography

CLAUDIA LINDÉN

> "At any rate, when a subject is highly controversial
> – and any question about sex is that – one cannot
> hope to tell the truth."
>
> Virginia Woolf,
> *A Room of One's Own*[1]

All history writing involves and actualizes different temporal structures, many of which are heavily laden with value judgements. The past can be constructed either as something primitive or as a lost origin. A central aspect of feminist critique of science has been the problematizing of how science traditionally writes history. The introduction of gender history into the discipline of history, like the comprehensive critique of the canon which has taken place in many humanities subjects, including literary history and the history of ideas, is an example of how historiography and the critique of science have been closely associated in research into gender theory. Feminist theory has been developed by means of the critique of science as well as an advanced and ongoing metacritique. Despite this, feminism's own historiography has remained a blind spot, above all, its account of the very recent past. Near-contemporary history is rarely experienced as history. Its narration can easily become a matter of where the narrator found himself or herself at a particular point in time. It becomes testimony rather than history writing, and, as such, difficult to problematize. Many of those active in the nineteen-seventies are currently writing their memoirs or journals.[2] Such personal observations and memories are perhaps not felt to be historical accounts. Yet that is precisely what they are. My aim here is not to open a debate over "what really happened" in the seventies, eighties, or nineties, but to ask why a *particular* history is narrated, and how it serves to confer a particular identity on the narrator.

As a literary scholar working with issues relating to gender, much of my work relies on some kind of criticism of the canon in which questions of inclusion and exclusion are continually at stake. Feminist theory must be able to reflect upon its own writing of history in order to avoid creating new ideologies of exclusion and inclusion. The subject of this article is a brief investigation into how Swedish academic feminism represents its own recent history, that is to say, between 1970s Second Wave feminism and the present. Which words are used, and which intellectual models structure the way we write history? My case material comprises a section of articles from anniversary or field-surveying special issues of feminist journals from the last few years.

A central problematic of my investigation relates to how we interpret discontinuity in the course of history. Dramatizations of historical moments as "breaks", "defeats", and "turning points" evoke the temporal models which govern our models of historical understanding. Yet my aim here is not to advance *one* correct historical account but to show how temporal metaphors operate in feminist historiography and what problematic implications they can have. Feminist philosopher Elizabeth Grosz has observed that feminist work relies on, and carries out, analyses of both the past and those present: "[T]o the extent that all radical politics is implicitly directed towards bringing into existence a future somehow dislocated from the present, our very object and milieu is time. We need to address these assumptions about the nature of time and its role in political (and biological) struggle".[3]

Gender and the construction of time

The representation of temporality is important because even temporality is often gender coded and consequently hierarchical. Rita Felski has noted that gender does not only affect the actual content of history, i.e. what is included and what excluded, but also "the philosophical assumptions underlying our interpretations of the nature of social meaning."⁴ Felski draws on Marshall Berman's analysis of Goethe's *Faust* as an example of how what is feminine in Gretchen is coded negatively as being older, indeed, as being precisely that which stands in the way of (masculine) modernity: "Woman is aligned with the dead weight of tradition and conservatism that the active, newly autonomous, and self-defining subject must seek to transcend. Thus she functions as the sacrificial victim exemplifying the losses which underpin the ambiguous, but ultimately exhilarating and seductive logic of the modern."⁵

Felski's analysis of Berman's association of masculinity with the modern, and femininity with conservatism, shows how a standard reading of modernity as forward-looking and progressive is tied to a temporal metaphoricity in which breaking with the past stands for innovation. Berman illustrates the way in which the gender coding of temporality also elicits hidden normative values and hierarchies, and vice versa. If even the temporal metaphoricity of historiography is gender coded, it is imperative that we remain vigilant with regard to how feminism's own history is written.

Our view of ourselves as modern is based on the conception of time that governs our view of history. In *Zeit und Tradition: Kulturelle Strategien der Dauer* (*Time and Tradition: Cultural Strategies of Duration*), literary historian Aleida Assmann, who has worked extensively on our cultural constructions of time, describes how our current conceptions of time emerged during the French Revolution. As a result, history was relieved of its exemplariness, instead becoming unique and irreversible: "When history proceeds by means of revolution, the past is forcibly detached from the present, and becomes antiquated. History, as Heidegger has it, is that which no longer happens."⁶ Such a model of history requires us to view the past as something alien and irreversible:

> What characterizes this model is the way that, alongside its explicit thematizing of temporal constructions, it remains wedded to a fixed temporal structure, namely, a linear and irreversible succession of events. This temporal model, which has emerged from narrative, is the backbone of all historiography. It forces us to emphasize change, development, and substitution as well as to *disregard contemporaneity in all that is non-contemporary.*⁷ (emphasis added)

The requirement to disregard contemporaneity in all that is non-contemporary is fundamental to twentieth-century Western culture. There is, I would argue, a connection between Assmann's analysis of the way in which our temporal construction forces upon us a definition of time, including the present, which can only exist in relation to that which does not exist, i.e. the *non-contemporary*, and the gender coding of the past as feminine and the present as masculine revealed by Berman's analysis of Goethe. What ties them together is the way they are defined by means of absolute exclusion of the other, making contemporaneity/modernity/masculinity a norm for how we understand the world.

In her historiographical investigation of historians of the early women's movement, Ulla Manns highlights the ideological dimensions of writing history. Manns also points out that historians of the women's movement have several functions: "repositories of memories, important "we"-creating instruments of socialization, and contributors to social debates of the day and to internal debates".[8] This double orientation, outward and inward, is characteristic of all feminist historiography. In this way, all feminist historiography, consciously or otherwise, makes a contribution to contemporary debates over questions of interpretation.

In a similar historiographical study of modern histories of the recent feminist past, British feminist Clare Hemmings shows how ideological even contemporary histories can be. Hemmings identifies a pattern whereby feminist history is evoked in terms of clear periods and thresholds, which principally coincide with the decades of the seventies, eighties, and nineties. For Hemmings, this involves its relation to poststructuralism. Either history is portrayed as a question of *development* from a naïve past, with the seventies representing essentialism and the nineties difference, or, alternatively, history is portrayed as a *defeat*, with involvement and politics becoming a thing of the past. Regardless of which history is being presented, poststructuralism is assigned the central role: "Yet, however inflected, the chronology remains the same, the decades overburdened yet curiously flattened, and poststructuralism animated as the key actor in challenging."[9]

Hemmings description of the technologies which have shaped "feminist storytelling" fit both with Assmann's description of a linear and irreversible structure of events, and Felski's analysis of the underlying gender coding at work in modernity's self-conception as the result of an irreversible break with tradition and the past. As I will show, Hemmings's description of feminist historiography as split between defeat and celebratory interpretations of the importance of poststructuralism well describes the situation in Sweden.

The temporality of generational conflict

A number of Second Wave feminists have written memoirs in the last few years. Explicit or implicit in these accounts is a critique of the present and of feminism today that makes reference to a loss of involvement and unity. Journalist Gunilla Thorgren's *Grupp 8 och jag* (*Group 8 and Me*) is an example. Yvonne Hirdman, Professor of History, has defended what she understands, with some irritation, to be the referent of "classic gender theory", i.e. the view that differentiation of masculine and feminine is a "fundamental pattern" in which masculine dominance is always the norm (rather, say, than placing the emphasis on heteronormativity). "Elementary, my dear Watson," writes Hirdman, and continues her critique of younger queer feminist: "But apparently it shouldn't be elementary. It should be muddled. These are the Muddle Ages."[10]

In recent years, Ebba Witt-Brattström, Professor of Comparative Literature, has clearly taken on the role of mouthpiece for the loss scenario. The fact that she has made this a question of generations, and hence a generational conflict, reinforces the impression that this relationship is based on temporality. In the sesquicentennial anniversary issue of the journal *Hertha*, she writes:

> Feminism finds itself in crisis. An historic unwillingness to understand and learn from history characterizes today's young feminists. Concrete politics are out. Instead of rallying living people on the street and in squares [...] we have the blogosphere's hysterical opinion-mongering, careerist media-feminism, and politically correct gender theory.[11]

In an article titled "When Sisterhood Was A Political Act", published in the Swedish newspaper *Dagens Nyheter* on International Women's Day, 8 March 2011, Witt-Brattström took up the subject again, citing journalist Inga-Lisa Sangregorio, another member of the original feminist "Group 8" who, according to Witt-Brattström,

> always hits her mark: 'I have never [writes Sangregorio] heard of anyone distancing themselves from their aberrations in the women's movement, we had fun, *we were right, and if they had only done as we said everything would have been much better today!*' (my emphasis).[12]

In Sangregorio's statement, the generational conflict becomes even more strained. It is now longer simply a question of defeat but of outright mistakes in the behaviour of younger feminists.

Witt-Brattström and Sangregorio are both examples of the history of lost involvement which Hemmings describes as one of the standard scenarios in feminist historiography: "A shift from the politicized, unified early second wave, through an entry into the academy in the eighties, and thence a fragmentation into multiple feminisms and individual careers, charts the story as one of loss of commitment to social and political change."[13]

In her article of 8 March 2011, Witt-Brattström sharpens the generational metaphor still further. Now it is not only a question of older and younger but of daddy's daughters rebelling against their mothers:

> The 'woman-mother' who lived in solidarity with her sisters had to make way for endless new versions of Pallas Athena, who had sprung from her father's head on a mission to restyle the goddesses of maternal retribution as the domesticated 'daughter-women' of paternal domesticity.[14]

When the conflict is described as being between mothers and daughters, rather than between different feminist positions, the generational metaphor serves to cement a temporality that is, as Assman puts it, "structured as an irreversible sequence of events".[15] That the stake here, as with the Anglo-American debate, is feminism's relation to poststructuralism, can clearly be seen from the fact that Witt-Brattström's *Hertha* article is criticizing a 1980s, postmodernist critique of the essentialist risks entailed by the term "woman". Strangely, since this was a critique which she herself helped initiate, she now describes it as a – false –artefact of modern gender theory:

> Many gender theorists in our universities cherish the bizarre notion that simply referring to someone as 'woman' or 'feminine' is an act of violence which legitimizes the global exploitation of women's labour and bodies.[16]

In Witt-Brattström's loss scenario, gender theorists and queer activists are identical.

Gender theorist Sara Edenheim has been specifically addressed, openly or covertly, in several of Witt-Brattström's articles as someone who, instead of moving women's experiences up the political agenda, "recommends the instant solution of leaving the prison of Woman."[17]

In a polemical article titled "A Few Words to My Dear Mothers In the Event That I Had Any", Sara Edenheim remarks that the nineteen-seventies are very much present on the curricula of gender studies departments, alongside "other feminist theoretical schools than yours."[18] Firmly rejecting the metaphor of generational conflict, Edenheim observes that this is a case of different theoretical traditions:

> But of course it may also be that you have an altruistic concern that we will need to reinvent the week. That is why I write to you now: have no fear. For we are not working on the same wheel. Indeed, this conflict has nothing to do with generations; you are not our mothers. Let me explain. The thing is, we do read and cite a great many feminists of your generation, just not *you*.[19]

Well aware of the dangers of defining feminism in terms of generations, periods, and breaks, Edenheim does not use a label to define her own position. However, she does point out in a footnote that the generational metaphor also seems to conceal a conflict over the validity of poststructuralism. Edenheim's analysis of Witt-Brattström's generational metaphor confirms that this is the very structure identified by Hemmings: "poststructuralism animated as the key actor" is the core of the problem:[20]

> The 'we' which I'm using here is not necessarily *de facto* the younger generation of feminist scholars but those of us who (against our will) have been interpellated by a portion of the older generation as being the *lost* generation, whereby our supposed deviation from the path stems from the fact that we spend far too much of our time on abstract

theorizing. This deliberately vague interpellation has led me to conclude that this 'we' in fact consists of both younger and older feminist scholars who explicitly base their research on poststructuralism.[21]

In Witt-Brattström's loss scenario, poststructuralism denotes a fall, or a loss of involvement. But for many others, it is a shift that should be celebrated, although this celebratory history often results in the same history of a break and the same temporal problematic.

Another history, the same temporality

Poststructuralism also plays a central role in an article by Mia Liinason, titled "Institutionalized Knowledge: Notes on the Processes of Inclusion and Exclusion in Gender Studies in Sweden" and published in the *Nordic Journal of Feminist and Gender Research*, as a tool for differentiating between conservative and progressive feminisms.[22] Liinason's article is an interesting indicator of how far the establishing of Gender Studies as a discipline has come. In barely two decades, a new university discipline has emerged, together with a definition of the discipline and a curriculum, and a canon may even be in the process of formation. There is thus every reason to discuss the starting-points of these new formations.

In her article, Liinason discuses the inclusions and exclusions which have been manifested in the historical account that has been established in introductory undergraduate courses on Gender Studies. Her aim is to show how Gender Studies is constructing a notion of heteronormative and essentialist femininity. For Liinason, the institutionalizing of feminist knowledge is also linked to a nationalist project:

> Perceiving the institutionalization of feminist knowledge in academia both as an effect of and a cause of a national project, I suggest in the course of this paper that the production of a particular understanding of gender in gender studies supports the idea of gender as it is re/produced in the national discourse in Sweden.[23]

Liinason seizes upon a textbook used in many departments of Gender Studies, Lena Gemzöe's *Feminism* (2002), which reviews the various strands of feminism. The book, which is also intended for a general readership, presents itself as an introductory overview. Liinason criticizes Gemzöe for creating a feminism which rests on a dualistic model of two sexes that fails to see the differences between women:

> Yet, in Gemzöe's feminist vision, women are infallible and cannot oppress each other. To her, differences between women are not significant, because the most important feminist struggle is the struggle against patriarchy. Accordingly, Gemzöe constructs women as universal category, subordinated under a similarly universal oppression, enacted towards 'women as mothers and sexual beings' (Gemzöe 2002:172). By way of this, Gemzöe reiterates a problematic slide of the national equality project 'in which sex is now gender is now sex is now woman's reproductive potential and the political battles over its control' as aptly phrased by Biddy Martin (1994: 107).[24]

Liinason constructs Gemzöe as an essentialist feminist who denies the differences between women and instead constructs women as a universal category, using an analogy between woman and nature in which motherhood is central and sexual difference the most fundamental category. Liinason needs to assign Gemzöe the role of essential feminist who believes in fundamental sexual difference and women as a universal category, in order to show, using Gemzöe's book as Exhibit A, that this position is identical with HSV's description of gender theory. Liinason can thereby describe how gender theory, based on a conception of sexual difference as the most fundamental social category, serves as the framework for both a national and an academic project which constructs men and women as binary opposites, "not only resulting in compulsory heterosexuality but also reinforcing the differences between the sexes."[25]

Using a series of analogies, Liinason in this way manages to construct gender theory as the locus of a conservative, heteronormative national project, and herself as the poststructurally-informed critic who questions identities, sexual and national alike.[26] My aim here is not to criticize her reading of Gemzöe (see instead Gemzöe's own response[27]) but to see how a poststructuralist approach is here used as a means of breaking with history. Hemmings observes in a follow-up article from 2007 that it is this very either/or description of "what happened" which has failed to discern the complexity in feminist history: "Further, these presentations, while narrated as mutually exclusive, combine to produce a remarkably similar account of what has been left behind, namely, unity under the category of 'woman.'"[28] Liinason's line of reasoning proves this point. Even when it is a case, not of defeat, as with Witt-Brattström, but of criticism in relation to a notion of development, unity behind the category of women becomes a decisive line of demarcation.

I am also interested in the temporal models which implicitly inform Liinason's argument. She concludes her article with a call to break with the teleology now inscribed in gender theory's proto-nationalist curriculum: "*Breaking* with the teleology that is constructed through references to a common past and a shared future" (my emphasis).[29] Using terms like "break" and "teleology", Liinason portrays gender theory as a solid and preordained construction which it is the task of gender theory's critics to smash. It is a historical account which produces "then" as the counterpart of the critic's "now", creating new varieties of inclusion and exclusion. From her perspective of a critical need to create "counter-stories", Liinason nonetheless creates a historiography which rests on the irreversibility that effectively prevents us from seeing what Assmann calls "*contemporaneity in the non-contemporary*".[30] It is also a way for her to relate to the past, which itself repeats Berman's gender coded description of tradition and modernity. In the process, and even when viewed from a poststructuralist perspective, the sexual difference that all gender theory wishes to do away with finds itself reinscribed at the level of temporality.

At the end of her article, Edenheim also notes that it is the metaphor of time which must be changed: "In a contingent temporality, feminist struggle can carry on without being forced to accept a beginning or an end, but merely trying different roads".[31] We have to get away from the notion of generations and succession because it erases both the difference between women and the similarities between ideas across time. Investigating technologies for feminist historiography, as Hemmings urges us, and seeing their connection to constructions of time and temporality, are both necessary if writing history is not simply to repeat old patterns of inclusion and exclusion.

Notes

1. Virginia Woolf, *A Room of One's Own*, Penguin, London & New York (1993) 4.
2. Recent books published on this topic in Sweden and in our Nordic neighbouring countries include: Bente Hansen, *En køn historie: erindringer fra kvindebevægelsen*, København: Lindhardt & Ringhof, 2004; Ida Blom, *Vi var med–: kvinnekamp i Bergen på 1970-tallet*, Bergen kvinnesaksforening (utgivare) Bergen: Bodoni forl., 2007; Pia Ingström, (red.) *Den flygande feministen och andra minnen från 70-talet*, Helsingfors: Schildt, 2007; Ebba Witt-Brattström, *Å alla kära systrar!: historien om mitt sjuttiotal*, Stockholm: Norstedt, 2010; Ingrid Sillén (red), *Tusen systrar ställde krav: minnen från 70-talets kvinnokamp* Stockholm: Migra, 2010; Gunilla Thorgren, *Grupp 8 & jag*, Stockholm: Pan, 2004; Kirsti Niskanen & Christina Florin (red.), *Föregångarna: kvinnliga professorer om liv, makt och vetenskap*, Stockholm: SNS förlag, 2010.
3. Elizabeth Grosz, "The Untimeliness of Feminist Theory", *NORA: Nordic Journal of Feminist and Gender Research* 18:1 (2010): 51.
4. Rita Felski, *The Gender of Modernity* (Cambridge, Mass. & London: Harvard University Press 1995), 1.
5. 5. Felski, *The Gender of Modernity*, 2. Felski also remarks that this logic is only one of several *possible* narratives of the modern. As an example, she mentions Gail Finney's analysis of the numerous heroines in literature at the turn of the twentieth century: "The so-called private sphere, often portrayed as a domain where natural and timeless emotions hold sway, is shown to be radically implicated in patterns of modernization and processes of social change." Felski p. 3.
6. Aleida Assmann, *Tid och tradition: Varaktighetens kulturella strategier* [Aleida Assmann: *Zeit und Tradition. Kulturelle Strategien der Dauer*, 1999] trans. Peter Jackson (Nora: Nya Doxa 2004), 76.
7. Assmann, *Tid och tradition*, 74.
8. Ulla Manns, "Så skriver vi historia. Den svenska kvinnorörelsen ur et historiografiskt perspektiv", *Kvinnovetenskaplig tidskrift*, 4 (2000), 8.
9. Claire Hemmings, "Telling Feminist Stories", *Feminist Theory*, 6:2 (2005), 116. Hemmings is criticized by Rachel Torr in "What's wrong with aspiring to find out what really happened in academic feminism's recent past?", *Feminist Theory*, 8:59 (2007). Hemmings replied in "What is a feminist responsible for?", *Feminist Theory*, 8:69 (2007).
10. Yvonne Hirdman, "Han och hon och dom – frågor i tidens töcken" in *Att göra historia – vänbok till Christina Florin*, ed. Maria Sjöberg och Yvonne Svanström, Institutet för framtidsstudier, Stockholm 2008, p. 43.
11. Ebba Witt Brattström, "Feminism i kris", *Hertha* 150 (2009): 65.
12. Ebba Witt-Brattström, *Dagens Nyheter,* mars 8, 2011, 8. Sangergori's statement is taken from Sillén, ed., *Tusen systrar ställde krav*. 2010.
13. Hemmings, 2005, 116.
14. Ebba Witt-Brattström, 2011, 8.

15. That generational metaphors are regarded as problematic, regardless of the age barrier, is *inter alia* evident from an article in *Dagens Nyheter* in which eleven feminists from different generations responded to Ebba Witt-Brattström's article of 8 March. See Malin Axelsson, Suzanne Osten, Maria Sveland, Farnaz Arbabi, Hanna Hallgren, Athena Farokhzad, Vanja Hermele, Birgitta Englin, Fataneh Farahani, Lawen Mohtadi, and Pia Laskar, "Generationskrig. Witt-Brattström skapar motsättningar som inte finns", *Dagens Nyheter*, mars 14, 2011, 5.

16. Witt-Brattström, 2009, 69.

17. Witt-Brattström, 2009, 69. See also Ebba Witt Brattström, *Å alla kära systrar* (Stockholm: Norstedts 2010, 191) in which she relates "the pipedream of contemporary postfeminism, that the very epithet 'woman' is an outrage."

18. Sara Edenheim, "Några ord till mina kära mödrar ifall jag hade några", *Tidskrift för genusvetenskap*, 4 (2010), 111.

19. Ibid., p. 115.

20. Gayatri Chakravorty Spivak, *A Critique of Postcolonial Reason*, London & New York 1999, p. 207.

21. Edenheim, 2010, 118.

22. The article is taken from Mia Liinason's doctoral dissertation, *Feminism and the academy: exploring the politics of institutionalization in gender studies in Sweden*, Lunds universitet. Centrum för genusvetenskap, 2011.

23. Mia Liinason, "Institutionalized Knowledge: Notes on the Processes of Inclusion and Exclusion in Gender Studies in Sweden", *NORA: Nordic Journal of Feminist and Gender Research*, 18:1 (2010) 39.

24. Liinason, 2010, 41.

25. Liinason, 2010, 45.

26. Liinason contends that 1970s and 1980s feminism constructed a specifically Swedish "'we-pride' produced in contrast to the outside world – in turn characterized by chaos, irrationality, and conflicts". Liinason, 2010, 44. Here, too, Liinason appears to emphasize her critique for polemical purposes. The claim that 1970s and 1980s feminism constructed an unproblematized category of inclusion ("we") is reasonable in itself, but, as Ulla Manns has shown in her analysis of research by Nordic women, this category was never national, but Nordic. It is precisely the idea of a given *transnational* community, stretching across the Nordic countries, that underestimated the linguisitic deficiencies and differences between women, as deconstructed by Ulla Mann in "En ros är en ros är en ros. Konstruktionen av nordisk kvinno- och genusforskning", *Lychnos* (2009).

27. Lena Gemzöe, "Faux Feminism? A reply to Mia Liinason's Position Paper", *NORA: Nordic Journal of Feminist and Gender Research*, 18:2 (2010), 122–128.

28. Claire Hemmings, "What is a feminist theorist responsible for? Response to Rachel Torr", *Feminist Theory* 8:69 (2007): 70.

29. Liinason, 2010, 45.

30. Assman, *Tid och tradition*, 74.

31. Edenheim, 2010, s. 117.

Atomic Hindsight: Technology and Visibility as Factors in Historical Periodization

TROND LUNDEMO

As the clouds briefly parted, the target became visible. At 08.15 on 6 August 1945, the US bomber *Enola Gay* dropped the atom bomb over Hiroshima, killing well over 100,000 people that day and a far larger number through injuries and radiation. Yet it also had hugely important consequences for the role of visual inscription in writing history, particularly historical periodization. Nuclear weaponry has influenced the formulation of several epochal shifts in history, among them, the end of the Second World War, the beginning of the Cold War, and, more central to my argument, the beginning of the Atomic Age. The race between the Third Reich and the United States to develop an atomic bomb during the Second World War produced a winner at the moment of detonation. However, it also created a new conception of warfare and a quite different understanding of the visual trace in photographic media.

This reconfiguration of the visual field in the aftermath of the first atomic bomb, during a long process of technological and social development, raises a series of questions about history and memory. What is the role of technical media for forming a 'social' or 'collective' memory of an event, and what role do they play in constructing historical periodizations? Can film and photography be understood as a 'witnesses' to historical events, and what are the limitations of such 'testimony' subsequently? Did nuclear energy usher in a 'new age', as some historical accounts have suggested, and how has it been re-contextualised following the introduction of other media technologies? Rather than answering every aspect of these questions, this overview aims to examine how the atomic bomb created new conditions for thinking about the inscription of historical events, and how these conditions form periodizations in recent history.

The 'Atomic Age' is an illuminating example of these processes of periodization and formation of social memory because it is an obsolete concept. The Atomic Age had wide currency as the denomination of the period after the Second World War but is no longer regarded as a meaningful term, forcing us to ask which mechanisms are at work in the formation of historical periodization, and how one periodizing category is replaced by another. I will here suggest that the Atomic Age was really the beginning of what would later be termed the Computer Age, and that the atom bomb was merely the 'content' of the new computer technology. For this reason, revision of the term has made it possible to see the end of WW2 as the beginning of the epoch defined by the technological features of society today. The atom bomb is connected to techniques of inscription and conditions of visuality that characterized the computer technology that is today ubiquitous.

A Reconfigured Visuality

The Hiroshima atom bomb was itself photographic.[1] In its intense white light the shadows cast by objects and bodies were seared onto walls and other surfaces in the city. When the bodies and objects turned to ash, their traces remained on the scene as unintended monuments of the detonation. While the bomb itself was photographic, with indexical and monumental properties, there were internal and external technological obstacles to its inscription. The blinding white glare of the bomb could only be witnessed at the cost of one's sight or life. The visual inscriptions of the bomb could only be made from its exterior, in the shape of a mushroom cloud at a distance. Because of the bomb's photographic light, only its after-effects could be represented. However, these kinds of representations were severely censored for a long time after the detonation. During the US occupation which followed Japan's surrender, all visual, aural, or verbal representations of the bomb and its consequences were censored in the Japanese media. Only after the end of the occupation in 1952 did it become possible to create cinematic re-enactments of this decisive event in

Japanese history. The technical conditions for forming an image of history are determined by a kind of *unrepresentability* at the level of the visual dispositifs and the political motifs necessary for forming a social memory of the events of the war.

The photographic light of the bomb reverses the traditional role of representation in the inscription of events. The bomb was 'archived' in the cityscape of Hiroshima but could not be visually described itself. It could only be represented as an all-effacing, blinding light whose radiation causes effects that are invisible. For this reason, only the *negatives* of things and bodies remain, reversing the polarity of light and shadow, life and death, inscription and erasure. As Akira Mizuta Lippitt has shown, the light of the bomb was a radiographic light: like an X-ray, it shows the inside of things.[2] This archive of inverted shadows shows only the absence of people and things, and the effects of invisible radiation. These effects became visible only after a long delay, as the diseases came to the surfaces of the bodies. Bodies decompose from the inside, a process visible only through radiography. Like nuclear radiation, X-rays lead to the decomposition of human tissue, as evidenced by the many casualties during their initial development. In keeping with the logic of the archive, the technologies of inscribing the body elicit the end of what they inscribe.

Lippitt doesn't develop his analysis of a 'shadow optics' in a historiographical direction, as he approaches Freud's writings and the X-rays as a similar mode of visuality as atomic radiation. His brilliant account of the interdependency and intersections between the visible and the invisible is linked to the whole of the history of cinema. However, a technological reconfiguration of visuality and indexicality takes place at around the time the first atomic bombs were detonated. Despite the inherent limitations of any account of epochal beginnings and endings, there is good reasons to make critical distinctions between the conditions of visibility in the early years of cinema and in the years of the Second World War. The science fictions of invisibility and the physical links to the X-ray in early cinema seem to be set in the quest for indexical inscription as such. At this time, the novelty of moving photographic images created a need for analyzing and charting the range and limitations of the material relation between the sign and its referent.

Instead, with the maximum visibility of the atom bomb, itself photographic and excessively luminous, visibility is invested with a shadow in its very mode of function and inscription. The light of the bomb is accompanied by nuclear radiation, which escapes visual observation, and the logic of photographic inscription is complicated by a spectral and mortal dimension. This point of rupture in the atom bomb is the critical moment of the image and the archive: the indexical aspect of the image undergoes a change. The bomb produced indexical traces in the city through the photographic light. These are images made by the bomb itself. Simultaneously, the effects of the bomb are unattainable for visual inscription. The bomb occupies the threshold of the indexical by reversing the logic of representation of the camera. While the transmissions of images, phantom rays and invisible men of early cinema belong to an affirmative stance to visibility, in the 'Atomic' Age and, later, the Computer Age, visual inscription exists only with an invisible dimension at its core, be it nuclear radiation or digital code.

Censorship and deferral

Just as the effects of atomic radiation only became visible after a time – the number of casualties from the after-effects of radiation greatly exceeds the numbers killed by the immediate impact of the bomb, which continues to claim victims even today – so, too, were its representations delayed until after the end of the US occupation. The US military produced a few information films for non-theatrical distribution to special audiences such as *A Tale of Two Cities* (US War Department 1946), mainly to downplay the after-effects of the bomb.[3] In general, the event of the bomb could only be confronted by the Japanese after the end of American occupation. What role did this delay – that is, the interval between detonation at ground zero and its effects in 1952 and beyond – have for public understanding of the event?

Representations of the atom bomb and its memorials remain highly contested. Several US authorities and organizations have argued that the Hiroshima Peace Memorial Museum provides insufficient background to the bomb, and much of the political engagement in

Japan in the 1960s and '70s departs from the claim that Japan has only continued with the same political culture, and often the same politicians, as in the totalitarian years. At the same time, this continuity in Japanese political life owed much to the US occupation, which felt a need to uphold traditional institutions such as the Emperor as a stabilizing force and a bulwark against communism. I will not examine these controversies in detail here even though they are highly significant for the ban on representations, which lasted until 1952, as well as for how the atom bomb was represented after the occupation. Nor will I offer a survey of how films such as the *Gojira* series and the *anime Atom Boy* (significantly renamed *Astro Boy* in the US) evoked the catastrophe after the ban was lifted.

This representational delay is highly significant for public understanding of the disaster's invisible aspect. For the purposes of comparison, we can consider three catastrophic events in Japanese history that reveal epochal shifts in the function of visual inscription. The Great Kanto Earthquake of 1923, which left most of Tokyo in ruins, follows a 'before-and-after' representational logic. Postcards and other photographic representations displayed the ruins of the great city alongside views of how it had looked before. Documentary films also followed this logic. The earthquake itself was not captured on film, and could only be reconstructed in the interval between 'before' and 'after'. This moment of change is also characteristic of the films portraying the reconstruction of the new city. The new age is symbolized by Ginza, which presented a contrast to traditional Edo culture in the Asakusa area of Tokyo. Similar oppositions between modernity and tradition proliferate in much Japanese cinema of the twenties and thirties.

After the Second World War, there were few such images of before and after. The ban on representations of ruins, rubble, or the occupying forces meant that representations of 'after' could only exist as reconstructions created long after the event itself. By the time the seven-year-long ban was finally lifted, public attention had shifted towards the long-term effects of radiation. This implies a change of representational regimes; the cities were being rebuilt but radiation continued to affect the country. The very invisibility of the radiation led to other modes of inscription, with temporal delay itself becoming a theme of images of the Second World War.

The ubiquity of digital cameras ensured that we have ample footage of the earthquake and tsunami of 11 March 2011 and their aftermath. Surveillance cameras, mobile phone cameras, and other devices show the effects of the disaster from every angle, ranging from official broadcasts to personal podcasts and YouTube clips. However, the disaster unites the ravages of the 1923 earthquake with the invisibility of the atomic radiation in 1945 insofar as radiation at the Fukushima nuclear plant remains invisible. The ubiquity of images shot by digital cameras has made the threat of a nuclear catastrophe of far greater interest than the earthquake and tsunami disaster itself, much to the discomfort of many observers in Japan. Alongside the inscription of the ravages of the tsunami, there is a 'dark margin', an invisible element of radiation, that seems more alluring to news reports exactly because of its invisibility. The potential threat of long-term effects of radiation cannot be inscribed visually, and thus leaves more room for imaginative speculation.

Whatever Happened to the Atomic Age?

The atom bomb's contested, paradoxical visibility led to the coining of an epoch that no longer exists: The Atomic Age. Not only has this period passed, its periodizing function has become obsolete. So pervasive was the concept in the years following the Second World War that a 1948 French TV documentary on the Lumière brothers (*Lumière*, directed by Paul Paviot, commentary by Abel Gance) could start with an image of a mushroom cloud and a commentary stating: "The Atomic Age was born with a blast in 1945. A long time ago, far away from the Pacific, it was the age of cinema . . . ." This counter-discourse tells us that these two periods are viewed as conflicting regimes of representation. Technological change is understood as an agent in historical periodizations, and the conditions for understanding the past have moved from the photographic inscription of cinema to a new, partly invisible, sphere.

The atom bomb has lost nothing of its psychological impact, even after end of the the Cold War. In the hands of Iran or Israel, North Korea or Pakistan, the nuclear weapons continue to be a threat, real or not, to the daily life of a lot of people. If the concept of the Atomic

Age has lost currency, it is because a much more comprehensive and ubiquitous technology has come to encompass the bomb. Allowing for a smooth narrative of one continuous process from the end of the Second World War up until today, the Computer Age has become a more compelling and persuasive periodization. Consequently, what used to be labeled the Atomic Age has become the Computer Age. As Friedrich Kittler provocatively puts it, the only information on the internet that really counts, is the atom bomb.[4] The internet was created to ensure that the military chain of command would remain intact in the event of a nuclear attack; in the meantime, we civilians are allowed to play with it. If the Atomic Age has been renamed the Computer Age, it is because the earlier concept mistook the content for the technology. The bomb is what affects people – ultimately, what kills people – but computer technology determines its construction, trajectories, and time of detonation.

The contested, paradoxical visibility of the Atomic Age has become even more pervasive as a feature of computers. Digital cameras are everywhere, capturing 'everything' while the function of the camera itself remains invisible. Images stored in digital code only become visible at the moment the file is opened, that is, as a surface effect, since digital code is to all intents and purposes invisible. The catchphrase 'What You see Is What You Get' is negated: what you see is something radically different. The invisibility, or even non-existence, of the image in digital technology has been contrasted with the photo-chemical image where the physical properties of the image, as a still negative or as a frame on the film strip, have always been optically verifiable. Many theorists of the photographical image have claimed the loss of the indexical to be the key feature of the digital image.[5] Even if this diagnosis rests on a reductive notion of the index, the invisibility of the digital signal as code prolongs the ambivalent status of visual inscription in the Atomic Age into the digital.

There are many reasons for locating the dawn of the computer age in the Second World War. Alan Turing's Universal Machine came into use, becoming famous for its part in the decrypting of Germany's Enigma machines. Konrad Zuse, working for the German government, constructed one of the first functioning mechanical computers (The Z1, Z2 and Z3) during the war. In the US, Vannevar Bush even described many principles for the functions of the internet in his article "As We May Think", written only a month before the detonation of the atom bomb in Hiroshima.[6] In it, Bush argues, first, that humans think using patterns that could be rendered as hypermedia links rather than by means of traditional 'tree structures' of categories and subcategories, and, second, that technology should provide machines adapted to human thought (The Memex). Perhaps most importantly, a proto-internet called ARPANET, developed from 1962 on, was devised as a command chain able to withstand a nuclear attack. The flexibility of the distributed computer networks now used every day is precisely based upon their ability to function in the aftermath of an atom bomb attack.

Periodizations and their names are always provisional. Any one era co-exists with overlapping periodizations and concepts. The Atomic Age was not the only name for the post-war years (a concept that already presupposes an alternative periodization), and it only applied to certain fields and disciplines. It could be objected that the Computer Age did not start with Hiroshima which had been predated by Alan Turing's and John von Neumann's theoretical foundations for the modern computer. The limitations of visual observation for accessing the 'real' had been scientifically established at a much earlier date, for instance, with quantum mechanics and n-dimensional geometry. Instead of debating illusory dates for beginnings and ends, I would argue that the atom bomb brought with it a reconfigured regime of visuality, in which what is visible has become even less the truth of things than it once was. The atom bomb invests the visible with its invisible counterpart; nuclear annihilation intersects with the long-term effects of radiation in the body to form a new configuration between the blinding white light of the bomb and its invisible shadow.

This is the way physical processes start to retreat from the visible, in so doing raising new questions for a theory of technical media. After the Second World War, the invisible life of atoms instituted a new period, named after the bomb. When many of the visual features of the bomb coincide with computer processing, the former periodization is written over by a new one. This process tells us not only about the changes of history, but also about the way in which historical periods are reconfigured. When one technological breakthrough, the atom bomb, is eclipsed by the emergence of a related technology with an even greater social pervasiveness, i.e. the computer, history is rewritten. An attention to technological ruptures is not to claim a technological determinism for processes of historical periodization. The obsolescence of the concept Atomic Age instead demonstrates that the social, economic, and political pervasiveness of the computer has come to overshadow and absorb the atomic blast into its configuration of the visual and the world. The determining factor of the social impact of the computer demonstrates how an epochal shift can be retrospectively reconceptualized when other machines have come to embody the shifts in a more powerful way.

Notes

1. Paul Virilio, *War and Cinema: The Logistics of Perception* (London: Verso, 1989), 81. Akira Mizuta Lippitt, *Atomic Light (Shadow Optics)* (Minneapolis: University of Minnesota Press, 2005), 50: "...the atomic explosions in Hiroshima and Nagasaki turned those cities, in the instant of a flash, into massive *cameras*; the victims grafted onto the geography by the radiation, *radiographed*."

2. Lippitt, *Atomic Light*, 92–95.

3. For a survey of representations of the atom bomb and its after-effects in postwar Japanese cinema, see Mick Broderick (ed.), *Hibakusha Cinema; Hiroshima, Nagasaki and the Nuclear Image in Japanese Film* (London and New York: Kegan Paul 1996).

4. Friedrich Kittler, *Grammophon, Film, Typewriter* (Berlin: Brinckmann & Boese, 1985), 7.

5. D.N. Rodowick, *The Virtual Life of Film* (Cambridge, Mass.: Harvard University Press 2007).

6. Vannevar Bush, "As We May Think", *Atlantic Monthly* July 1945, reprinted in T. Druckrey (ed.), *Electronic Culture; Technology and Visual Representation*(New York: Södertörn Philosophical Studies

Södertörn Philosophical Studies is a book series published under the direction of the Department of Philosophy at Södertörn University. The series consists of monographs and anthologies in philosophy, with a special focus on the Continental-European tradition. It seeks to provide a platform for innovative contemporary philosophical research. The volumes are published mainly in English and Swedish. The series is edited by Marcia Sá Cavalcante Schuback and Hans Ruin.

Index

Adorno, Theodor W. 65, 79, 92, 243, 246, 279, 288
Ahmed, Sara 292, 299
Agamben, Giorgio 248, 255
Alencar, José de 134
Alighieri, Dante 77
Améry, Jean 15, 237, 241–244, 246
Amoedo, Rodolfo 134
Anaximander 52
Anderson, Benedict 106, 134, 135, 138, 190, 197
Andrade, Mario 129
Anghie, Anthony 174, 178
Appiah, Kwame Anthony 117, 118
Arendt, Hannah 247, 254, 255
Aristotle 34, 41, 51–53
Assmann, Aleida 73, 84, 93, 303, 304, 310, 311
Assmann, Jan 13, 94, 106
Auerbach, Erich 88, 94
Augustine 51, 53–56, 60, 171, 177

Bach, J. S. 97
Badiou, Alain 280, 286–289
Bagge, Axel 114
Barthes, Roland 44, 148, 151
Baudrillard, Jean 144, 151
Beck, Ulrich 188
Benjamin, Walter 64, 65, 71, 73, 140, 148, 149, 151, 233–235, 254, 255
Bergson, Henri 57
Berman, Marshall 303, 304, 310
Berry, Chuck 97
Blake, William 83, 89

Blanchot, Maurice 67, 68, 73, 94
Blaut, James M. 269, 271, 272, 275, 276
Bloom, Harold 80, 82, 92, 93
Bonaparte, Napoleon 45, 224
Boisseau, T. J. 296, 299
Bourdieu, Pierre 79, 88, 92, 93
Brémond, Claude 43, 49
Burke, Edmund 230, 235
Bush, George H. W. 143
Bush, George W. 157
Bush, Vannevar 319–321
Butler, Judith 170, 177
Byron, G. G. Lord 90, 227, 228

Casanova, Pascale 89, 94
Castells, Manuel 193–195, 198
Celan, Paul 15, 74, 83, 247, 249, 255
Chakrabarty, Dipesh 221, 226, 299
Cicero 78
Coleridge, Samuel T. 90
Comte, Auguste 156, 218, 225
Condorcet, Marquis de 156, 164
Curtius, Ernst Robert 77, 78, 88, 92, 94

da Cunha, Euclides 15, 217–223, 225, 226
Damrosch, David 89, 90, 94
Dayan, Daniel 140, 150
Deleuze, Gilles 15, 73, 197, 257–263, 265
Descartes, René 110
Derrida, Jacques 15, 51, 57–59, 71, 73,

INDEX

74, 94, 151, 195, 235, 247–250, 253, 255
Dienst, Richard 140, 150, 151
Dostoyevsky, Fjodor 46
Dreyfus, Alfred 279
Duchamp, Marcel 24, 25, 28
Dugas, Gaëtan 156

Edenheim, Sara 307, 310, 312
Edensor, Tim 121, 127
Eliot, George 229, 235
Eliot, T. S. 89, 94
Elsaesser, Thomas 148, 149, 151, 152
Erdogan, Recep 211
Eze, Emmanuel 110, 117, 118

Felski, Rita 302, 303, 305, 311
Fitzgerald, F. Scott 15, 257–265
Fogelklou, Emilia 185, 188
Foucault, Michel 9, 22, 28, 36, 73, 107, 195
Frazer, James 112, 113, 117, 118
Freud, Sigmund 237, 239, 244, 245, 288, 315
Frye, Northrop 42
Fukuyama, Francis 156, 164

Gadamer, Hans-Georg 24, 25, 28, 65, 71, 73, 83–87, 91, 93, 94, 179, 187
Gaddis, John Lewis 142, 147, 151
Garner, Margaret 233
Gemzöe, Lena 308, 309, 312
Ginzburg, Carlo 250, 252, 255
Godard, Jean-Luc 140
Goethe, J. W. 303, 304
Goodman, Nelson 169, 177
Graça, Antônio Paulo 134, 135, 138
Grotius, Hugo 173, 177
Grosz, Elisabeth 302, 311
Grever, Maria 291, 293, 298, 299
Gripenberg, Alexandra 15, 291–299
Guattari, Félix 197, 258, 261, 262, 265
Guillory, Paul 82, 88, 91, 93, 94

Gül, Abdullah 207, 211
Gunder Frank, Andre 269, 271, 272, 275, 276
Gustav V, king of Sweden 99
Gustavus I, king of Sweden 109

Habermas, Jürgen 36, 73, 93
Halacoğlu, Yusuf 206, 207, 212
Hardenberg, Friedrich von, see Novalis
Hardt, Michael 190, 197
Hauch, Adam W. 111, 112, 118
Hazelius, Artur 109
Hegel, G. W. F 24–27, 105, 107, 142, 144, 156, 164, 280, 283–289, 294, 299
Heidegger, Martin 51, 52, 56–59, 67–69, 73, 87, 94, 303
Hemmings, Clare 304–307, 309–312
Hildebrand, Emil 114
Hirdman, Yvonne 305, 311
Hitler, Adolf 99, 122, 123, 198, 245
Ho Chi Minh 161
Hobbes, Thomas 281
Hölderlin, Friedrich 72, 74, 105, 107
Holzer, Jenny 26
Homer 52, 78
Horace 78
Horkheimer, Max 279, 288
Hugo, Victor 160
Hume, David 36, 110
Husserl, Edmund 51, 52, 55–58, 67, 73, 126

Ieng Sary 159, 160

Jameson, Fredric 28, 140, 150, 190, 198
Joyce, James 78
Jürgensen Thomsen, Christian 111, 112, 114, 118
Juvenal 78

INDEX

Kafka, Franz 83
Kant, Immanuel 9, 22, 28, 56, 64, 73, 86, 88, 110, 115, 177, 180–182, 187, 188, 280–289
Katz, Elihu 140, 150
Keats, John 90
Key, Ellen 179, 182–188
Khieu Samphân 159, 160
Kittler, Friedrich 319, 321
Kolbas, E. Dean 81, 92, 93
Koselleck, Reinhart 22, 28, 30, 31, 38, 58, 155, 158, 159, 164, 165, 179–181, 235
Kosuth, Joseph 26
Kracauer, Siegfried 194, 198
Kristeva, Julia 239, 245
Kropotkin, Peter 160

Lange, Christian 186
Laub, Dori 147, 151
Levi, Primo 248, 249, 255
Lévi-Strauss, Claude 43, 44
Levinas, Emmanuel 61, 288
Lewald, Fanny 15, 227–235
Lewis, Wyndham 19
Liinason, Mia 308–310, 312
Lilla, Mark 281, 288
Lippitt, Akira Mizuta 315, 321
Lloyd, Llewellyn 113, 118
Locke, John 281
Lon Nol 162
Longinus 88, 94

Machiavelli, Niccolò 36
Mack, Michael 283, 288, 289
Malthus, Thomas R. 273
Martens, Renzo 191–193, 195
Marx, Karl 156, 164, 229, 233, 235, 269, 270, 288
Matthew 259
Mégret, Frédéric 174, 175, 178
Meinzer, Michael 157, 158, 164
Mendelssohn, Moses 281, 282, 288

Mink, Louis 39, 40, 42, 49
Montesquieu, Baron de 36, 160
Moraes, Antônio Carlos Robert 133, 138
More, Thomas 103
Morgan, Lewis Henry 112, 118
Morrison, Toni 233
Mozart, W. A. 97
Musil, Robert 42

Nancy, Jean-Luc 67, 68, 73
Negri, Antonio 190. 197
Neumann, John von 73, 320
Newton, Isaac 53
Nietzsche, Friedrich 22, 28, 34, 35, 38, 97, 237, 238, 245, 263, 288
Nilsson, Sven 111–113, 117, 118
Nolte, Ernst 239, 240, 245
Nora, Pierre 140, 150
Norodom Shianouk 159, 160
Noun Chea 159, 162
Novalis (Friedrich von Hardenberg) 104, 107

Olsen, Bjørnar 121, 127
Ovid 78, 105

Paine, Thomas 157, 164
Paul 283, 286–289
Patočka, Jan 69, 70, 73
Peirce, C. S. 49
Plato 38, 47, 144, 180
Pol Pot (Saloth Sar) 159–162, 165
Polk, James 157
Polybius 35, 36
Pomeranz, Kenneth 269, 271–277
Pomian, Krzysztof 100, 106
Prince, Gerald 40, 49
Propp, Vladimir 42, 43, 49
Proust, Marcel 83

Ramos, Alcida 134, 138
Rebelo, Aldo 135, 136, 138

INDEX

Renan, Ernest 118, 134–136
Ruhnken, David 76, 78
Ricoeur, Paul 52, 58, 61, 73, 141–144, 150, 151, 198, 235, 238, 245
Robespierre, Maximilien de 160
Roosevelt, Franklin D. 99
Rosendahl Thomsen, Mads 89, 93, 94
Rousseau, Jean-Jacques 160
Rupp, Leila J. 297, 299
Rüsen, Jörn 107, 238, 245
Rushdie, Salman 217, 225

Sachs, Nelly 63, 73
Said, Edward 269
Shelley, Percy B. 90
Schelling, Friedrich 22, 105, 107
Schiller, Friedrich 253
Schlegel, Friedrich 104, 105, 107
Schleiermacher, Friedrich 63, 73
Schmitt, Carl 172, 173, 177
Schreiner, Olive 15, 217–221, 223–226
Shakespeare, William 85
Short, Philip 160, 165
Skinner, Quentin 155, 177
Smith, Adam 269
Son Sen 159
Speer, Albert 122, 123, 128, 248
Spencer, Herbert 218, 224, 225
Spinoza, Baruch 288

Spivak, Gayatri 195–198, 220, 221, 226, 312
Stagnelius, E. J. 83
Stalin, Josef 99, 161
Stein, Edith 56
Stieglitz, Alfred 25
Szondi, Peter 148, 151

Therborn, Göran 190, 198
Thucydides 36
Tilly, Charles 36
Todorov, Tzvetan 248, 255
Trotsky, Leon 288
Turing, Alan 319, 320
Turner, Ted 141
Tylor, Edward B. 112, 118

Virgil 77, 78, 94

Weber, Max 269
White, Hayden 13, 38–40, 42, 44, 45, 49, 50, 58, 140, 142–147, 151, 164
Wilson, Woodrow 157
Winch, Peter 169, 177
Witt-Brattström, Ebba 305–308, 310–312
Woolf, Virginia 301, 311
Wordsworth, William 90

Žižek, Slavoj 137, 138, 280, 286–289
Zuse, Konrad 319

Authors

Peter Aronsson is Professor of Cultural Heritage and the Uses of History at Linköping University

Jens Bartelson is Professor of Political Science at Lund University

Mats Burström is Professor of Archaeology at Stockholm University

Staffan Carlshamre is Professor of Philosophy at Stockholm University

Staffan Ericson is Associate Professor of Media and Communications at Södertörn University

Andrus Ers is PhD and Researcher in History of Ideas at Södertörn University

Victoria Fareld is Assistant Professor of History of Ideas at University of Gothenburg

Kristina Fjelkestam is Associate Professor of Comparative Literature at Linköping University

David Gaunt is Professor of History at Södertörn University

Johan Hegardt is Associate Professor of Archaeology at Uppsala University

Stefan Helgesson is Professor of English Literature at Stockholm University

AUTHORS

Alf Hornborg is Professor of Human Ecology at Lund University

Stefan Jonsson is Professor at REMESO – Institute for Research on Migration, Ethnicity and Society at Linköping University

Dan Karlholm is Professor of Art History at Södertörn University

Rebecka Lettevall is Associate Professor of History of Ideas at Södertörn University

Claudia Lindén is Associate Professor of Literature and Gender at Södertörn University

Patricia Lorenzoni is Assistant Professor of History of Ideas at University of Gothenburg

Trond Lundemo is Associate Professor of Cinema Studies at Stockholm University

Ulla Manns is Professor of History of Ideas and Gender Studies at Södertörn University

Anders Olsson is Professor of Comparative Literature at Stockholm University

Johan Redin is PhD and Researcher in Aesthetics at Södertörn University

Hans Ruin is Professor of Philosophy at Södertörn University

Marcia Sá Cavalcante-Schuback is Professor of Philosophy at Södertörn University

Irina Sandomirskaja is Professor of Cultural Studies at Södertörn University

AUTHORS

Fredrika Spindler is Associate Professor of Philosophy at Södertörn University

Jayne Svenungsson is Associate Professor of Systematic Theology at Stockholm School of Theology

For more information, see: www.histcon.se

Södertörn Philosophical Studies

Södertörn Philosophical Studies is a book series published under the direction of the Department of Philosophy at Södertörn University. The series consists of monographs and anthologies in philosophy, with a special focus on the Continental-European tradition. It seeks to provide a platform for innovative contemporary philosophical research. The volumes are published mainly in English and Swedish. The series is edited by Marcia Sá Cavalcante Schuback and Hans Ruin.

www.ingramcontent.com/pod-product-compliance
Lightning Source LLC
Chambersburg PA
CBHW031313160426
43196CB00007B/518